TRADITIONAL HOME ™

# ROSE GARDENING

Elvin McDonald

Meredith® Books
Des Moines

Meredith® Books

*Traditional Home*™
ROSE GARDENING
Writer: Elvin McDonald
Senior Editor: Marsha Jahns
Art Director: Linda Vermie
Copy Editors: Sharon Novotne O'Keefe, Mary Helen Schiltz
Special thanks: Edith Manning and Stephen Scanniello, for sharing the love of roses; Eleanore Lewis, Anne Halpin, Jerry Sedenko, Marion Lyons, and Mary Uhrbrock, for rose writings


Vice President and Editorial Director: Elizabeth P. Rice
Executive Editor: Kay Sanders
Art Director: Ernest Shelton
Managing Editor: Christopher Cavanaugh


President, Book Group: Joseph J. Ward
Vice President, Retail Marketing: Jamie L. Martin
Vice President, Direct Marketing: Timothy Jarrell


*Traditional Home*®
Publisher: Deborah Jones Barrow
Editor in Chief: Karol DeWulf Nickell
Art Director: Matt Strelecki
Managing Editor: John Riha
Garden Editor: Senga Mortimer


President, Magazine Group: Christopher Little


Meredith Corporation
Chairman of the Executive Committee: E. T. Meredith III
Chairman of the Board and Chief Executive Officer:
    Jack D. Rehm
President and Chief Operating Officer: William T. Kerr

All photographs by Elvin McDonald except for the following: All-America Rose Selections (page 102), King Au (page 61), Cathy Wilkinson Barash (page 137), Pamela Blackburn (page 13), Ernest Braun (pages 28, 29, 83, 118, 123, and 185), Kim Brun (pages 27, 40, and 41), Steve Cridland (pages 30–31 and 32), Richard Felber (pages 10–11 and 16, top), Randy Foulds (pages 46, 72–73, and 87), George de Gennaro (pages 16, bottom, and 33), Jay Graham (page 47), Karlis Grants (pages 18; 19, bottom; 48–49; 51; and 181), Hedrick Blessing (page 58), William Hopkins (pages 52–53; 56–57; 59 bottom; 74, center and right; 75; 76–77; 78; and 167), Terry Husebye (page 38), Jackson & Perkins (pages 72, far left, and 153, top), Jon Jensen (page 55), Mike Jensen (page 81), Dency Kane (pages 39, 195, and 204), Peter Krumhardt (pages 155, top, and 173), Andy Lyons (pages 22–23), Maris/Semel (pages 43, 88, and 186), Memphis Commercial Appeal (page 45), PHOTO/NATS, Inc. (pages 117 and 135), Marilyn Pindar (page 154, right), The Conard Pyle Co. (pages 190–191), Eric Roth (page 19, top), Susan A. Roth (pages 67, 122, and 125), Semarco Inc. (page 20), Bill Stites (pages 15, 17, and 187), Mark Thomas (pages 59, top, and 60), Thomson (page 103, right), and Judy Watts (pages 24–25 and 62–63).

All of us at Meredith® Books are dedicated to providing you with the information and ideas you need to garden successfully. We guarantee your satisfaction with this book for as long as you own it. If you have any questions, comments, or suggestions, please write to us at:

MEREDITH® BOOKS, Garden Books
Editorial Department, RW 240
1716 Locust St.
Des Moines, IA 50309-3023


If you would like to order additional copies of any of our books, call 1-800-678-2803 or check with your local bookstore.

Roses are a universal symbol of the beautiful and the noble. They have historically been cultivated by every class, their beauty recognized by all who see, sense, and feel the life spirit manifest in the ephemeral rose flower. It is our goal through these pages to shed a light both timely and timeless on a subject eternal: Encouraging a creation from nature to achieve its purpose, thereby enriching all we hold dear.

# Table of contents

# 96 Rose husbandry

Exploring for New Roses
Selecting the Perfect Rose

# 104 An encyclopedia of roses

Wild or Species Roses
Gallica Roses
Damask Roses
Alba Roses
Centifolia Roses
Moss Roses
China Roses
Tea Roses
Bourbon Roses
Noisette Roses
Hybrid Perpetual Roses

Large-Flowered Bush Roses
Cluster-Flowered Bush Roses
Modern Shrub Roses
Dwarf Cluster-Flowered Bush Roses
Miniatures
Ground-Cover Roses
Climbing and Rambler Roses
English Garden Roses

# the history of the rose

Roses have excited the imaginations of men and women since the dawn of history. To start growing these ancient flowers in your own garden is to enter into a lifelong romance.

**3.5 million years ago**

First fossil records of the rose.

**70 million years ago**

No fossils of rose blossoms found, but distinct impressions of leaves and thorns.

**3000 B.C.**

In what is now Iraq, the Sumerians write about roses for the first written record.

**1700 B.C.**

Frescoes of roses appear on the walls of the Cretan palace of Knossos, along with iris and lilies.

**600 B.C.**

Sappho, in her "Ode to the Rose," refers to the rose as the queen of flowers.

**30 B.C.**

Romantic to the end, Marc Antony asks Cleopatra to strew his grave with roses.

**27 B.C.**

Party time in Rome means tons of rose petals, most of which are grown by the millions near Paestum.

**60 A.D.**

Nero shows he knows how to have fun by ordering the equivalent of $150,000 worth of roses for one banquet.

'Empress Josephine'

| 1187 | 1277 | 1455-85 | 1485 | 15th century | 16th century | 1590 | 17th century |
|---|---|---|---|---|---|---|---|
| Saladin defeats the crusaders and orders 500 camel loads of roses, distilled into rose water, with which to cleanse the mosque of Omar of the presence of the infidels. | The "rose of Provins," probably *Rosa gallica officinalis,* raised by the square mile near Paris. The fact that its fragrance is carried in the petals, even when dried, makes it an important medicinal flavoring. Edmund of Lancaster takes it back to England and adopts it as the emblem of the House of Lancaster. | The House of York, whose emblem is the white rose, engages in the longest British civil war with the Lancasters. We know this period as the Wars of the Roses. Later, a crimson-and-white-striped rose is found and the York and Lancaster rose comes into being. | The Lancasters prevail under Henry Tudor, who accepts Elizabeth Plantagenet, a Yorkist, as his bride. She brings him white roses, and the rose becomes the emblem of England. | Damask roses appear, a probable cross of *Rosa gallica* and other old roses. | Brought by colonists, the rose is probably the longest-cultivated European plant in North America. Likely cultivated in medicinal gardens, one can't help but think that sentimentality had more than just a little to do with it. | Musk roses introduced into European cultivation. There is some mystery as to just where and what these large climbers, really are. The name lingers on in the category of hybrid musks. | Centifolia roses appear, especially in Dutch still-life paintings. Also known as cabbage roses and roses of Provence, they are probably crosses of alba and damask roses. |

# the history of the rose

| 1725 | 1792 | 1798 | 1804 | 1805 | 1807 | 1809 | 1822 |
|---|---|---|---|---|---|---|---|
| The rose 'Common Moss' appears. First found in southern France, this sport of a centifolia produces scented fuzzy growths on sepals and leaves. Other mosses appear in short order. | A major breakthrough occurs when 'Slater's Crimson China' is found in China. It bears double flowers and blooms periodically all summer. | Empress Josephine acquires her palace at Malmaison and begins the serious collection of roses. The most remarkable rose garden ever planted, it includes every variety known at the time (about 250) in an estimated 4,500 acres. | *Rosa multiflora* sent from Canton. Not grown in Britain until 1975, it is now a major pest in certain sections of the United States, and planted by the millions along highways, owing to its virtues of being "horse-high, ox-strong and goat-tight." | 'Parson's Pink China' becomes the parent of a new race of miniature roses. | The violet-scented Lady Banks rose arrives from China. Somewhat tender, it seems that every protected wall in Britain sprouts at least one. Now planted along highways in the American Southwest. | 'Humes' Blush Tea-Scented Rose' sent from India by Alexander Hume, factor of the East India Company in China. The fragrance is unlike anything else, and special arrangements are made between warring French and English navies for safe transport to Josephine. | A chance seedling from a cross of an autumn damask and a China rose found on and named for the Ile de Bourbon, now Reunion, in the Indian Ocean. Fragrance and constant bloom were big plusses, and others were created intentionally. |

## 1795

Another repeat-blooming China rose is discovered, 'Parson's Pink China,' and roses will never be the same.

| 1824 | 1870 | 1899 | 1910 | 1920 | 1935 | 1970s | 1990s |

**1824**
'Park's Yellow Tea-Scented Rose' sent from China. Led to many pale pink and yellow roses.

**1867**
Blending hybrid perpetuals (a mixed bag of heritage) with a tea rose gives the silvery-pink 'La France,' the first acknowledged hybrid tea, still popular today.

**1870**
First polyanthas, descendants of *Rosa multiflora*.

**1890**
The pillar rose 'Mme. Plantier,' of indeterminate parentage, is all the rage. Vita Sackville-West will later train it into old fruit trees at Sissinghurst.

**1899**
Founding of the American Rose Society, whose main purpose is the rating and sharing of knowledge of growing roses throughout the United States.

**1910**
Climbers derived from the glossy-leaved *Rosa wichuraiana* hit the market. Some of them, such as 'Dorothy Perkins' and 'Dr. W. Van Fleet,' still remain, although the original gardens may be long gone. Later, a recurrent sport of 'Dr. W. Van Fleet' is named 'New Dawn.'

**1920**
Hybrid teas dominate the market, likewise today.

**1935**
Floribundas, derived from polyanthas, officially recognized.

**1945**
The most popular rose of all time, 'Peace,' is released after having been smuggled to the United States from occupied France.

**1970s**
David Austin of England introduces his "English Roses," combinations of modern hybrid teas and old roses. They're mostly recurrent, with old-rose forms and fragrance, but in "modern" colors, including peaches, apricots, and strong, clear yellows.

**1990s**
Miniature and modern shrub roses have become well established within the American Rose Society ratings sytem as well as that of the commercial All-America Rose Selections. Landscape roses are favored as well as those that are self-reliant.

'Peace'

'Dynasty'

# designing a rose garden

Roses, more than any other flower, should be shown to their best advantage. Whether you have one, ten, or hundreds of roses, the context in which they are planted contributes to both their cultural and visual success. The design of a rose garden is as important as the flowers it contains.

The beautiful rosebush in a roadside hedgerow. The charming wild or species roses beside an old barn. The voluptuous old garden rose in the yard of a rusticating abandoned farmhouse. There is in each of these examples the fundamental lesson about roses and design: Simplicity is what becomes them most. Implicit is their need for space to develop naturally, for free air movement, and for lots of sun. Climbers and ramblers, in particular, also require some means of support.

Although the words "yard" and "garden" can be used interchangeably, there is a distinction. Roses are embellishments to yard spaces, integral to charming the outdoor aspects of a dwelling as surely as creature comforts and beautiful accessories make interior rooms livable.

By contrast, roses play both major and minor roles in gardens. The purist rosarian often grows the roses alone, bedded-out in a straightforward arrangement with nothing more than swept-earth paths or strips of lawn surrounding. Roses also may be framed more formally by low, clipped hedges or mixed with other flowers, woody, herbaceous, annual and perennial, in casual borders that can be curved and asymmetrical or straight and symmetrical.

Because roses come in all sizes and habits, from bushes that are really creepers or trailers to climbing giants, they offer untold possibilities. The goal always is to select the right rose for the right place so that the total effect represents more than the sum of its parts.

**The design of this garden accommodates the human element as well as the vegetation. Everywhere the eyes are drawn to beauty, down an inviting path flanked by roses, clematis, and assorted perennials.**

# Creating a garden with style

In either case, there are basically two ways to achieve the design. One is to work it all out in advance on paper; the other is to design on the site by actually moving the plants around until the result is satisfactory. Gertrude Jekyll at her most sensible said the all-blue garden needn't be all blue, merely beautiful, and thought nothing of transplanting something in bloom if it happened to clash with neighboring bedmates. Unless you are familiar with the roses themselves—their habit, size, and color—planning first on paper will almost inevitably save you time and effort later and produce more spectacular results.

## Winter is for planning

The winter season is ideal for rose gardening on paper, a time when this pursuit can be enjoyed leisurely. It has three specific activities:
- studying catalogs to see what is available,
- working out the design, and
- writing out orders as appropriate.

Eager gardeners often skip the second activity and end up wild-eyed and sweaty in the fever of spring planting, fraught with uncertainty as to which plant should go where but aware that bare-roots need to be set in the ground without delay. Even a rough diagram or the simplest plan of action is better than nothing at all.

Rudimentary drafting tools and supplies make the design work more enjoyable. These include a T-square, a triangle and straightedge, a supply of graph paper, pencils, and erasers. Depending on the space and your preliminary ideas about the design, an S-curve and a compass also may be helpful. Choose a workable scale for your garden design; often ¼ inch on a sheet of graph paper is used to represent 12 inches in actual garden space. If plants of different heights and varied profiles are being combined, try sketching them in elevation based on how you have arranged them in your bird's-eye plan. A set of colored marking pens will also come in handy when you start envisioning color schemes and relationships.

It is a generality, but formal gardens tend to be easy to design but difficult to maintain. Informal or casual gardens require a certain design finesse to succeed, but their upkeep is likely to be less demanding.

## Formal rose gardens

Because of their specialized cultural requirements, roses have traditionally been grown in separate beds. Probably for efficiency's sake, as well as an older esthetic, these beds have taken on formal designs. Some of the hallmarks of this formality are geometry, symmetry, structure, and focal points.

Square or rectangular beds divided by pathways comprise the simplest formality. Transected circular beds are more difficult to infuse with formality. From this point of departure, embellishments can become elaborate to any degree. Whatever form you choose, you'll do well to plan the garden first on paper. You'll be able to get a sense of proportion and space that will be appropriate for your garden.

**Clipped dwarf boxwood in a formal parterre frames stylish tree-form standard roses at Longue Vue Gardens, in New Orleans. This design concept is French-inspired.**

**Roses needn't be set in formal beds unto themselves. In the island bed opposite they mix companionably with cottage-garden varieties of flowers.**

# Creating a garden with style

Any garden should invite you into it, offering various ways to enjoy the scene as you move through it. A pergola provides shade and a little bit of mystery, with glimpses between the supports of the rest of the garden. A well-placed stone jar, statuary, or other feature at one end gives a pergola a sense of purpose and destination.

Benches are a must in any garden, particularly formal ones. They not only add to the symmetry of the place but allow a chance to sit and really appreciate the beauty of the garden.

Attention needs to be paid to color in every garden. White structures look crisp, and dark green gives a sense of low-key permanence. Rustic work of bark-covered poles is the most nostalgic, all the more charming with old-fashioned lax-growing rambling roses. It's the design more than the materials that creates formality.

Beds flanking a generous pathway of manicured grass or stone or brick paving set the tone. This axis can end at a hedge or wall of treillage, with a thoughtfully placed statue or other art object to bring the whole thing into focus.

The formal framework of the garden can be delineated further by the use of low hedges. Boxwood is the classic material for this. The effect can be accomplished faster with dwarf lavender, santolina, or germander, all of which take to shearing like cloth to scissors. Remember, when establishing your hedges, clip them back as they grow to make them dense. Waiting until they reach full size before shearing gives a sparse, puny effect.

Structures continue the theme of firm lines in the rose garden. Arches and gates are naturals, and a trellis-covered bench makes a fascinating bower of privacy. A gazebo makes a wonderful spot for conversation and lemonade. It can be as simple as posts holding up a roof.

**A strategically placed bench, above, adds to the symmetry of a formal garden and offers a quiet spot for reflection.**

**A delight for the senses, the garden opposite, top, welcomes human and wildlife visitors alike.**

**'New Dawn' and floribunda roses spill over an antique trellis, which serves as the focal point for the fragrant rose garden opposite, bottom.**

# A rose for every yard

Add a touch of whimsy to a rose garden with a birdhouse or other outdoor artwork, craft, or found object.

Use roses in new and imaginative ways. Here they camouflage a dog run, deftly turning a yard from ordinary to charming.

Nearly every town of substantial size has a municipal rose garden, usually part of a much larger park, devoted to a series of beds of roses of a kind. Portland, Oregon, the American Rose Society Gardens in Shreveport, Louisiana, and Butchart Gardens outside Victoria, British Columbia, are all examples. These extensive collections are wonderful places for inspiration; see a complete listing of public rose gardens on pages 208–215 of this book.

More to the point for the individual rosarian is a scaled-down version of the public rose garden, with a few plants of favored cultivars. It's a question of scale (and finances). The smaller the space, the less jumbled a bed of roses should be. If your garden has only space for a half-dozen hybrid teas, you can make each one different, but try to keep the colors harmonious. A brilliant pink next to a tangerine could be jarring. The other option is to choose all the same variety. This can give impact and show off design but probably won't satisfy the collector's urge to have at least one of everything.

With a little imagination, you can grow roses in some nontraditional ways. Large ramblers can be trained up into trees. Seeing their blossoms lacing through the branches toward the sky is a unique experience. For rose-bedecked entryways, use less thorny varieties—the sweet-scented 'Zephyrine Drouhin,' for example.

Collecting the daily mail can be a joy when roses are planted at the base of the mailbox support. Make them lower-growing floribundas or miniatures. Line the driveway with roses, but near the entry to the house, plant something for winter effect—holly or pyracantha—because roses usually look forlorn in January.

A circle of roses cut from the expanse of a paved patio does much to relieve the view of what could be an oppressive, hot wasteland in August. Make a collection of small and miniature roses in pots, classic terra-cotta or whatever your sense of order dictates. Group them around some hybrid teas and add a tree-form rose or two. Even if you have no soil to garden, there are ways of having roses grace your life.

A porch railing is dressed up with climbing roses: white 'Sombreuil,' red 'Crimson Glory,' and pink 'Aloha.'

# Companion plants for roses

Although beds of just roses may be the classic way to grow them, roses assort well with a host of other plants. Whether carpeted underneath with ground covers or in a mixed-border setting, roses will look more settled—at home—with companionable bedmates.

Because roses don't have much to offer in early spring, plants like forget-me-nots, sweet violets, and primroses add some interest. They need sun at this season but appreciate the shade of the rosebushes during summer.

To keep down weeds and maintain tidiness, choose carpeters to help cover the naked bases of hybrid teas. *Artemisia stellerana* covers the spaces between the plants with a 2-inch-high silver filigree, but doesn't interfere with the well-being of the roses. Dusky-leaved Labrador violets seed about gently, never becoming a pest, and look uncommonly pretty with roses in bright, sunset hues. Perennial violas do best in cool-summer or mild-winter areas, rewarding with weavings of bright little pansy faces. Even Johnny-jump-ups fit charmingly beneath rosebushes.

You'll get a finished, neat look by edging your beds with low hedges. Clipped ones of dwarf box or lavender are traditional, but any low, dense plant will do. Slightly less rigid are santolina and lamb's-ear. Both are silverlings, which sets off any color rose, and the fuzziness of the lamb's-ear invites stroking, for a different textural look. If you find its flower stalks a bit gawky, plant the noon-flowering variety 'Silver Carpet.' Armerias go nicely with roses. They all have drumstick flowers borne on sturdy wiry stems, but because their foliage, particularly the dwarfs, is a dead ringer for a tussock of grass, plant them next to paved surfaces to avoid confusion and heartbreak with the lawn mowing.

Old roses, with their loose, shrubby form, are naturals for mixed plantings. Herbaceous perennials, coming and going all season, fit the bill wonderfully. What you want is not just a collection of plants but a real garden, where things blend and complement one another. Cushiony roses need the contrast of firm line, like the spikiness of crocosmias or species gladiolus. Stately delphiniums in that most elusive color in the garden—true blue—are a time-honored combination with roses. Lighten

Mix roses with compatible annual, biennial, and perennial flowers and with other shrubs and vines. They'll quickly look settled in and promising.

the garden with color and texture by including some nonrunning artemisias. 'Lambrook Silver' and 'Powis Castle' are two of the best. Lilies can be tucked in the smallest spaces, to tower mouth-wateringly over the garden. The clumping asters give a punch to late summer and fall. Indispensable is *Aster* x *frikartii*, whose lavender-blue daisies go on for months.

Don't forget to mix in some of the later-blooming *Clematis viticella* varieties with your climbers, especially if the roses are once-bloomers. Avoid a tangle by cutting them annually nearly to the ground.

Embellishing expanses of lawn with beds of roses and other flowering plants can actually reduce your maintenance chores.

A border of roses and other flowers along a driveway or walk adds instant appeal.

## Flowers that thrive with roses

### Perennials
*Alcea* (hollyhock)
*Armeria* (thrift)
*Artemisia* (mugwort)
*Campanula* (bellflower)
*Dianthus* (pinks)
*Geranium sanguineum* (cranesbill)
*Gypsophila* (dwarf baby's-breath)
*Helianthus* (sunflower)
*Lilium* (lily)
*Oenothera* (Missouri evening primrose)
*Primula* (primrose)
*Scabiosa* (dwarf scabious)
*Thymus* (dwarf thyme)
*Veronica* (speedwell)
*Viola* (violet)

### Annuals
*Borago* (borage)
*Consolida* (larkspur)
*Dianthus* (Chinese pinks)
*Eschscholzia* (California poppy)
*Iberis* (candytuft)
*Ipomoea tricolor* (morning glory)
*Linaria* (toadflax)
*Lobelia*
*Lobularia maritima* (sweet alyssum)
*Myosotis scorpiodes* (forget-me-not)
*Petunia* (petunia)
*Phlox* (phlox)
*Tropaeolum majus* (nasturtium)
*Reseda* (mignonette)
*Viola tricolor* (Johnny-jump-up)
*Verbena* (verbena)

# Choosing your rose

When you visit a garden center or nursery in spring or look through the colorful pages of mail-order catalogs in late winter, you're likely to become overwhelmed. So many roses in so many sizes and colors. How do you begin to narrow your choices to fit your garden space and gardening time?

## Select for site

First, you really should know where you're going to plant a rose (or roses—seldom will one do!). Once you have read the information on the many ways you can use roses in a landscape, take a good look at your landscape. Is there a slightly shady spot for an old-fashioned hybrid musk? Do you have space between the driveway and house for a hedge of one of the new shrub roses? An entry to the backyard that could be improved by the addition of an arbor? A hilly section you'd prefer not to mow, where a ground-cover rose would combine erosion-control with colorful flowers? Or simply a sunny plot of ground you want to turn into a true rose garden? Thinking of site first—before color, fragrance, or habit—will help you control your impulses.

## Look for performance clues

Roses that have stood the test of time, those that are growing well in local private and public rose gardens, award winners that have been tested across a wide range of climatic and soil conditions—all of these clues can help to ensure your success.

Old-garden or heritage roses, many raised in gardens for centuries, may bloom only once, in spring, just as rhododendrons and azaleas do. Some may repeat bloom. The fact that they have been cultivated for so long gives you a clue to their vigor and disease resistance. You have to decide whether one glorious show

**One of the new shrub roses that almost take care of themselves, 'Carefree Wonder' won an All-America Rose Selections award in 1992. Whether grown in the ground or in containers (inset), it will cover itself with dark pink/white reverse blooms all season.**

of blooms coupled with ease of care warrants giving them a place in your garden alongside other spring-blooming shrubs.

If you want a longer flower show, and you're partial to modern hybrids, look first for those that have won awards for garden performance. Roses that receive an All-America Rose Selections (AARS) award, for example, have undergone stringent two-year trials in test gardens across the country. Each year, two or more roses qualify for an award (1990 was an exception, when only one rose, the floribunda 'Pleasure,' received the accolade).

Through the American Rose Society, rosarians take part in a survey of roses that perform well (or not so well) for them. Based on a point system that indicates better-than-average disease resistance as well as exceptional form, color, fragrance (if any), and abundance of blooms, the roses are rated in the Society's annual handbook. Roses rated 8 and above could readily find a place in your garden.

The Society's Award of Excellence recognizes outstanding miniatures, some of which also garner AARS awards.

## Buying your rose

Most roses are sold bare-root; some are sold in containers. Bare-root roses are offered in early spring and are sold in a dormant state (no green leaves). Their roots are usually wrapped in a protective covering of moss and then packaged in a plastic wrap or cardboard box, which shows the name, type, and color of the rose, and often gives planting directions.

Roots should be numerous, long and firm, and generally unbroken. Canes should be green or reddish, not gray, shriveled, or dried out. No. 1 grade roses, the best you can buy, should have at least three plump canes, each approximately ⅜ inch in diameter.

With container roses, you have the advantages of being able to plant almost any time from spring through fall and to get a head start on gardening because the roses will be leafed out and growing actively. The disadvantages are higher cost and fewer varieties from which to choose.

# roses in your landscape

Roses are expected to provide visual and other delights in the garden. They also yield a harvest rich in colors, smells, textures, and forms that can be a source of indoor pleasures.

Think of rose gardening as a lifestyle, one in which you will regularly invest time and energy in a sort of savings account from which you can draw all kinds of benefits as they are needed in your home. Potted miniature roses have become almost commonplace in the last quarter of the 20th century, something to be enjoyed momentarily, brought from a grower's range, or grown in a sunny window or under fluorescent tubes.

Cut roses are among life's nicer moments, one bud or a whole bouquet fresh from the garden. They also can be dried, simply tied by the bunch, and hung, later to be enjoyed this way or worked into an arrangement or dried rosebud topiary.

There is also the tradition of enjoying roses for their fragrance. Rose water may provide the first written history of humankind's seduction by the rose. Rose scents vary, from light to heavy, and they are never better than when fresh. If potpourri smells stale or unfresh, add it to your compost pile and enjoy making a new batch.

Another aspect of the rosarian's life at home is the need for a place to store rose books, catalogs, and periodicals. It is also beneficial to have a garden work center where gardening activities can be accomplished at a counter of the appropriate height.

Besides bringing roses into your home, there is also the obvious joy in having them grow well in various roles outdoors, each bringing to the garden room its unique color, appearance, and scent. Remember, roses are far more than two-dimensional in the garden; they are multifunctional.

**Roses can enhance a landscape in many ways—as foundation plantings, as borders along walks or drives, massed against fences or walls, and clambering over arbors and trellises, to name just a few.**

# Roses on arbors say welcome

Can anything evoke the lushness of an old-fashioned country garden like an arbor overflowing with roses? Wherever it's set—on a front walk, at the entrance to an herb, vegetable, or rose garden, over a path leading from front to rear yard—an arbor is a nearly irresistible place to plant roses. It also reminds visitors to relax, to set aside momentarily the stresses and cares of the day. Placed at the end of a path with a bench beneath, it becomes a secret haven for dreaming.

## The structure of arbors

An arbor not only provides a place to grow and enjoy roses with upward mobility, it also gives the garden a pleasant appearance during the times of year when the plants are dormant.

An arbor is basically a simple latticework structure in the shape of an inverted U or V, of sufficient width and height to pass through comfortably. It can be constructed of wood, metal, plastic, or wire; finished wood painted white or a shade of green is traditional. Rough-hewn logs and twigs can be picturesque—and inexpensive. Bamboo tied with twine or nylon cord in the Japanese manner is another inexpensive option.

An arbor doesn't have to be constructed; it can be formed naturally by trees or tall shrubs that arch over, forming a leafy shelter beneath. It's possible to train one or two vigorous roses and other climbing, vining plants on this living structure for a true bower of roses. Supports and lattice can be used in tandem with the living arch for added strength.

Climbers and ramblers need very little encouragement to cover an arbor. Strongly upright growers, they will naturally arch over from the weight of their canes. All you have to do is plant them next to the frame and guide the canes as they grow so that they rest on and intertwine with the overhead trellising. Traditionally, a strong climber is planted on one side of the arbor and a pillar-type rose is set on the opposite side, but there are no hard-and-fast rules.

**An inviting spot to linger, this arbor was created with ginkgo trees. Thousands of tiny white blossoms of *Rosa soulieana*, a Chinese species, climb up the sides and over the canopy.**

# Roses on arbors say welcome

This arbor as pergola boasts an open structure of posts and overhead twigs for climbing roses along a walk at the Old Westbury Gardens, Old Westbury, New York.

Unlike arbors, which need not lead anywhere, pergolas should lead someplace, even if it is only to a bench. A pergola "ought to lead distinctly from some clear beginning," wrote Gertrude Jekyll in 1902 in her book on roses, "to some definite end. . .otherwise it merely looks silly." It should be level and straight and situated so that it is seen from all sides—a design that gives the roses plenty of air, space, and light.

Over the years, garden design has become looser and, therefore, more natural looking. A straight pergola is no longer de rigeur. Curved walkways are far more pleasant to amble along and even more pleasing with a fragrant, flowering cover. If there's a change in level, however, you should follow the old style: Don't angle the connecting beams up or down. Better to interrupt the even flow of the pergola by adding steps (as many as necessary) and raising the posts at the steps to the length of the higher ground or, leaving the steps uncovered, beginning a new pergola at the top of the rise.

If you select roses that bloom only once in spring—'Excelsa,' 'Lady Banks,' 'Paul's Himalayan Musk Rambler,' or 'White Cherokee Climbing,' for example—you also may want to plant a flowering vine, such as clematis, that will provide blooms for the rest of the warm season.

## Pergolas

Like a series of arbors, a pergola consists of pairs of uprights spaced a few or several feet apart and connected with beams, the overhead of lattice or poles joined together. The result is a tunnel-like structure sturdy enough to support the more vigorous climbers and ramblers. Spring- and fall-blooming 'Cecile Brunner Climbing' and 'Mermaid' with its 20- to 30-foot canes—any of the old garden ramblers, in fact—are ideal choices for the strong pergola whether rustic or formal.

A pergola is the perfect spot for repeat-blooming and fragrant roses, as well as vines such as wisteria, clematis, honeysuckle, and passionflower.

## Arbors as focal points

Set at some distance from the house, an arbor not only can divide one area from another but also provide a focal point in the garden. Catching sight of it from windows and through doorways is a delightful experience, recalling halcyon moments and bygone or future hopefulness.

In its own space in the garden, an arbor or pergola becomes an outdoor room, with latticed walls and a "ceiling" open to the elements but strong enough to support climbing roses.

A simple wood arch at the top of steps leads from a garden-bordered walk to the front entry of a clapboard house. It speaks of intimacy and relaxation with its cover of roses.

# Roses on fences

Roses clambering over a fence look as pleasingly romantic and old-fashioned as those scaling a trellis or an arbor. Weathered split rails, crisp white wrought iron, jaunty pickets, expanses of ubiquitous chain link—all become better dressed with the addition of one or two rosebushes. Roses on fences combine beautifully with vining plants, such as clematis, honeysuckle, and bittersweet, to create a flower garden in a very narrow space, because their canes are trained up-and-along rather than out.

With at least 3 feet of width, a border garden along a fence can accommodate perennials as well as roses to give you a cottage-garden look. Cottage-type perennials that complement roses include delphiniums, hollyhocks, artemisia ('Silver Queen' or the low-growing, more contained 'Silver Mound,' and the newer, medium-size, lacy and fragrant 'Powis Castle'), peonies, fall-blooming asters, and Japanese anemones.

Climbing and rambling roses are not the only types you can use on a fence. Any rose that produces long canes will work, even if it isn't known as a climber. The ground-cover rose 'Alba Meidiland,' with its clusters of small, very double white blooms, shoots out canes as long as 6 feet. Inappropriate on the chunky frame of a split rail, it is

exquisite meandering along a delicate black wrought-iron fence or peeking through unfinished, naturally weathered wood or rustic twig pickets.

Because a rose doesn't climb the way a clematis does (with tendrils or twining stems), training a rose along a fence requires tying the canes to the fence, using ordinary string or plant ties. For a profusion of flowers, tie the canes in an arched or horizontal position. That way every bud will produce a flowering branch. As the canes grow, you can twine them around rails or pickets or along the top of a fence without tying. The sharp thorns on some, notably the old garden roses, will help the canes "grab" the support, but don't rely solely on them.

**A rustic fence affords the perfect setting for the informal plantings of the cottage garden opposite.**

**With its colorful and ever-changing blossoms, 'Joseph's Coat,' right, can be trained against a wall or fence in mild climates.**

# Roses on slopes

If you have sloping or hilly ground, eliminate grass that has to be mowed and plant ground-cover shrubs and perennials. Terraced or not, the slope becomes a focal point instead of an eroding eyesore. Your aim, in addition to beautifying a piece of awkward land, is to prevent further erosion.

Ground-cover roses, especially the snowbank white 'Alba Meidiland,' can cover bare soil in less than a season. Planted 4 feet apart, 'Alba' grows only 2 to 3 feet high but produces canes from 5 to 6 feet long with masses of bloom in early summer and repeat-bloom until frost.

Climbing and rambling roses, unsupported, will arch over and cover a large space as well. They can become very unkempt, however, if you don't prune them annually and guide their canes into some semblance of order. Instead of allowing them to sprawl, you can fashion low (one-rail) supports on which to train them. In effect, you "terrace" the slope without building actual levels.

## Terracing a slope

If a slope is quite steep (more than 45 degrees), you may need to terrace it before planting to prevent soil erosion and drainage problems. The art of terracing dates back centuries to Italian and French gardens and to the ancient Incas in what is now Peru. Formal or informal, depending more on the kinds of plants incorporated than on the type of material used to build up the beds, terracing is the solution for providing garden space where you thought there was none.

Think of each level of a terrace as a modified raised bed, with each level or step no more than 3 to 4 feet wide and as long as your slope. Like a raised bed, each step can be anywhere from 1 to 4 feet deep. The depth depends on the steepness of the slope and the number of terraces you want to build.

**Sweeping in a semicircular arc, this rose garden terraced with stones showcases more than 100 varieties of hybrid teas.**

# Roses on slopes

**Backed by tall roses, the terraced garden opposite is hidden from view of the house and becomes a delightful surprise, an outdoor room to discover on leisure walks.**

Fieldstones, brick-in-cement, railroad ties, and rot-resistant lumber can be used to frame the steps and contain the soil. While you're building the terraces, but before planting, install drip irrigation lines to make watering the garden easy and efficient.

During the building phase, modify the soil and provide shelter for specialty plants—wildflowers, for example, if you're planting a combination garden. Tuck pockets of soil into the retaining walls as you build so you will have a place for spreading or vining plants that will help camouflage the supporting structure of the garden.

To make each level easily accessible, consider putting in steps made of the same material as the retaining wall, or use the material for the risers and closely clipped grass for the steps. The latter is very effective with wide terraces.

To lessen a steep slope and help solve drainage problems, this garden's contoured plant beds are bordered by Sonoma moss stone and high desert flagstone.

## Garden style

The plants you use will reflect the style of your terraced garden.
• Combining evergreen shrubs, roses, and perennials creates a country-style garden.
• A planting of roses-only presents a traditional, formal one.
• Alternating sodded levels and planted levels offers a very European, as well as a more formal, look. Hybrid teas are stunning planted in this manner.

• Wildflowers with ground-cover roses that spill over the containing walls give a natural, unplanned look.
• An edging around each terrace of boxwood or other low-growing evergreen shrub provides winter interest and form to what might otherwise be barren-looking in the off-seasons.

# Roses for small spaces

**Small can be grand! This townhouse yard is bursting with color from dozens of roses.**

You don't need large amounts of space to grow beautiful and healthy roses. Although hybrid teas and heritage roses can require 5 feet or more around each bush, floribundas and miniatures can fill a smaller space and provide much satisfaction and lovely color for the ardent rose lover.

If you have your heart set on hybrid teas but don't have much room, you can still plant roses. Just remember to be extra-conscientious about pruning the bushes for an open center and about keeping an eagle-eye out for pests and diseases. A debris-free garden is most important when space is limited.

# Planning your space

Small yards can yield good-size gardens if you keep lawn areas to a minimum. Make walkways narrow and sodded: grass paths, just wide enough to run a lawn mower along and show off roses and other plants to flattering advantage. Because most roses require full sun, limit the number and mature size of the trees you plant —or retain, if you're renovating a landscape.

Rambunctious, very vigorous roses are difficult to maintain in small yards. Check the ultimate spread of the roses you want to plant. You can prune most roses quite heavily to keep them in a more confined space, but are you prepared for the extra care? How much easier to select plants that do not require that effort.

Height is also a consideration, unless you're growing a climber. Roses that naturally grow 6 or 7 feet may dwarf your space if they're set anywhere but at the edge of your property or with other equally tall shrubs.

## Designing with roses

When planning for roses in a small space, consider the following:
• Specimen plants. Use one bush as a focal point in your yard. Your best choice is a heritage rose such as a perpetual or repeat-flowering bourbon ('Louise Odier' or 'Souvenir de la Malmaison') or one of the gallicas (*Rosa gallica officinalis* 'Belle de Crecy').
• Perimeter plants. Add a hedge of floribundas ('Betty Prior' or 'Europeana'), landscape roses ('Bonica' or 'Sevillana'), or hybrid musks ('Felicia' or 'Ballerina') around your property line.
• Border plants. Edging a driveway or walk, miniatures ('Rainbow's End,' 'Rise 'n' Shine,' and 'Starina') are delightful. Because most miniatures are grown on their own roots, they are less likely to be irreparably damaged by the extra weight

of snow piled along the edge of a wide drive or walkway. If the weight "prunes" them to the ground, they'll resprout from their roots in spring.
• Combinations of plants. Incorporate one or more bushes in a perennial border. Miniatures make excellent edgings for a border; floribundas ('French Lace,' 'Europeana,' 'Sweet Inspiration') enhance the middle, especially mixed with gray- or dark-green-leaved perennials.
• Spot plants. Use bushes to face-down taller, leggier shrubs. Landscape and floribunda roses do well in this situation; so do polyanthas ('The Fairy') and some of the smaller David Austin roses ('Mary Rose,' 'Wife of Bath,' 'English Garden').
• Arbor plants. Train a rose up and over a support. In addition to climbers, bourbons 'Honorine de Brabant' and 'Madame Isaac Pereire' adapt well to arbors and walls.

**Roses in this garden are staked for the straight stems required in an exhibition rose. The only space not devoted to roses is occupied by lawn-mower-wide grass paths.**

# Roses for small spaces

It is a matter of public record that Phillip J. Bondi, rose gardener extraordinaire, grows big roses that win blue ribbons for their perfection. Perhaps less known is how simply it is done in a very small garden around the Bondi home in western Pennsylvania. Except for a paved walk and narrow paths of lawn, every inch of yard—front, side, and back—is devoted to the cultivation of large-flowered hybrid roses. The retired barber's passion for roses is long-standing; Bondi has been a consistent winner in amateur rose competitions for at least 40 years. There have lately been a spate of "Queen of Shows" and the accompanying silver trophies. Inside the narrow townhouse, a compelling love of the rose is everywhere apparent in pictures, paintings, wallpaper, slipcover fabrics, china and silver patterns, books, and garden catalogs.

**Phillip J. Bondi freely shares rose lore and culture. Velvety red 'Olympiad' is a Bondi favorite.**

## Winter roses bloom under lights

Downstairs, most of a half-basement room is given over to the needs of a rosarian who loves his hobby and wouldn't dream of completely closing up shop because of inclement weather or season. In one corner, 40-watt fluorescent tubes in ordinary commercial reflectors ("shop lights") are suspended about 6 inches above the tops of the roses, which grow and bloom all winter. Bondi tests several new, as yet unnamed roses, each year and has made it a practice to grow these in 14-inch pots so he can observe them outdoors in summer sun and indoors in winter fluorescent light for 16 hours daily. Another corner houses a desk and writing table where Bondi can dream over catalogs and make out orders and cultivar name tags. The wall behind is covered with ribbons and newspaper clippings attesting to the rosarian's long-running success at the show table.

## Hilling up saves bushes

A double door facing south opens directly into the backyard filled with roses that in early fall are taller than their keeper. Here, too, are receptacles for collecting what the roses themselves cast off, such as spent petals and normally yellowed leaves that can be safely composted and wood prunings and diseased leaves that must be destroyed. A bin filled with the porous earth awaits a hard freeze, usually by Thanksgiving in this area, when it will be used to hill up the bushes.

Before hilling up, Bondi arbitrarily cuts all stems back to 2 feet. The mostly leafless branches remaining are drawn together and tied so that a plasticized wire-mesh collar 12 inches high by 18 inches in diameter (which he has individually stitched together for this purpose) can be conveniently dropped around each bush, then filled with the porous earth to a depth of 1 foot.

Come spring, at about the time the forsythia is blooming in his neighbors' gardens, Bondi removes the collars and returns the earthy hilling-up material to its bin in the backyard. Each bush in turn is untied, then pruned, first to get rid of any wood killed by winter, and second to favor the development of a shapely plant, open at the center and without crossing branches. When all of the bushes have been uncovered and pruned, fresh mulch of bark chips or cocoa bean hulls is applied evenly over the beds to a depth of 2 inches.

## Secrets of success

Besides a sloping, well-drained site that is airy and mostly sunny, without any infringing tall trees or greedy-rooted shrubs, the Bondi rose beds are enriched at planting time with mushroom compost. The consistent use of organic mulch also serves to increase the soil's desirable tilth. Fertilizing is done every two weeks mid-spring through summer using gallon-size plastic jugs and alternating between fish emulsion (three tablespoons per jug of water) and chemical granules with NPK of 23-21-17 (one tablespoon per jug of water). Insects such as aphids and spider mites are doused with rose spray as indicated, but not on a rigid schedule. Any sign of powdery mildew or black spot is immediately treated with a fungicide; the occasional diseased leaflet is removed and destroyed, never left on the ground or added to the compost pile.

## Growing roses for show

A rose destined for the show table must appear in all its perfection at the top of a perfectly straight 24-inch stem. Bondi is apparently an eternal optimist for on the day of our visit every blossom and bud throughout the garden stood erect, each tied precisely to its own cane by figure-8 loops of green jute cord. Besides straightness, staking the thorny stems individually helps prevent their blowing against each other, which can snag holes in otherwise faultless petals. As the dates for a given show draw near, Bondi assesses which buds show the most promise for being at their peak the moment of meeting the judges' eyes, then for a time most of his attention will be devoted to these select few, including the placement of makeshift umbrellas and individual plastic "bonnets" to variously shield from potentially damaging rain, hail, and sun, or to increase heat and humidity in order to hurry the blossoming process.

A visit with Bondi recalls an observation made by Liberty Hyde Bailey in his 1928 book *The Garden Lover*: "He admires his plants alone when nobody is looking, and loves to be with them for companionship in all odd hours. . .When not in bloom they are his, at morning, noon and night. With discernment and discrimination he talks about them now and then with sympathetic friends."

Below, individual blossom stems of 'Tiffany' are tied to bamboo canes with a figure-8 of green jute cord.

Bondi has devised a plastic bonnet, above, to cosset a possible show winner of 'Color Magic.'

# Roses, an accent for special places

Just as cut roses breathe life and beauty into every room in a house, as bushes outdoors they can provide striking accents in the yard. Gone are the days when gardeners automatically set roses in a garden of their own, partly because roses seem less work-intensive if they are planted with other flowers and shrubs. For gardeners with little time, caring for one beautiful specimen rather than a number of less-than-ideal bushes may be the solution to satisfying their rose-gardening urge. Used as an accent or focal point, one large rose can be impressive; three or more miniature roses, exquisite.

## Accent roses

Anyone who has grown a rose knows, however, that one is never enough, that no matter what area is to be landscaped, the design can always be improved with a few rose-bushes.

• Miniatures planted 12 inches apart will edge a driveway, walk, or patio with low mounds of color.

**Wrapped around a bench, the dense hybrid musk shrub rose 'Belinda' creates a quiet corner for contemplation or simply soaking up the view.**

• Grown as standards, miniatures can anchor the corners of an herb garden or provide a focal point in the center.

• Old garden roses, planted singly in a corner of the yard or in front of dark green evergreen shrubs or trees, are stunning early summer masses of bloom. "Any trees of dark or dusky foliage serve well as rose backgrounds, whether of the greyish tone of the common juniper or the richer greens of Thuya or Cypress, Yew or Holly," said Gertrude Jekyll almost a century ago, and her observation has stood the test of time.

• Roses with fragrance are extra special. The old garden roses such as damask and moss, new hybrids like David Austin's Eng-

**Many antique and shrub roses are hardier than their modern counterparts. 'The Fairy,' 'Iceberg,' 'Queen Elizabeth,' 'Betty Prior,' and 'Europeana' flourish in the high desert garden opposite.**

lish roses, hybrid teas such as 'Double Delight' and 'Mister Lincoln'—all should be planted where you can enjoy their scents in the garden as well as cut for bouquets. That means by an entry, below a window that's often open, or near a patio or deck.

• Rugosas, with their "awesome" thorns, will create an impenetrable hedge in one or two seasons if they are planted 3 feet apart.

• Because of the thorns, one or two rugosas will offer appreciable security under a first-floor window and, unlike the ubiquitous barberry, display lovely flowers at the same time.

• Rugosas are sturdy enough to flourish at the seaside, where sand, wind, and salt-spray make rose-growing difficult.

• Shade-tolerant roses (there aren't many) can brighten yards with mature landscaping: Most hybrid musks and rugosas, the bourbon 'Honorine de Brabant,' the albas, and ramblers do quite well in light shade.

# Roses in a natural setting

The "back forty" may have shrunk to a 75 x 100-foot plot, but that doesn't mean natural or country-style and "wild" plantings have to disappear, even where roses are concerned. Here is where the species roses, as well as climbers and ramblers, modern shrub and floribunda roses, especially those with single blooms, come into their own. Hybrid teas are out of place in a natural setting.

## Species roses

Species roses are very hardy and pest and disease resistant. They provide marvelous cover and food for birds and other wildlife. Their single blooms in shades of white, red, rosy pink, coppery red, and yellow appear in late spring, followed by large, colorful hips in late summer.

Plant them in a corner where their sometimes rampant growth can proceed unhindered. To keep them scaled down somewhat, prune out old canes and be on the alert for layering—canes that root where they come in contact with the ground.

Among the species and their hybrids are: Sweetbriar rose, *Rosa rubiginosa* (*R. eglanteria*), with very fragrant foliage; 'Austrian Copper' (*R. foetida* 'Bicolor'), a rose that predates the 15th century and produces medium-size, copper-red blooms with yellow reverses; newer rugosas such as red 'Linda Campbell' and yellow 'Topaz Jewel' (stems of the latter are covered with very sharp thorns); an older rugosa, pink 'Frau Dagmar Hastrup,' which is compact enough for small gardens; and yellow 'Father Hugo's Rose' (*R. hugonis*), a medium-size shrub introduced in 1899 and still much loved.

## Modern roses

Shrub and landscape roses perform without intense care, which makes them excellent candidates for "naturalizing." Plant them on the edges of fields, as a cover for old tree stumps, and in the foreground of wooded areas.

Modern shrub roses owe much of their initial development to the German company Kordes and their further popularity to the French House of Meilland. Some of the best are: 'Fruhlingsmorgen,' a single pink; 'Carefree Wonder,' a double pink with white reverse; 'Alba Meidiland,' a white ground-cover rose; 'Betty Prior,' a dark pink floribunda; and 'The Fairy,' a pink polyantha often grown as a hedge but well suited to a wild setting.

**Small and large roses alike have a place in naturalistic landscaping. It is possible even to combine numerous wild roses so that they alone make a natural garden.**

**Roses, except the rigidly upright large-flowered hybrids, fit easily into mixed naturalistic beds bursting with native as well as exotic plantings.**

# Roses in containers

Better than setting roses around a patio is planting them in containers on a patio, deck, or terrace. Miniature roses may come to mind first, and they are excellent for pots, but floribundas, hybrid teas, and some of the Meidiland roses also can be grown in containers. Standards, whether miniature or full size, have traditionally been raised in pots.

Roses in containers offer many advantages for gardeners.
• They can be moved around to get as much sun as possible or to decorate an area for a special occasion.
• Weeds aren't a problem, especially if you mulch the soil surface or plant low-growing or trailing plants around the perimeter of the pot. (It helps to start with a clean, weed-free potting mix.)
• No matter what your garden soil is like, container soil can be specially mixed, in smaller quantities, for perfect drainage. Use a blend of one part pasteurized or packaged soil, one part peat moss or other organic matter, and one part sand or coarse horticultural vermiculite.

For containers on a terrace or rooftop, a ready-made soil-less mix is best because it's lightweight. (Balconies often have a 50-pound-per-square-foot maximum for container gardens.)
• With the new container drip-irrigation systems, watering is not time-consuming, and the systems get the water to the roots without wetting foliage. You can also feed at the same time. Alternatively, add a polymer (available at garden centers) to your soil mix. Polymers expand to hold many times their weight in water and release it as the soil dries.
• Winter protection for container-grown roses is simply a matter of moving the pots into a sheltered, frost-free spot.

## Consider the containers

Containers for roses can be redwood tubs, glazed pottery, porous terra-cotta, or plastic. Unglazed clay pots aren't recommended for miniatures because air can get through the pot walls and dry out feeder roots too quickly.

**Large-flowered hybrid bush roses and climbers grow in a New York City rooftop garden, opposite. The metal-reinforced wood containers are automatically watered.**

Containers must have holes in the bottom or lower sides for adequate drainage. Porous containers should be soaked in water for 30 minutes before being planted so they don't absorb moisture from the soil.

Miniatures grow well in pots 6 inches in diameter and 8 inches deep. For a lush effect the first season, group three pots in a larger tub; when the plants get too large ('Child's Play,' for instance, grows to 2 feet tall and wide), unearth the pots and move them to another setting on their own.

Full-size roses require a tub at least 18 inches in diameter and 14 inches deep.

When you plant, set the rose in the container so that the root ball is lightly covered with fresh soil.

**A collection of miniature roses in ordinary unglazed clay pots looks beautiful but requires special watering care during hot, dry weather to keep the roots nicely moist.**

# Climbing roses

What wonderful things you can do with roses that shoot out long canes! That's basically what differentiates climbers and ramblers from bush roses, although some bush roses, notably 'Reine des Violettes,' also have a tendency to vigorous, upright growth and can be used as climbers.

## Into the trees

You can amaze your neighbors and make them just a bit envious when you train a climbing or rambling rose up into the branches of a tree or over and through a shrub. The technique is a great way to disguise a dead tree, but living trees or shrubs (holly, yew, rhododendron, and willow, for example) also benefit.

Low-branched trees and tall shrubs provide ready support for the canes; with other trees, you may have to assist the canes. For the latter reason, it's a good idea, if you can, to plant the rose on the windward side of the tree, although at a good distance from the trunk. The wind will actually help the rose into the branches as it shoots up in search of sun. New growth will come from the older wood high up instead of near the ground. If a particular cane isn't going where you want it to, it's fairly easy to redirect it with a long pole.

'Paul's Himalayan Musk Rambler' and *Rosa multiflora* readily climb into trees; the older varieties have more pronounced thorns (those on 'Paul's Himalayan Musk Rambler' are actually hook shaped) that help them grab at a support. Other climbers for tree-training include 'Improved Blaze,' 'Golden Showers Climbing,' 'Lady Banks,' and 'Mermaid.'

## Up a house wall

"No plant is more helpful and accommodating in. . .providing living curtains of flowery drapery for putting over dull. . .places," wrote Gertrude Jekyll about climbers. Even if your house walls aren't exactly dull, they can take on the look of a rose-covered cottage with one or more climbing roses mounting a trellis very firmly anchored in the ground next to the house. Because climbers possess an inherent upward thrust, they'll also do their covering act on hooks or mounts placed strategically across and up a wall.

For easier maintenance with clapboard houses that will need painting, train the roses on a trellis that can be swung away from the wall. Brick, stucco, and cedar shake houses do not present that problem.

When planting a rose to climb the wall, set it far enough away that it will not be directly under an eave; otherwise, it will never receive the proper amount of moisture.

If you have a roofed front porch, you can plant a climber below each or every other

**A rustic post-and-beam design provides support for a climbing rose that helps disguise the utilitarian aspect of a rear entry, left.**

**Also called 'Beauty of Glazenwood,' the very fragrant amber-yellow blooms of 'Fortune's Double Yellow' tumble over a wall, opposite.**

# Climbing roses

pillar and within two to three years, the roses will have clambered up and begun to ramble along the roof. This technique gives the best effect if you remember to prune out old canes so that new growth comes from the base and keeps the bush looking full and lush.

Climbers for covering walls include 'Cecile Brunner Climbing,' 'Excelsa,' 'Joseph's Coat,' 'Mermaid,' and 'Pinata.'

## On a pillar

Many climbing roses with somewhat shorter canes are well suited to being planted by freestanding pillars or lampposts. Because of their strong upright tendencies, pillar roses—'Aloha Climbing,' 'Don Juan Climbing,' 'Joseph's Coat Climbing,' 'Pinata'—often don't need an actual support; they will grow basically upright to 6 feet or more on their own.

Pillar roses create eye-catching statements at the corners of a flower or herb garden. They also do well on each side of an arbor, with taller, more vigorous climbers trained up and over the top arch.

## Over the ground

You can allow climbers to roam free over slopes, low walls, stumps, or anything unsightly or simply too bare. Keep the bush in bounds by pruning back new growth and cutting out older canes occasionally.

When landscaping with roses in this manner, you need to bear in mind that the roses won't provide attractive cover in winter because they aren't evergreen. They will, however, offer some protection and bright rose hips as food for winter birds and other wildlife—not a bad trade-off.

Alternatively, plant your climbers with one of the evergreen ground covers, though not ivy, which has a tendency to overwhelm anything in its path.

**A climbing rose grows freely among the branches of a tree at the end of a sunny double border. A focal point in its own right, it marks the beginning of a shady woodland garden.**

49

# Roses to grace the garden

Human interpretations of the rose as Queen of the Flowers notwithstanding, it is a plant that gets on well in every circumstance that can be imagined: city, suburb, or country. Formal, informal, or nearly wild. At the curb, on a rooftop, spilling over a balcony, or hiding the compost. Potted or in the ground, indoors, outdoors, or in-between.

The rose has a grace that by its very presence makes us glad. It comes as no surprise then that a hedge of roses can be at home in a kitchen garden, in a farmer's truck patch, in formalized beds of civic plantings, or in English borders and cottage gardens. Or how about a big earthen pot of one or more roses at the place where two paths cross in a garden? Such a planting might even include a tree-form standard rose and a small collection of micro-miniatures arranged around it at the base.

## Compatible companions

Because roses need a half day or more of direct sun, along with well-drained soil and plenty of water during droughts, they also do well accompanied by a host of other favorite flowers, including delphiniums, hollyhocks, foxgloves, carnations and other dianthus, lavenders of all kinds, sages culinary and otherwise, lilies, daylilies, peonies, veronicas, penstemons, clematis, jasmine, honeysuckle—the list has no end.

It does pay always to keep rose bedmates at sufficient distance to allow air to circulate freely. If another plant grows unexpectedly rank and starts to shade out a rose, don't hesitate to prune back the invader. A rosebush in a kitchen garden is always vulnerable to hostile takeover by a galloping squashvine unless you assert the rose's air and sun rights.

**Roses fit into all kinds of gardens—formal, informal, or casual, for show or for work. Here they are a delight with towering sunflowers and rows of sweet corn.**

# bringing roses inside your home

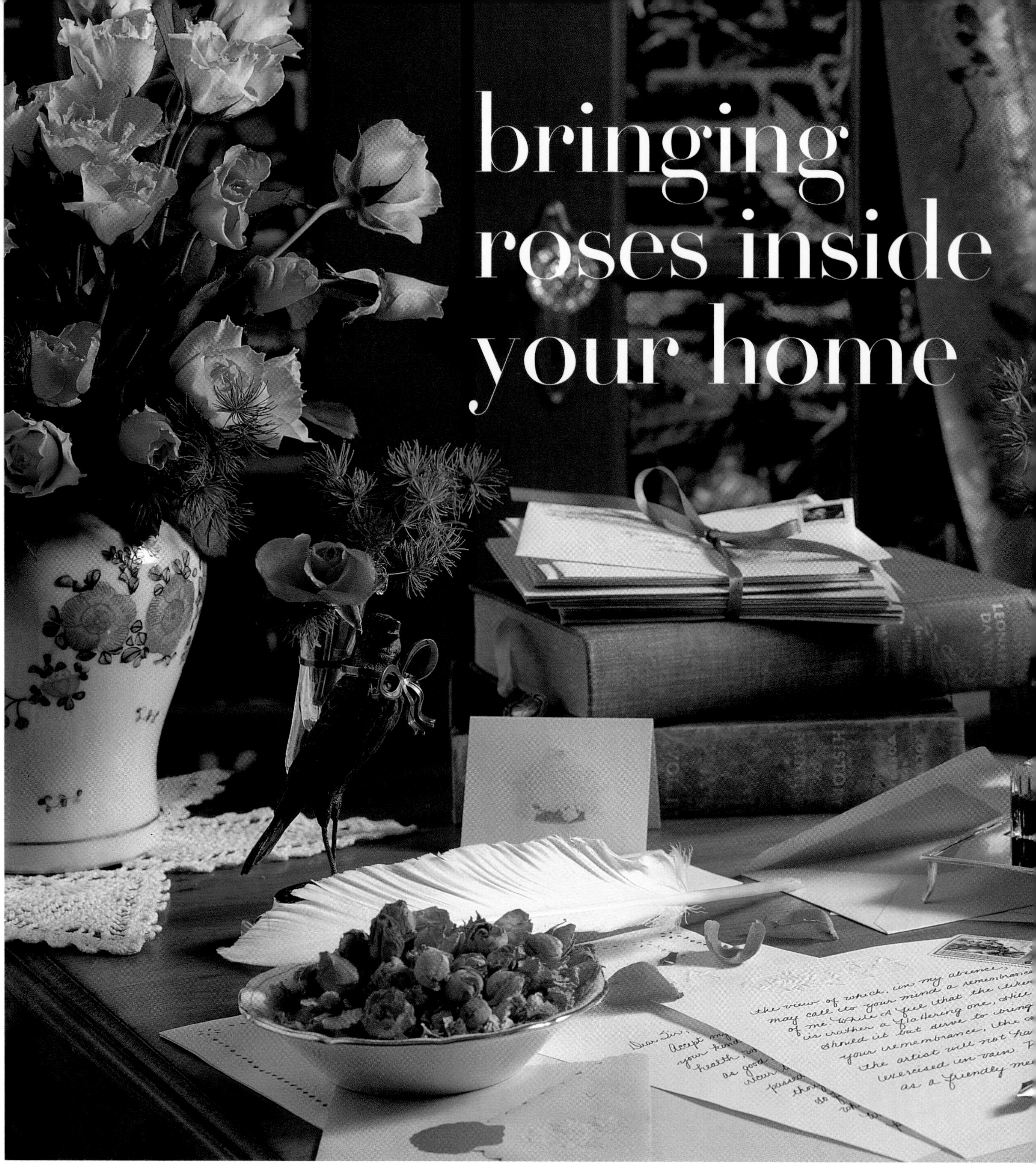

Throughout the ages the glory of roses has been enjoyed in sumptuous bouquets and everlasting arrangements, in sachets and scents, and even in delectable sweet treats to eat!

The beauty, fragrance, and wonder of roses have been enjoyed for centuries. It is believed they were the first plants cultivated for pleasure. From the dawn of Western civilization, the rose was considered the queen of flowers. Records from Mesopotamia note the use of rose oil. The rose was sacred to Aphrodite, and Greek poets extolled the beauty of roses. Wealthy Romans bathed in rose water. In fact, roses were so associated with excesses of the Roman Empire that early Christians refused to allow them in their churches. In 15th-century England, roses were so valued by the nobility that the white rose became the emblem of the House of York and the red rose of the House of Lancaster in the War of the Roses.

Roses also have served as nourishment for the body and soul. Fossil evidence confirms the presence of roses on earth long before the evolution of Homo sapiens—cave dwellers probably included the flower in their diet. Roman legionnaires carried them in their baggage for a variety of medicinal purposes, thus spreading roses throughout Europe. Pliny lists 32 remedies made of rose petals and leaves. Later, medieval gardens included many roses for use as food, as medicine, and as an ingredient for making rosary beads.

Roses have always been prized for their enchanting fragrance. Rose petals are the source for attar of roses, the fragrant essential oil that is one of the most valuable of the volatile oils for making perfume.

Roses are cherished today as much for their beauty in the home as in the garden. They have a presence all their own in a vase in the living room. And they can live on indefinitely in dried bouquets, wreaths, potpourri, and many other everlasting keepsakes you can make for yourself and for gifts.

The beauty, color, and fragrance of roses can be enjoyed indoors, as well as outdoors in the garden.

# Roses to have and hold

The joy of roses doesn't end in the garden. It's wonderful to enjoy the blooms in your living room or to place an arrangement on the dining table for any meal. A vase of freshly cut blossoms makes the whole room come alive with their delicate, velvety beauty, and the fragrance that can be nearly intoxicating or merely uplifting.

When cutting roses for your home or to share with neighbors, choose blooms from well-established plants. First-year bushes should be allowed to grow and produce blooms, so it's best not to be tempted to harvest their flowers, at least not on long stems.

If bouquets of roses are an everyday amenity, it will help to use a stem stripper, a unique tool for efficiently removing thorns and leaves from rose stems. Just be sure that you keep any part of the stem from which a leaf or thorn has been removed under the water line in the vase. If you don't, air will enter and rapidly dry out the blossoms and cause premature wilting.

Floral preservatives will prolong the freshness of the flowers. They contain three basic ingredients: an antiseptic to discourage microorganisms that could clog stems and prevent their intake of water; a substance that promotes the uptake of water through the stems; and a carbohydrate such as sugar for nutrition. The old practice of putting an aspirin in the vase discourages bacteria from proliferating by acidifying the water.

**Large-flowered hybrid roses, daisies, and other garden flowers bring the beauty of nature indoors.**

An interesting, fairly scientific experiment was conducted at a floral exposition near San Diego, where cut roses of the same variety and source were tried in a number of preservatives, both folk and over-the-counter preparations. The best results were from a can of clear carbonated beverage sweetened with sugar to approximately one quart of clear water. (A cola sweetened with sugar might work as well for prolonging flower life, but dark coloring would travel by osmosis into the petals, at best giving them a macabre appearance.)

**Cutting roses for bouquets is one of the joys of growing them.**

# Gather ye rosebuds

Even when the last rose of summer has faded, you can celebrate the beauty of the queen of flowers with a dried rosebud wreath or trinket box.

The wreath pictured below is made by gluing dried rosebuds, tips up, over the entire surface of a straw- or moss-covered wreath form. Start in the center of the wreath form, and cover the sides of the form as well. Place the buds as close together as possible. When the glue is completely dry, trim the wreath with a satin bow.

For the trinket box, stain and varnish a box. Next, glue dried rosebuds to the lid, starting in the center and working out toward the edges. Glue the buds as close together as possible. When the glue is dry, trim the edge of the box with lace or gold braid.

# Roses as keepsakes and gifts

cover and let them continue to dry. Don't leave the flowers too long in the gel or they will fade and fall apart.

When flowers are ready to be removed, slowly pour off the gel and cup your hand under the flower head. Gently shake off the drying compound and remove stubborn granules with an artist's brush.

A microwave oven can dry flowers and leaves (without stems) more quickly than the silica-gel method. It also preserves their color and shape.

Select flowers that have a firm shape; cut stems to within 1 inch of the blossoms. Bright, light colors are preserved better than darker hues.

Pour about 1½ inches of silica gel or a mixture of two parts cornmeal to one part borax into a bowl. The gel should be at least 2 inches below the top of the bowl. Place a single flower, blossom up, on top of the gel. Don't let it touch the sides of the bowl. Using a fine mesh sieve, gently sift gel granules over the top and completely cover the bloom.

Fill an 8-ounce measuring cup with water, and place it in a corner of the microwave oven. Put the gel-covered flower in the oven. Do not cover the container. Dry one flower at a time. Turn on the oven. The color of the gel will change from blue to pink as moisture is absorbed and the flower dries. Drying times range from several seconds to three minutes, depending on the blossom's size and texture and your oven's heating capacity.

When the timer stops, remove the bowl from the oven and set it on newspaper. Do not touch it for 20 minutes; allow the gel to cool. Pour off the top layer of gel. Gently lift out the flower, which will be limp; place it on top of the gel until it is firm enough to handle (five to 20 minutes). Once the gel is cool, it is ready to reuse. Brush excess granules off the flowers with an artist's brush. Let the blooms rest overnight, if you are going to attach florist's wires for making wreaths or nosegays.

Tuck a bouquet of dried roses into a pouf of lace and ribbon, and a gift box, above, becomes a keepsake. Shown below is a tussie-mussie, or large nosegay, favored by Victorian ladies to refresh their sensibilities. You might like one in a vase or basket.

**Highlighting the collection of wreaths opposite is an extravagant whimsy in a Victorian style, which is fashioned only of red rosebuds.**

# proper care
## of roses

Although we usually imagine roses being pampered by countless generations of gardeners, they are one of the most remarkably resilient plants and have managed to survive in a wild state in nearly every corner of the world.

The rose as we know it has had no trouble gaining the adulation of countless generations of gardeners. It seems only natural, therefore, that the basic rose plant should need only the simplest of attentions and conditions in order for it to succeed.

Light is the first requirement. Most roses need a half day or more of direct sun. If this can occur in the morning, so much the better. More sun in the afternoon is usually next best—better than sun only through midday. Some roses are more shade tolerant than others; they are discussed on page 76 and throughout this book as appropriate.

Second is the need for soil that is well drained and reasonably free of greedy roots from encroaching trees and shrubs. If the endemic soil is poorly drained, you will have to dig and install a drainage system or arrange for raised planting beds. If you opt for the latter but are undecided on the best material to use for raising the beds, consider temporarily installing inexpensive pine boards from your local building supply, using 12-inch stakes for hammering them in place. Incorporate the soil amendments and additions, and plant your roses. Later, you can install a permanent edging from stone, bricks, or some other material.

Roses also need water. Some can get by on less than others, but in general they need generous soil moisture at the time of planting and while roots are becoming established. In colder areas, it is also especially important to their survival that they be given an adequate supply of soil moisture before a hard freeze.

Finally, roses may need some pruning and protection against predatory insects and diseases. Your best protection is a healthy rose in healthy soil.

**Roses can be low-growing or tall, ground covers, wall drapers, trellis lacers, or festoon makers.**

# The cultivation of roses

Although siting your roses properly and giving them the basics of soil, sun, and water are important, another crucial factor is the initial purchase of your plants. Roses are either on their own roots or grafted onto a rootstock. Own-root roses, even if they're killed to the ground by cold, will resprout given the appropriate variety. If they are frozen below the bud union, grafted roses will instead put forth shoots of the rootstock, not at all what you had in mind.

If you order your roses through the mail, order only from a firm whose reputation merits your trust. If you purchase bare-root roses at a nursery, you usually can examine the plants, making certain there are no deformities, disease or insect infestations, unhealthy canes, or puny roots.

Choosing naturally disease-resistant varieties or those suited to your climate also precludes many problems. For instance, bourbon roses perform beautifully in southern California but are slaves to disease in the Northwest. In some climates, particularly rainy ones, your roses may grow fine, only to have the buds degenerate into nonopening wads of mush called "balling." Your local rose society should be able to provide guidance to help you get your roses off to a good start.

As with most things, an ounce of prevention is worth a pound of cure. Keeping water off the foliage as much as possible will help, so roses are naturals for drip irrigation, which not only conserves water but also keeps the water where it belongs. If your chosen site drains poorly, plant your roses in raised beds. An 8-inch height should be adequate.

Another valuable consideration is a layer of mulch. It not only keeps spore-laden water from splashing on the foliage, but also controls weeds, elminates surface cultivation, and stabilizes soil temperatures during winter freezes and summer heat waves, thereby preventing frost heaving and stressed summer roots. Mulch, in its decomposed state, replenishes the organic content of the soil and keeps worms and beneficial bacteria happy. As if this weren't enough, mulch also puts a neat frame on the picture.

Stroll through your garden every few days with an eye toward any irregularities on the leaves. Two of the most common infections are mildew, a gray powdery fungus that distorts leaves and canes, and black spot, a fungus that creates unsightly splotches on the foliage and can cause the bulk of the leaves to drop.

Slightly less common is rust, which leaves orange pustules on the foliage. If you notice anything amiss, don't delay treatment. Controlling the first signs of mildew or black spot often stops the disease in its tracks. Bugs, too, need early control. Often the best thing for them is a systemic pesticide, which elminates sucking and chewing critters from within but doesn't hurt your ladybugs.

If you notice a yellowing throughout the plant with veins etched in green, you may be witnessing chlorosis, a problem with nutrient uptake of iron in alkaline soil. This is usually easily treatable with an acidifier.

Roses are heavy, or gross, feeders, but if you live outside Zones 9 or 10, stop feeding them on Labor Day—or even earlier if you live in an extra-cold region. Stimulating growth that late in the season is flirting with disaster from an early freeze. Also, don't be in a rush to winter prune. Wait until the worst of winter is over and buds are swelling, or a late cold spell can create havoc. The added stem length means that, even if the worst happens, the damaged portions are farthest out on the canes, and you can cut back to healthy wood.

In mild areas, foliage may last through the winter. Don't let it; disease organisms love it. Pull off and destroy (do not compost) the old leaves, and clean up any plant debris from the ground.

If you have a windy garden, consider a hedge or mesh fencing with vines. Fences are best for keeping dogs in and people out, but they don't make good shelters because the force of the wind creates much turbulence on the lee side of the structure. A looser, nonsolid hedge is more effective in baffling the wind.

Finally, don't be intimidated by all this culture. You can do little but control disease and still have roses. They just won't be the *best* roses.

**Roses require attention dictated by the seasons. Keep appropriate tools in a handy spot such as this mailbox.**

# Sunlight

**Roses keep company with vegetables in these raised beds. A sunny location like this one is best for roses.**

Generally speaking, roses grow best with as much sun as you can give them. They need at least six hours of full—or almost full—sun every day. The more sun the better. Experts universally agree that morning sun is a better choice than afternoon sun.

Sun in the morning allows the dew to evaporate promptly from the leaves, decreasing the chance for black spot or mildew to develop on wet foliage. Providing some shade in the afternoon will afford the plants some relief from intense summer heat, especially in warm climates. It also will slow the evaporation of moisture from the soil, promoting better growth. Moreover, the

flowers hold up better when they are not exposed to full sun during the hottest part of the day.

As you go about selecting a location for a new rose garden, keep in mind that nearby trees and shrubs, if not fully mature, will create more shade as they grow taller and may eventually cast shadows over the garden if you put it too close to them. The wide-ranging root systems of trees and shrubs also can compete with your roses for moisture and nutrients. If possible, keep the rose garden well outside the root zone of trees and shrubs.

# Roses for shade

Although roses are sun lovers, most will bloom if they receive shade for part of the day. Many will tolerate half shade, which is usually defined as morning or afternoon sun, or intermittent periods of sun and shade throughout the day. Half shade also can mean a location that is shady for four or five hours during the brightest part of a summer day, between the hours of 10 a.m. and 6 p.m. Half shade might be found at the edge of a shrub border along a lawn, or to the east or west of a hedge, wall, or building.

Climbers and hybrid musk roses are the best types of roses for shady locations. If they receive plenty of sun in spring, when they are setting their buds, the plants will even bloom in more than half shade in the summer. *Rosa wichuraiana* also will adapt to a shady location.

Hybrid musk roses are especially appealing because of their heavenly fragrance, disease-resistant foliage, and lovely soft colors, as well as their shade tolerance. Hybrid musk roses may take the form of bushes, shrubs, or climbers. Some have colorful hips in fall when not deadheaded.

First developed in England early in the 20th century by a clergyman named Joseph Pemberton, hybrid musk roses tend to take a while to establish themselves in the garden, but give them a season to settle in. They usually will grow vigorously during their second season, and your patience will be amply rewarded.

Here are some hybrid musk roses you may wish to consider for shady locations:

**'Buff Beauty,'** introduced in 1939, is a shrub that grows to 6 feet tall, with fragrant double flowers in a soft blend of apricot and yellow that harmonizes well with many other colors. Plants bloom early to midseason, repeat in fall, and have good winter hardiness.

**'Cornelia,'** developed in 1925, is a vigorous shrub that grows to 6 feet tall and can be trained as a climber or a hedge. The fragrant flowers are small, semidouble, and creamy pink with glowing golden stamens. Plants are winter hardy and bloom in mid-season, with repeat blooming until autumn.

**'Erfurt,'** developed in 1939, is vigorous and bushy and grows to 6 feet tall with good winter hardiness. Its semidouble flowers, deep pink with a cream-colored eye, are very fragrant and appear throughout the season.

**'Kathleen,'** introduced in 1922, is a tall, vigorous shrub that can be trained as a climber, reaching 8 or more feet tall if left unpruned. The sweetly fragrant single flowers are pale pink with a deeper pink reverse to the petals.

**'Lavender Lassie,'** a relative newcomer among the hybrid musks, was introduced in 1960. It can be grown as a 5-foot-tall bush or a 10-foot-tall climber. Its cool pink—not lavender—blossoms are highly fragrant, carried in large clusters, and appear in mid-season with good repeat.

**'Penelope,'** from 1924, is a 5- to 6-foot-tall shrub, winter hardy, with very fragrant semidouble flowers of pale blush pink to creamy yellow. Blossoms appear in large clusters intermittently all season.

'Penelope'

Other good hybrid musk roses include 'Ballerina,' pink with a white eye; 'Felicia,' peachy pink fading to cream; and 'Vanity,' dark cherry-rose.

# Air quality

For all their demanding loveliness, roses can be surprisingly tough. They apparently possess a reasonable tolerance for air pollution, as their presence in so many urban gardens seems to attest. One of the most important rose gardens in the United States—the Cranford Rose Garden in the Brooklyn Botanic Garden—thrives in New York City, only a short subway ride from the heart of Manhattan. Just because they can grow in city air does not mean that air quality is not important to roses, however.

Roses, unfortunately, are prone to attack by the organisms that cause powdery mildew, black spot, canker, rust, and many other fungal diseases. These diseases are especially problematic when many roses are grown together, as they so often are. In a closely planted garden, where all plants are prone to disease, the disease organisms can spread rapidly from plant to plant throughout the garden. In still, humid air, as is found around the Gulf of Mexico, the problem is exacerbated.

To help minimize the risk of infection and to slow the spread of disease if it attacks your plants, good air circulation is essential. If fresh air can circulate freely around and between plants, it becomes more difficult for pathogens to take hold and spread. Air circulation is essential whether or not you follow a regular spray program of fungicides and insecticides in the rose garden.

If you live in an area where summer weather tends to be hot and humid, or where fog is common, carefully consider how to maximize air circulation in the rose garden.

Try to find an open, airy location for the garden, but don't pick a spot that is exposed to frequent strong winds. If you live by the sea, plant a windbreak of salt-tolerant shrubs and trees that will slow, but not exclude, the breeze.

If you want to enclose the garden for privacy or intimacy, surround it with a fence of open construction rather than a solid brick or stone wall.

Probably the most obvious way to provide air circulation is to pay close attention to spacing when designing a rose garden. Never crowd roses together. Spacing for bush roses—hybrid teas, floribundas, and grandifloras—varies with the climate. Northern gardeners can plant roses more closely together than is advisable in warm-climate gardens.

## Too much of a good thing

Although air circulation is essential for roses, too much can cause damage. Strong winds can dry out rose canes, especially in winter. Cold winter winds are a primary cause of winterkill. If the long canes of climbers or ramblers become detached from their supports, strong winds will whip them about, possibly injuring the tissues. Wind-damaged and winter-killed roses will have to be pruned back to healthy tissue (see page 79). Check climbers and ramblers periodically throughout the year to make sure the canes remain securely fastened to their supports.

## Spacing for roses

Below is the average recommended spacing for different types of roses in different regions:

• In the coldest parts of New England and in the North Central states (Zone 3), plant hybrid teas, floribundas, and grandifloras in a sheltered location, $1\frac{1}{2}$ to 2 feet apart. Give them plenty of winter protection.

• In parts of the Northeast and North Central region (Zone 4), space rosebushes 2 to $2\frac{1}{2}$ feet apart.

• In the Mid-Atlantic area and in the South Central states (Zones 5–7), plant hybrid teas and grandifloras $2\frac{1}{2}$ to 3 feet apart and floribundas 2 to 3 feet apart.

• In the mild to warm climates of the Deep South, Southwest, West Coast, and Pacific Northwest (Zones 8–11), space hybrid teas and grandifloras 3 to 4 feet apart and floribundas $2\frac{1}{2}$ to $3\frac{1}{2}$ feet apart.

• In any zone, plant climbing and rambling roses no closer than 5 feet apart. Allow 2 to 3 feet of space between shrub roses if you want to use them as a hedge. Miniatures can be set 1 to 2 feet apart.

**A hybrid form of the anemone rose, *Rosa laevigata* is lovely trained against an old brick wall. Gardeners in humid climates should plant roses no closer than 2 feet from such a wall to allow for better air circulation.**

# Soil

Roses need well-drained and well-aerated soil to thrive. They will not grow well in soggy, poorly drained soil. If the soil in your garden is heavy clay or is slow to drain, you can lighten its texture by working in lots of organic matter or sharp builder's sand. If drainage is very poor, consider growing your roses in raised beds instead of trying to amend the soil. Make the beds at least 8 to 12 inches high and fill them with a fertile, crumbly soil mix such as a blend of three parts good topsoil, one part well-rotted livestock manure, and one part compost or peat moss. Or, if you prefer level planting beds and are not afraid of hard work, you can excavate the soil and install drainage tiles.

Clay soils, which contain a high proportion of tiny clay particles, tend to be heavy and slow to drain, although they usually contain a good supply of nutrients. As long as they are not too dense, clay soils are generally fine for roses. Work in compost, leaf mold, peat moss, and well-rotted manure, with gypsum or ground limestone to improve soil texture. If the soil is still too dense, work in sharp sand or coarse vermiculite to increase porosity.

Sandy soils, which contain a high proportion of large sand particles, can be too loose and low in nutrients for roses, but organic matter can help. Work in lots of it, up to half the volume of soil in the bed in extremely sandy soils. Organic matter gives sandy soil more body and improves its water-retention capacity.

Some growers with sandy soil plant in beds that are sunk several inches below the level of the surrounding soil. Sunken beds will capture more moisture for the plants, and they make it easier to mow grass around the edges of island beds. Roses in sunken beds are more difficult to maintain, however, especially in cold climates, where plants in sunken beds require more winter protection than plants growing in level ground or raised beds. Air stagnation can be a problem, too.

## Soil types

LOAM

CLAY

SAND

## pH by degrees

A pH around 6.5 is ideal for roses, although they can tolerate a fairly wide range, from acid to alkaline. It is a good idea to test soil pH when you are preparing a new rose bed and every few years in established gardens. If the pH is below 5.5, add ground limestone to bring it up to a more acceptable level. If you have a soil analysis performed through your local county extension office, follow recommendations on how much lime to add. The amount varies between 3 and 10 pounds of lime per 100 square feet of garden, depending on the level of acidity.

If the soil pH is 7.5 or above, you can lower it by adding powdered sulfur, approximately 3 pounds for every 100 square feet of garden.

Assuming the pH falls within acceptable limits and drainage is adequate, just about any reasonably fertile garden soil will support roses.

## Preparing soil for planting

It is best to prepare the soil several months before planting to allow time for the ground to settle and mellow, and for organic soil amendments to begin releasing their nutrients. If you plant roses in spring, try to prepare the soil the previous autumn.

Loosen the soil to a depth of 1½ feet when preparing a new rose bed. To ensure a healthy content of organic matter, spread a layer of compost, leaf mold, or well-rotted manure—or a combination of all three—1 to 2 inches deep over the entire surface of the bed. Dig or till the organic matter thoroughly into the soil. If you prepare the soil in fall for planting in spring, you can leave the surface rough over the winter. There's no need to level and smooth it until you are ready to plant. If a recent test has shown the soil to be deficient in nutrients, you will need to add nutrient sources (see pages 24 and 25). Unrefined or natural fertilizers such as rock phosphate, granite dust, and bonemeal are best added when you prepare the soil. Synthetic plant foods such as 5-10-5 can be applied at planting time.

If your winters are usually wet, and the soil is slow to warm and dry out in spring, your rose beds may not be ready for planting when the best time for planting bare-root roses arrives. To help get the soil in shape, stretch a sheet of clear plastic over the bed a month or two before planting time. Anchor the plastic securely around the edges. If you have a decent amount of sunny weather, the plastic cover will act as a solar collector and help the soil warm more quickly. This solarization technique should be used only in new gardens or in parts of established gardens where nothing is planted. The heat would be very detrimental to plants already in the ground.

## Maintaining soil wellness

With a little bit of attention each year, soil in good condition will stay that way, providing an excellent growing medium for your roses season after season. Follow the suggestions below to keep your soil in peak condition.

In late autumn or winter, after the growing season has drawn to a close, spread a 1- to 2-inch layer of compost, leaf mold, or well-rotted manure on top of the soil. If the ground is not frozen, dig the organic matter into the soil. Work very carefully around the plants to avoid injuring roots. Do not dig organic matter into the soil any closer than 1 foot from the base of each plant. Instead, use the compost or manure as a topdressing in the area immediately surrounding the bases of plants.

If you are gardening in heavy clay soil, you may need to spread gypsum or ground limestone at least for the first few years. To avoid raising soil pH in gardens where the pH is already at the high end of the acceptable range for roses, add an acidic soil conditioner to balance the alkalinity of the lime or gypsum. Powdered sulfur is one good acidifier. Other acidic materials include leaf mold made from oak leaves, cottonseed meal, and pine needles. If you are adding acid or alkaline or both to the soil, it would be wise to test the pH again in spring at the start of the growing season.

If your soil is very dense and poorly drained or even compacted, grow your roses in raised beds. Blend an ideal soil mix to fill the beds.

An established rose garden benefits from additions of organic matter each year to keep the soil in excellent condition. This thriving, well-tended garden, enclosed by a wood fence, is an elegant entry to the yard of this Spokane, Washington, home.

71

# Planting roses

Bare-root and packaged roses and roses in plantable cardboard boxes are put into the ground while the plants are still dormant. Plant them in early spring as soon as the soil can be worked or in fall at least a month before you expect the first frost. Gardeners in warm climates can plant in winter.

Container-grown roses can be planted any time during the growing season when weather conditions are not too stressful. In most parts of the country, spring and fall are the best times to plant container-grown roses.

If you are unsure about when it is safe to plant roses in spring, here are two guides to use. First, to find out if your soil is ready to work, scoop up a handful of earth from the bed in which you will be planting. Squeeze your hand into a fist, then open your fingers. If the soil stays in a big ball, it is still too wet to work. If the ball of soil crumbles when you open your fingers, it has completely thawed and dried out enough for planting. The other clue you can use is to watch for forsythia to bloom in your yard. Generally, when forsythia flowers the danger of heavy frost is past, and it should be safe to begin planting bare-root roses.

## Delayed planting

Mail-order nurseries routinely ship roses as bare-root plants with the roots protected by packing material. Bare-root roses should be planted, if at all possible, within 24 hours after you receive them. If you cannot plant them for a few days, open the packages and sprinkle the plants, including the roots, with water. Reclose the package and set it in a cool place.

If you have to wait more than a couple of days before planting, take the roses out of their packages and soak the roots in water for a few hours, but no longer than 24 hours. Then, heel them into an empty spot in the garden. To heel in plants, dig a shallow trench and set the plants into the trench on an angle. Cover the roots loosely with soil. Do not hold the plants longer than two weeks before planting.

If you buy preplanted bare-root roses in a biodegradable carton, you can hold the plants in their boxes for up to a week before planting. Regularly check the moisture of the medium in which the roots are packed. If it dries out, you will need to water. Soak bare-root roses in a bucket of water for up to 24 hours before planting.

If you cannot plant container-grown roses immediately, set them in a shady spot and water whenever the soil in the containers feels dry an inch or two below the surface.

Adequate spacing is important for roses to minimize the risk of disease. Before planting, see the section on air quality on pages 68 and 69 for information on spacing distances for different types of roses in various parts of the country.

If you will be planting climbing or rambler roses, have the trellis or other support in place before you plant.

Before you plant, inspect the roses carefully. With a sharp knife or pruning shears, cut off any broken, damaged, or shriveled canes. On bare-root plants, check the roots as well, and cut off any that are damaged. Most roses will have been pruned before you buy them, but if you are planting unpruned roses, cut back long canes to 12 inches above the bud union. Remove any canes that are thinner than a pencil and canes that cross over one another as well.

Dig planting holes before removing plants from their containers or packages. The planting hole must be deep and wide enough to hold comfortably all the roots without bending them. On an average, the hole will need to be approximately 1 to 1½ feet deep and 1½ to 2 feet wide. If you will be planting container-grown roses, make the hole at least 6 inches larger than the container in all directions.

Toss a shovelful of compost or well-rotted manure into the bottom of each hole and mix it with the soil. If you are planting bare-root roses, make a mound of soil approximately 8 inches high in the bottom of the hole, firming the soil with your hands.

Planting depth is important for roses, especially hybrids grafted onto different rootstocks, as most plants are. If you live where winter temperatures drop to 0°F or lower (generally Zones 3–7), plant your roses with the bud union an inch or two below the soil surface. In warm climates, the bud union should be an inch or two above the soil surface. The bud union is the point—recognizable as a knob or swelling—where the green top meets the brown rootstock.

**After initial bed preparation and planting, roses are surprisingly self-reliant, often less trouble than an ordinary front lawn.**

# Planting roses

## Roses in containers

After digging the holes, remove the first plant from its container. Loosen the soil ball by laying the pot on its side and tapping the outside of the pot on all sides with the handle of a trowel. Tap the bottom of the pot as well. Grasp the plant around the base of the stem and gently slide it out of the pot. If tapping on the pot does not loosen the plant, you may have to cut the container to remove the plant without damaging the roots. If the plants are in metal containers, have the containers cut open at the nursery before you bring the plants home. Then get the plants into the ground as soon as you get them home.

Holding the plant at the base of the stem, pull off the pot with your other hand, then support the root ball as you transfer the plant into the hole. Center the plant in the hole, hold it upright, and check the position of the graft union to be sure it is at the correct level (see page 73). If it is not, remove the plant, adjust the depth of the hole, and reposition the plant. When the depth is correct, fill the hole with soil, working it around the root ball.

Water well, and add more soil, if necessary, to fill any air pockets. Water your new plants regularly, keeping the soil moist but not soggy, for the first three weeks after planting, while the plants establish themselves.

## Bare-root roses

To plant bare-root roses, begin by removing the packaging. If the plants are preplanted in biodegradable cardboard cartons

## Planting bare-root roses

Roses are assured of a good start in life when they are planted properly.

1 Soak the roots of bare-root roses in a bucket of water before planting. Let the plants soak overnight, for up to 24 hours.

2 Set the plant on top of the soil mound in the bottom of the hole and check the position of the bud union. Adjust the planting depth if necessary.

that are meant to go into the ground with the plants, cut or tear the sides of the box before you place the plant in the hole. This will allow the roots to grow out easily into the surrounding soil in the event the cardboard carton is slow to decompose after planting. Follow the instructions on the box regarding planting depth for preplanted roses.

After removing a bare-root rose from its package, set the plant on the soil mound in the bottom of the hole, and check the depth by noting the position of the bud union. When the depth is correct, make sure the roots are spread evenly over the sides of the soil mound, with none of the main roots overlapping one another.

Begin to fill the hole with soil, steadying the plant with one hand while you work soil around the roots with your other hand.

When the hole is half-filled with soil, fill the rest of the hole with water to settle the soil around the roots. When the water drains, fill the hole with soil, gently rock the plant back and forth a few times, and water well.

If you live in a northern climate, where the weather is still quite cool, or if you are planting in fall, it is a good idea to make a mound of soil around the base of the stem immediately after planting. For spring plantings, the mound will help hold moisture and allow the plant to make an easier adjustment to the garden. In fall, the mound will provide some winter protection for the new plants. Gradually, over a week, remove the soil mound when the plant starts to grow.

Water new plants regularly to keep the soil evenly moist but not soggy during their first few weeks in the garden.

3 Set the plant in the hole, fill halfway with soil, add water to settle, fill the remainder of the hole, and water again. Mound soil around the base of the plant for protection.

4 A loose mulch will help conserve moisture and keep down weeds around newly planted roses. Crumbled compost, leaf mold, and aged manure are all excellent mulches.

5 If the plants were not pruned by the nursery before you purchased them, cut back the canes to 12 inches above the bud graft union.

# Nutrients

Roses benefit from regular applications of fertilizer. For novice rosarians, figuring out what to feed the plants can seem a rather daunting task. Is it best to use an all-purpose fertilizer or a special formula? Chemical or organic? When should it be applied? How much do you use?

The first step is understanding what roses need. Plants require three major nutrients to fuel their growth and development: nitrogen, phosphorus, and potassium. Each is identified in the horticultural world by its chemical symbol. Nitrogen (N) is important for healthy leaves and promotes photosynthesis. Plants need phosphorus (P) for flower formation, for ripening fruit and seeds, and for root growth. Potassium (K) improves the overall vigor of plants and assists in fruit formation and the development of tubers.

The three numbers you see on a fertilizer package indicate the percentage composition of the major nutrients in a plant food. The first number gives the percent by weight of nitrogen in the fertilizer. The second number is the percent of phosphorus. The third number indicates the percent of potassium.

In addition to the three major nutrients, plants require smaller amounts of secondary minerals, such as iron and calcium, and tiny amounts of trace elements, including boron and magnesium for vigorous development.

A good soil test will tell you whether your soil is deficient in any of the major or minor nutrients. If your soil is deficient, you will have to add the missing nutrients before planting. In all soils it is helpful to replace the nutrients taken up by growing plants to ensure a constant supply throughout the growing season and from year to year. That's what fertilizers are for.

Plant foods are available in several forms. The term "organic" is given to nutrient sources applied to plants in a more or less natural form. Organic materials break down gradually in the soil to release their nutrients to plants over a period of time. The goal of organic gardening is to build healthy soil. "Feed the soil, not the plant," organic gardeners say. They aim to supply a balanced complement of nutrients. The advantage of organic fertilizers is that they are far less concentrated than the chemical products. It is more difficult to overfeed with organic materials, so the risk of pollution-causing nutrient runoff is minimized.

Traditionally, organic fertilizers have been applied to soil individually or in combinations chosen by the gardener. In recent years a number of packaged, preblended granular or powdered organic fertilizers have come on the market. They are convenient to use, but if you want a genuinely organic product, read package labels carefully and look for ingredients such as those in the table opposite. Terms such as "organic" and "natural" can be used purely as marketing ploys.

The other type of fertilizer is widely referred to as "chemical," which really means that the materials are synthesized—man-made—or that their form is altered from the way it occurs in nature. Chemical fertilizers are, in general, very concentrated. They are given to plants in small doses, and their nutrients

**To apply a dry granular or powdered fertilizer, sprinkle it in a ring around the base of the plant, and lightly scratch it into the soil.**

become available quickly, except in the case of specially designed timed-release formulas.

To apply dry fertilizers, spread them in a ring around the base of each plant, 6 inches out from the stem. Scratch the fertilizer lightly into the soil, then water it in. In dry weather it is a good idea to water the day before you fertilize.

In addition to dry fertilizers, liquid and water-soluble plant foods are available. Liquid fertilizers are best used as occasional boosters for most roses, although they can provide the main source of nutrition for miniatures and plants in containers. Liquid fertilizers must be applied frequently—every couple of weeks—which is a time-consuming process if you have many plants. When dissolved or diluted in water according to the directions on the package, liquid fertilizers can be watered into the ground or sprayed onto leaves as a foliar feed.

In addition to the various chemical formulas available, organic liquid fertilizers such as fish emulsion and seaweed concentrates are also on the market. Some growers swear by a solution of Epsom salts (one tablespoon) in water (one gallon) to encourage more basal shoots and, thus, more flowers.

You might decide to use a combination of organic and chemical fertilizers. Whatever products you choose for your roses, carefully follow the package directions regarding application rates, especially for chemical fertilizers. Overfeeding plants stimulates fast but weak growth that is very susceptible to disease and pest damage. Too much chemical fertilizer may burn plant tissues, and the runoff from excess fertilizers eventually finds its way into the ground water, polluting streams and even water supplies. Avoid getting fertilizer on the bud union.

## When to fertilize

Incorporate dry organic fertilizers into the soil where you will be planting new roses several months ahead of planting. If you expect to plant in early spring, apply the fertilizers the preceding autumn. In established gardens, apply organic fertilizers in spring and again in late fall when plants are dormant.

If you prefer a dry chemical fertilizer, apply it to newly planted bushes after the first flush of bloom and once a month thereafter until six to eight weeks before you expect the first fall frost.

## Organic and inorganic nutrients

Roses need a balanced supply of nutrients, but as flowering plants they have a particular need for phosphorus. Avoid high-nitrogen fertilizers such as those intended for lawns.

Chemical fertilizers: Use a rose formula such as 8-12-4 or 6-6-4, or an all-purpose formula such as 5-10-5 or 15-30-15.

Organic fertilizers: Use any of these in whatever combination you choose, making sure you supply plenty of phosphorus, or use a packaged organic fertilizer.

Nitrogen sources: Dried blood, bonemeal (contains a small amount of nitrogen), cottonseed meal, fish products, and livestock manures. Be sure the manure is composted or well-rotted before using.

Phosphorus sources: Dried blood (contains a small amount), bonemeal, colloidal phosphate, fish products (small amount), guano, and phosphate rock.

Potassium sources: Fish products (small amount), granite dust, greensand, and wood ashes.

Trace element sources: Seaweed and algae products, Epsom salts (magnesium), and household borax (boron).

In warm climates, do not apply it before you begin to induce dormancy by removing old leaves.

Feed established roses in spring, four to six weeks before the plants begin to bloom. Fertilize monthly thereafter until six to eight weeks before the first frost.

If your soil is in good condition, you can cut back a bit on how often you fertilize. Feed the plants once in spring right after pruning, a second time after the first flush of bloom, and a third time in summer six to eight weeks before the first frost.

# Pruning and Training

Gardeners who grow roses to exhibit them need to produce the largest possible blooms on tall, straight stems. For bigger blooms, allow only one bud of a cluster to develop. Pinch out smaller, secondary buds.

Regular deadheading is important for promoting rebloom. Cut off faded flowers about ¼ inch above the nearest leaf with five leaflets and an outward-bound bud.

It's important to prune roses. Regular pruning results in a well-shaped plant, better flowers, and growth of the vigorous basal shoots that produce the best blooms. If you're growing roses for show, you will want to prune the plants severely to produce fewer, but larger, flowers. Exhibition growers also remove some of the buds, but to enjoy your roses in the garden and as cut flowers, prune as described in this section to get the most flowers throughout the blooming season.

## Deadheading

Deadheading—removing spent flowers—is really a form of pruning and is important for encouraging roses to rebloom. Even roses that bloom only once a year, however, benefit from deadheading. To deadhead, cut off the stems of faded blossoms about ¼ inch above the nearest leaf with five leaflets. On reblooming roses, this cut will stimulate the dormant bud just below the cut to produce a new flowering stem.

Some roses, such as rugosas, produce large, colorful hips after they bloom. Do not deadhead roses if you want hips to form for fall color or rose-hip tea.

## When to prune

Roses are best pruned late in their dormant period, just before the buds begin to swell and before new leaves appear. In regions with cold winters, the best time to prune is early spring—March or April in much of the United States. Warm-climate gardeners prune in winter—December or January—for shapeliness and to induce a rest.

If you can't prune your plants at the right time, and new spring growth begins, it's better to prune late than not at all. Canes in active growth will bleed sap when pruned, but bleeding is preferable to the disease organisms and overwintering insects that may be present in old, unpruned wood.

## How to prune

Use a good, sharp pair of pruning shears. Older plants with thicker canes may require lopping shears or a small pruning saw.

Make all pruning cuts on an angle, and cut about ¼ inch above an outside bud or outward-facing leaf. The new growth will develop in the direction the bud or leaf is facing, so pruning

When the canes of climbing roses such as 'Altissimo' are trained to grow horizontally, they will produce more lateral, flowering stems.

to outside buds will result in an open growth habit that allows good air circulation around the canes.

If you need to control the growth of a plant that is spreading too vigorously, prune to inward-facing buds.

## Pruning established plants

Unless you are an experienced rose pruner, it is best to work from the top of the plant downward when pruning.

Begin by removing dead, diseased, and damaged growth. Cut back winter-killed and frost-damaged canes to healthy tissue, which you will recognize by the white pith in the center of the stem. (Dead wood has a brown pith.) Cut back diseased wood at least a couple of inches below the infected tissue.

Next, remove twiggy growth and all canes thinner than the diameter of a pencil. Cut off at the bud union older canes that produced weak growth and no flowers last year.

For bush roses, the final step in the basic pruning process is to eliminate all canes except those that will form the plant's foundation. Leave four to eight canes, depending on the size and age of the plant. Older, vigorous plants can support more canes than young plants. Your goal is a plant that is symmetrical and balanced.

# Pruning and training

In general, you will want to remove the oldest canes in order to stimulate new canes to grow from the bud union. Old canes usually are lined and cracked, dull and grayish in color, with grayish thorns. Young canes are smooth-surfaced and reddish brown in color. Cut back to the bud union when removing old canes. Cut back the older canes you will leave on the plant to a lateral stem. Do not cut into thick, old wood unless removing the cane entirely. Shorten younger canes as directed below for various types of roses.

Finally, thin out branches growing into the center of the plant and crossed branches. To prevent new growth into the center, rub off buds facing in that direction.

Sometimes rosebushes send up suckers from the rootstock, which must be removed. Their foliage is different from that of the other canes. Remove soil around the base of the plant to uncover the point where the sucker emerges from the rootstock, then remove it completely, even if you have to cut into the root.

If a bush develops "candelabra canes"—shoots growing from the bud union that are markedly taller and stronger than the other canes—you can control them by pinching off the growing tip when the shoots are about 15 inches tall.

Following are tips on pruning particular types of roses that have been in the garden for at least one full season.

•Hybrid teas and grandifloras: Cut back young canes by one-third to one-half. Prune yellow-flowered hybrid teas less severely.

•Floribundas: Cut back new canes by one-fourth to one-third and 2-year-old stems by half; remove 3-year-old canes at the bud union.

•Climbers: Remove canes more than 4 years old at the base. Leave any first-year canes that have not yet bloomed. Cut back blooming stems to two or three eyes for varieties that bloom once, three or four eyes for everblooming varieties. Tie canes in

## Where to prune

*Angle cuts:*
**Make all pruning cuts at a 45-degree angle.**

*Weak growth:*
**Remove all canes thinner than the diameter of a pencil.**

*Frost damage:*
**Cut back frost-damaged and winter-killed growth to healthy tissue.**

*Remove suckers:*
**Suckers growing from the rootstock must be removed completely.**

**Nothing adds so much to a garden as the verticality of a lattice arbor with climbing roses and a place to sit.**

a horizontal position to encourage growth of lateral (flowering) stems.

•Ramblers: Remove 2-year-old canes, unless the plant has only a few. In that case, shorten the laterals and cut off the old wood above the laterals.

•Shrub roses and old-fashioned and species roses: In most cases, prune only lightly to shape plants and remove dead and damaged growth. Prune old tea roses like floribundas, and hybrid perpetuals like hybrid teas.

•Miniatures: Cut back by about half.

•Tree-form roses: Cut back a few older canes to the bud union. Shorten younger canes by about half, or to 12 to 15 inches. Thin growth and remove buds to keep center of plant open. If the standard is new, remove undesirable lateral shoots from the main cane during the growing season to encourage growth at the top of the tree.

## Pruning at planting time

Most roses will have been pruned by the nursery before you buy them. Here's what to do if you are planting unpruned roses.

**Hybrid teas, grandifloras, old tea roses, and hybrid perpetuals:** Prune canes and roots hard. Remove any canes not producing strong shoots and canes thinner than a pencil.

**Floribundas and polyanthas:** Prune back to 6 inches.

**Climbers:** Do not prune climbers at planting; simply remove any dead tips. Tie the canes in a horizontal position to encourage the growth of lateral stems on which flowers will be borne.

**Ramblers:** Cut back to 3 feet.

**Shrub roses and old-fashioned and species roses:** Trim lightly if not pruned by nursery.

**Miniatures:** No pruning needed at planting.

**Tree-form roses:** Remove any dead or damaged wood. Cut stems back to four to six eyes.

# Watering frequency

Roses are notoriously thirsty plants. Most of them need regular, even moisture in order to bloom well. Roses growing in containers need to have the potting medium kept constantly moist in order to grow and bloom to their full capacity. Roses that suffer water stress respond with shriveling shoot tips and dying leaves. Even if a plant is water-stressed just once, the plant will show the strain if the soil becomes dry enough.

Although roses need even moisture, they will not thrive when their roots stand in water for extended periods of time. That is why well-drained soil is so important to their good health. Putting containers of roses up on "feet" or blocks will ensure that excess water can drain quickly. Never plant roses in containers that have no drainage holes in the bottom.

As with all rules, there are exceptions to the "thirsty roses" rule. Some roses tolerate or even prefer conditions on the dry side. Two native Americans, *Rosa virginiana,* which is native to the eastern part of the country, and *Rosa stellata* var. *myrifica,* which hails from the Southwest, tolerate dry conditions. They are good choices for seashore and desert gardens respectively. Rugosas also are recommended for dry gardens. Their deliciously fragrant flowers and big, colorful hips make them delightful additions to seaside gardens.

Except for these few hardy types, most roses must have water frequently and in abundance. The general rule of thumb for watering roses is: When nature doesn't supply water, the gardener must—once every week to 10 days. In light, sandy soils during hot, dry weather, roses may need watering more often. In heavy soils they may need it less frequently. If you're unsure when it is time to water, poke a finger into the soil. When the ground feels dry a couple of inches below the surface, it's time to water.

Avoid giving roses frequent light waterings. When only the top few inches of soil are moistened, plants tend to concentrate their roots there. Plants with shallow roots are more susceptible to damage during hot, dry weather. Because roses tend to be shallow-rooted, it's important to water deeply to encourage the plants to send some roots deeper into the soil.

Roses growing in containers will need to be watered more often than plants growing in the ground because the smaller volume of soil they contain dries out quickly. Miniatures planted in small pots are especially at risk on hot summer days. Depending on weather conditions, container sizes, and the porosity of the growing medium, potted roses may need to be watered every day in summer.

You can help containerized roses avoid water stress by planting them in a medium rich in organic matter. Humus-rich soils retain moisture while allowing excess moisture to drain away. Mulch also helps. Another way to conserve moisture is to rig up some sort of device that will shade the pots during the heat of the afternoon, while allowing the plants themselves to be in the sunlight. This also will keep the soil cooler.

Whether your roses are growing in pots or in the ground, water them early in the day if possible. If you cannot water them in the morning, try to do it late in the afternoon, when several hours of daylight remain. The goal is to allow enough time for the foliage to dry before nightfall. Roses are more susceptible to the fungal diseases that plague them when their leaves are wet at night.

It's also not advisable to water at midday, when the sun is most intense. Watering is least efficient at this time of day because more of the moisture is lost to evaporation than it is earlier or later in the day. Also, water droplets clinging to leaves can act like tiny lenses that concentrate the sun's rays and can burn the foliage.

Another important time to be sure roses have sufficient moisture is when the soil begins to freeze in winter. Roses need to be well supplied with moisture going into winter because they will not be able to draw water from the soil after it freezes. If plants are dried out, they are more likely to suffer winterkill. Water your roses well when the soil starts to freeze, and mulch them after it is frozen.

Gardeners in warm climates should check their roses periodically throughout the winter to be sure the soil does not dry out. Water if necessary during periods of dry, sunny weather.

**Hybrid roses like these need regular, uniform moisture in order to thrive. A good mulch conserves soil moisture and keeps the soil temperature cooler.**

# Watering and conservation

## Mulching to protect plants

Roses benefit greatly from a loose, organic mulch during the growing season. Mulch helps slow the evaporation of moisture from the soil. In summer, it keeps the soil temperature cooler, which, in turn, promotes better flowering. A summer mulch also keeps down weeds, which means weeding chores will be reduced or eliminated. This is beneficial for shallow-rooted plants like roses, whose roots are easily damaged by cultivation. Mulches like bark chips and cocoa bean hulls look attractive in the garden, too.

In winter, mulch helps to prevent frost heaves that occur when the soil alternatively freezes and thaws by keeping the soil cold during winter warm spells. Frost heaves can push roots right out of the ground, where they can be killed by exposure to wind and cold temperatures.

Mulch your roses when they begin to send out new growth in spring and the protective soil mound is removed from new plants. Spread the mulch in an even layer 2 to 4 inches deep. It's best to keep the mulch away from direct contact with the plants. Leave a few inches of bare soil immediately around the base of each plant.

## Mulching options

Here are some recommended mulches for roses:
• Bark chips, attractive and available in several sizes, are brown initially, then turn gray with age. Lay down 1 to 2 inches of small chips or a 2-inch layer of larger chips. Add some nitrogen fertilizer to the soil when the bark chips begin to decompose.
• Cocoa bean hulls are handsome but expensive, and they really do smell like chocolate. Apply 2 inches deep.
• Compost also makes a good mulch and improves soil as it decomposes. Spread it 2 to 3 inches deep.
• Shredded leaves can be used as a mulch. Apply a 4-inch layer in summer, a 6-inch layer in winter.
• Salt hay is an excellent mulch in areas where it is available. It isn't as good-looking as wood chips or cocoa bean hulls, but it adds trace minerals to the soil, and it will not pack down. Spread a 2- to 3-inch layer.

## Watering methods

Traditionally, gardeners have watered their plants with handheld hoses or overhead sprinklers. Although those methods offer the advantages of cleaning foliage and cooling the air, they are not very efficient.

Overhead watering wastes a lot of this precious resource. The water is spread over a large and not very well-targeted area, and substantial amounts of moisture are lost to evaporation. And with roses, wet foliage is always risky, especially at night, when mildew thrives.

A better way to water roses is to deliver the water directly to the root zone with soaker hoses or drip irrigation systems.

Soaker hoses are made of canvas or fiber, and some now are made from recycled tires. Water trickles slowly through small pores along their walls. The faucet needs to be turned on only partway, and very little water is lost to runoff. Soaker hoses must be laid through the garden every spring and brought indoors over winter, but they are relatively inexpensive and very effective at delivering water only where needed.

Drip systems have slender plastic tubes with small holes in the sides. Lengths of tubing are connected with couplings and installed under the surface of the soil. You can buy individual components or a kit for a complete system. Automatic timers are available, too. There are even drip systems for container gardens. Drip irrigation equipment is costly and fairly labor-intensive to install, and the tubing sometimes clogs up. These systems are efficient and convenient, however, and they do not detract from the garden's appearance as do soaker hoses and sprinklers.

**The yellow roses in this garden take on an ethereal glow when backlighted by the sun. The abundance and quality of the flowers could not be achieved without plenty of water.**

# Rose chores—Spring

A metal arbor supports climbing roses and gives this garden added visual appeal in all seasons. Thin out any twiggy growths.

After the gloom of winter, life returns anew in the garden. Now is the time to get the jump on problems. Inspection of each rose plant comes first, followed by whatever pruning seems advisable. Wait to prune roses that bloom once a year until after they finish flowering.

When buds are swelling, begin your feeding program. Many growers recommend three feedings a year. The spring feeding might be the most important because the production of vigorous new canes is greatest during this season—and vigorous canes produce abundant flowers.

Granular fertilizer is probably best now as soil is moist and will dissolve and disperse nutrients efficiently, with little worry of chemical burn. Don't be put off by such fertilizer terms as NPK ratio. That's just chemistry shorthand for nitrogen, phosphorus, and potassium, the three basic requirements for growth. Their ratio usually is expressed as 10-5-3, or some other combination of numbers in that order referring to the parts per hundred available in the fertilizer (see page 76).

Nitrogen is for leafy growth and, therefore, photosynthesis, which is the conversion of light and nutrients into plant energy. Phosphorus benefits roots, and because a plant is only as good as its uptake system, this nutrient is essential. Potassium produces sturdy stem growth and vigor. Commercial rose food will show the NPK ratio on the face of the product, and it will be properly balanced for your roses.

After application, check your drip-irrigation system and put down a layer of mulch. Two inches of humus, finely chopped leaves from last fall, bark, or just about anything vegetable will preserve soil moisture and preclude most weeds. Let's face it—weeding thorny roses is no picnic!

Keep a close watch for pests of all kinds. Controlling the first wave of bugs, like Japanese beetles, will stop succeeding generations from running amok. Aphids can spread virus and deform buds, but a strong spray of water from the hose will keep small populations in check. Disease control should not lag. At this often rainy season, controls may have to be applied frequently and repeatedly. When nights are cool and days are warm, powdery mildew almost always makes an appearance.

'Yellow Lady Banks' gives a shower of delicately scented small roses for several weeks in spring. The rose also is suited to training up into a tree.

# Summer

This, the season of reveling in roses, is not without its unpleasant tasks. All those gorgeous blossoms, for example, need to be removed when spent. If not, they make a mess and furnish a foothold for disease. Certain varieties are almost as attractive for their seed capsules—hips—and these should be retained after the petals finish. These types are often once-bloomers, but with continuous-blooming plants, developing hips take the energy required to make more blossoms.

Go over your roses every few days, pruners in hand, and try to remove spent blossoms before the petals drop. Otherwise, gathering up fallen petals from the ground can become an onerous, thorny problem.

Where to cut is often a mystery to the novice rose gardener. A good rule of thumb is to cut just above the first leaf bearing five leaflets. Where the leaf joins the stem, a dormant bud appears at the base of the leaf. Make your cut at an angle, with the bud just below the upper end of the cut. To avoid tangled bushes and the disease that they can harbor, choose an outward-pointing bud. Roses are extremely directional in their growth, so cutting to an inward-facing bud causes canes to grow together in a confused mass.

You may notice extra-vigorous canes shooting up from the base of a plant. Some varieties are more prone to this than others. Determine if this is the variety you want or if it's the rootstock trying to take over. The first thing to be aware of is the foliage. If the leaves look like the rest on the bush, you're probably all right. If the leaves are smaller, with more leaflets per leaf, chances are it is the rootstock. This applies only to grafted roses, because there is no rootstock with own-root roses. If the shoots originate below the thickened knobby bud union, you must remove them. Don't cut, however, or you will stimulate the dormant adventitious buds at the base of each shoot and create a bigger problem. Instead, don a pair of sturdy gloves, and break off the shoots, also known as suckers, at their point of origin. This may require digging down to the base of the sucker, but do it very carefully, because a damaged root is even more prone to throwing suckers.

Climbers need to have their long new canes tied in place as they grow. Horizontally trained shoots will produce many more flowers than upright ones, so try to fan out the canes. If your

For color in the garden all summer long, combine an array of roses and annual flowers.

climber is a rambler, with long, lax shoots that bloom only once, after flowering remove the bloomed-out canes to the ground because their job is done.

Continue to watch for insects and diseases, and make sure your plants have ample water, especially during hot, dry spells, but mostly, this is the season to enjoy the bounty, the fragrance—everything you love about your roses. One way is to cut some for the house. Long stems are easiest to place in a vase and, if you prefer quality to quantity, pinch off any secondary flower buds from the stem, permitting the terminal bud to develop into one perfect rose. You may want to make the second application of fertilizer following the first round of blooms.

# What's wrong with my roses?

When a rosebush has grown strong from having completely favorable conditions, predatory insects and diseases are less likely to attack. Life as a bed of real roses, however, almost inevitably will yield an occasional problem. Illustrated here are some of the likely invaders and clues as to what may be wrong. Where diseases are concerned, the best line of defense is to site the plants so they receive good air movement. Promptly remove from the soil surface any diseased leaves and blighted petals that may have fallen. Bury these in an out-of-the-way corner of the garden. Don't add them to the compost pile. There was a time when every good rose gardener sprayed or dusted once a week whether or not there was any sign of insect or disease. Now, the rule is to monitor for problems, to think prevention, not treatment. At the outset, consider the degree of wellness that will make you happy with your rose garden, or at what point sickness is causing poor results. Some gardeners see only the blossom; others can't help noticing if the stems are clothed or bare.

to favor cool weather. Ignore them and some blossoms and upper leaves may be disfigured, but the entire season is not lost. The primary damage is from loss of vital sap through the aphids' sucking. Secondarily, honeydew from the insects gives a sticky coating on leaf surfaces that provides an ideal place for the establishment of disease spores such as sooty mold and powdery mildew. If you have only a few roses and not too many aphids, they can be removed by hand and any remains knocked off with a stiff spray of water from the hose nozzle. Many organic sprays as well as petrochemicals labeled specifically for treating aphids on roses also are available. These may be applied as sprays or dusts or to the soil as systemics.

## Aphids

Plant lice is another name for an aphid. These are small, soft-bodied, usually wingless insects that may be green, brown, black, pink, or yellow. They almost always cluster on the tenderest new shoots and flower buds. Their presence isn't really a sign of neglect or wrongful practice but rather a natural part of the growth process. It's true that an excess amount of nitrogen in the fertilizer formula may entice more aphids than usual. They also tend to be cyclical and

## Balling

Botrytis is the blight responsible for balling, a malformation seen in buds that are trying to open. It often occurs in the fall when a period of cool, wet weather changes abruptly to warm and sunny. Observed in the earliest stages, the blighted petal edges tightly hold the ever-fattening bud beneath. It is possible through a deft motion of thumb and forefinger to release the constriction, thus permitting the flower to unfurl without much damage. Otherwise, the interior petals soon decay, leading to a rotting, collapsing, and unsightly mess that needs to be removed promptly to stop the spread of the disease. Old and modern roses are subject to balling, especially those with large flowers and tightly packed petals.

## Bent rose neck

A rosebud or blossom may droop from lack of water, cooler temperatures, or too much oxygen at the roots. If the condition can be corrected in time, the starch will come back, and growth will assume its normal state of uprightness. A bud definitely bent over, yet turgid, suggests a metabolic problem caused by low temperatures during early development. This often leads to some sepals elongating more than others. The shorter ones pull the bud over and produce the bent neck. It's also possible that a midge has damaged cells just below the bud.

## Black spot

Beginning in midsummer and continuing into fall, a rosebush that shows yellow foliage must be inspected to see if the yellowed parts are centered by inky black spots, which are likely at this stage in the season. The black spot disease cannot be cured, but it can be prevented by diligent spraying or dusting with a fungicide. Hygiene is critical to keeping this disease at bay. Keep all infected leaves promptly picked. After you handle diseased

leaves, don't put your hands on healthy parts of the rose. Don't add diseased parts to your regular compost pile; bury them elsewhere to the depth of your spade. Black spot tends to attack older leaves first. It's essential that its spread be halted before the younger leaves succumb, for they sustain the bush.

## Japanese beetles

There is no mistaking these glistening, bronze-winged, ½-inch beetles. They chew on flowers and foliage and seem to prefer large white and yellow roses. If not routed at this stage, they will lay eggs in the ground—usually turf—and the larvae will overwinter. Total control is impossible, but here are some treatments you might try:

• Hand-pick or brush beetles into a bucket of kerosene.
• Chemical or electric traps are effective, but don't use them unless your neighbors also join the fight. Otherwise, all the beetles around will be attracted to your rose garden in numbers greater than the traps can accommodate.
• Contact sprays such as pyrethrum or rotenone are reasonably helpful.
• Apply an inoculant bacterium to surrounding lawn turf that will kill the grubs.

# Waste management

An old-fashioned shrub rose at Rosedown Plantation in St. Francisville, Louisiana, is surrounded by fallen petals waiting to be raked up. They can be disposed of by putting them on the compost pile.

In the not-so-distant past, garden waste—everything from rose petals and canes to falling leaves—was packed into big, heavy-duty plastic bags and left for the trash collector or hauled to the local landfill. Not today. The earth has run out of room, and we can no longer bury or burn this debris, but we can readily put most of it to good use at home.

The quickest way to dispose of dead canes is to put them in a chipper-shredder and grind them into valuable mulch, which you can spread immediately around your roses or store in a neat pile for future use. Mulch is beneficial because it helps retain moisture in the soil, keeps down weeds, and protects plants from winter cold.

To turn deadheaded blossoms as well as worn-out leaves and canes into useful organic matter, compost them. Composting is easy, safe, clean, and tidy. Before you start, get organized so you can routinely separate out diseased leaves, flowers, and canes and bury them, if you have the room. If not, send them to the municipal dump. The rest of your garden waste can go straight to the compost pile.

Composting is the process by which grass, leaves, and other organic material from your yard and garden are placed on a pile to be decomposed, over time, by microorganisms. You can also add vegetable leftovers from the garden or the kitchen to the pile. Coffee grounds and egg shells are acceptable, but meat scraps attract unwelcome scavengers. Temperatures inside the pile will be quite warm (up to 160°F) as the microbes go to work. In time, a brown, fluffy soil-like material is formed that is known as humus or well-rotted compost. In addition to organic material, the process requires moisture and air.

Finished compost has many uses in the garden. Spread it around plants as a mulch, or work it into the soil as an amendment (be sure, however, not to disturb plant roots). It also can be used to enrich the soil of plants in containers. When you mix compost into garden soil before planting, it helps correct deficiencies in the texture of the soil, breaking up thick clay and improving the moisture-holding capacity of sandy soil. You also can use compost as a topdressing for the lawn, but it's best to sift it first through a ¼-inch screen to remove large particles. Return the large pieces to the pile or use them as mulch.

The ideal place for your compost pile is in a level, well-drained location near a source of water. It doesn't matter if it's in sun or shade, but the area should be convenient and, preferably, inconspicuous. If you have ample space, simply pile your yard and garden refuse in a heap. The optimum size for such a pile is 5 feet wide and 3 feet high; length is unimportant. Don't locate it next to a wooden structure, such as your house or garage, which could rot.

If you have a small yard and don't like to see an untidy heap, or if you want to speed up the time required to make compost, there are many manufactured compost bins available in garden centers and hardware stores. You can choose from tumblers,

A day's collection of deadheaded roses and spent canes and leaves fills a bin destined for the compost pile at Longwood Gardens, Kennett Square, Pennsylvania.

wooden bins, and wire or plastic bins. An effective inexpensive container is an adjustable bin made of perforated polyethylene that is connected at its ends to form a freestanding unit. When the pile is composted, you can easily lift off the container.

Left on their own, most materials would turn to humus in one to two years. The process can be cut to a few weeks if you tend the pile closely. Beneficial steps include shredding materials so they break down faster, stirring the pile occasionally to ensure that it stays moist and receives oxygen, and making sure there are plenty of microorganisms available by adding a few shovelsful of earth or compost to the pile occasionally to bolster the level of microbes. When the compost is done, it will be dark brown and have a crumbly texture and a fresh, earthy odor. Use it liberally because you can always make more.

# rose husbandry

Despite scientific advances, breeders continue their search for the perfect rose. Out of 1,000 attempts, one rose may be selected, even while the breeder continues to look to other, as yet unnamed, seedlings for the one perfect rose that will outperform all others.

Although roses have been part of the garden scene for centuries and the first hybrid tea was recognized in the 1860s, it was not until the 20th century that roses became the subject of so much hybridizing and testing. Until recently, breeders focused on hybrid teas. They were looking for characteristics such as better disease resistance, striking color and color combinations, compact growth habit, and show quality. If you're in the Wasco area of California, near Bakersfield, you'll see evidence of all these breeding attempts—acre upon acre of roses in various stages of production. Even some of those roses, however, won't make it onto the pages and shelves that tempt us every spring.

It is, in fact, mind-boggling to realize that a breeder may plant and observe 100,000 seedlings in order to produce one that may be a winner in the eyes of the public. That one will go through about 10 years of testing and production before it's ready to take on a proper name and leave the nursery. Along the way, it may be abandoned for any of a number of reasons, from a tendency to black spot during one season to flowers that don't hold up in another season's severe weather.

All of the hybridizing and testing will be for naught if the rose doesn't sell. That's where the importance of its type and name comes in. More research is being done now on landscape roses—floribundas, ground covers, and shrubs—than on hybrid teas because their ease of care and hardiness make them more appealing to the public and to those who buy for mass plantings than the work-intensive tea roses.

As for naming roses, that's a tricky business. The name has to sell the rose almost indefinitely. It has to be memorable, as 'Mister Lincoln' is, so that you can identify the rose's particular assets or differences compared with all other, often similar, roses. The bold color and stature, for instance, of 'Mister Lincoln' uncannily match our image of the man.

'Bonica' was honored with an All America Rose Selections award in 1987.

# Exploring for new roses

Most of the hybrid roses on the market today were bred in this century by firms such as Kordes in Germany, Meilland in France, and Jackson & Perkins and Nor'East Miniature Roses in the United States. A few gifted amateurs also have had the joy of hybridizing excellent roses: Jerry Twomey ('All That Jazz' and 'Sheer Elegance,' AARS winners in 1992 and 1991, respectively) and Frank Benardella ('Tinseltown,' the first human-hybridized striped hybrid tea) are two outstanding examples.

'Sheer Elegance,' an All-America Rose Selections winner in 1991, is one of the few award-winning roses bred by an amateur breeder, Jerry Twomey.

Anyone can hybridize a rose. Doing it on a mass, commercial scale is something else. Consider: Every seed in a rose seedpod will grow into a different (however slightly) plant, with somewhat unknown characteristics of flower color, plant height and spread, leaf color, disease resistance, and fragrance. Every seed, therefore, must be planted if the breeder isn't to miss out on the possibility of a special find.

## Picking the parents

This is where experience and imagination come to the fore. So does practicality: If a rose that's to be crossed is, for instance, known to produce dozens of seeds per pod, it will be used as the seed parent rather than the pollen donor. The breeder will have that many more hybrids from one cross to grow on and evaluate.

A breeder can select two parents from any of the hundreds of roses available today. Although patented plants cannot be asexually propagated, they can be used to sexually propagate—the seeds they develop will not grow into exact replicas of the parents. Breeders don't enter blindly into hybridizing; they are knowledgeable enough about various roses and their genetic makeup to have an idea of what specific crosses may yield. A breeder may select one rose for its fragrance and a second for its vigor and interesting flower color.

What a breeder gets from such a cross may be surprising: Some plants may not bear fragrant blooms, others may have different shades of color, and still others may be rank-growing. One or two may not be worth naming and producing commercially but be sufficiently new and different, or in some minor way special, to warrant using them as seed parents for further crosses. ('All That Jazz,' pictured opposite, is the product of a cross between an unnamed seedling and a named plant, 'Gitte,' a fragrant hybrid tea with admirable vigor.)

## Making the cross

Commercially, field workers do the actual labor at the direction of the breeder. Thousands of crosses are done each year in a short span of time. Before they have a chance to mature and release pollen grains, the stamens are removed from the flower that will be the female parent so that it doesn't pollinate itself. The stamens from the male parent flowers are removed when they reach a pollen-producing stage; then they are dried and kept in a closed container until the stigmas of the female parents are ready to be pollinated. Pollen from the same male parent may be used to fertilize many different female varieties. (As a home garden hybridizer, you don't have to dry the stamens because you won't need the large amount of pollen that a breeder does.)

Using a sterilized camel's-hair brush, the field worker dips into the stamens and transfers the pollen to the stigma by brush-

**A shrub rose, 'All That Jazz' was an All-America Rose Selections winner in 1992.**

## The beginning of a new rose: seeds and breeding

**Parent plant**
Each rose blossom contains male and female parts. The pollen-bearing stamens (male) are removed from the female parent so the remaining stigma is ready to receive pollen from the rose chosen to be the male parent.

**Rose hip**
If all goes well, the female parent will produce a seedpod, technically a fruit (in rosarian terms, a hip). When it is ripe, the color changes. There may be anywhere from one or two to nearly 100 seeds inside.

**Rose seeds**
The seeds are removed from the hip and cleaned of residue. They are mixed with moist peat and sand in a plastic bag or glass jar and kept at about 42° F. for six weeks. Then they can be planted. First blooms are possible in 90 days.

# The beginning of a new rose: cuttings and grafts

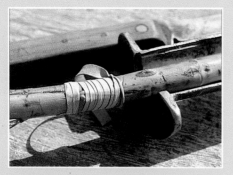

**Bud grafts**
Promising roselings are multiplied as quickly as possible by grafting each viable bud onto a rootstock, resulting in many genetically identical roselings. A rose chosen for introduction is then replicated in large numbers by the same process outdoors.

**Cuttings**
Cuttings for rootstocks are stuck directly in the fields. They are irrigated and monitored with care. Tree-form standard roses require a rootstock in the ground topped by a trunk that may be the same but still requires a separate graft.

**The new plant**
Here are tree-form standard roses in the diminutive patio size, about 24 to 28 inches tall. These are at the end of three years' training, ready for harvest in late fall or early winter for distribution the following season.

# Exploring for new roses

ing gently across it. Some hybridizers simply brush the stamen over the stigma, as can you.

The pollinated flower is tagged with a number corresponding to the recorded parentage and may be covered or not with a plastic bag. For breeders, seldom does a cross fail and invite the chance pollination by a visiting bee, so they usually don't bother to cover the flower. In the home garden, you may want to cover it; a sandwich bag will do.

If the pollination has taken, a seedpod (hip) will begin to develop in two to three weeks, at which point the bag can be removed. When it has ripened, indicated by a change in color to yellow, orange, red, or reddish brown, it's harvested, by hand. Most rose hybridizing, from pollination to the field production stage, is done by hand; equipment used was adapted over the years by the rose growers themselves from farm machinery.

## Sowing the seeds

Seeds are removed from the hip and cleaned. Then they are stored in a plastic bag filled with moist peat moss and sand in darkness at a temperature of 38° to 42°F. You can use your refrigerator but not the freezer. Stored for six to eight weeks, the seeds are then ready to be sowed, to the depth of their thickness, in a seed-starting medium.

You'll want to transplant the seedlings to individual pots when they have a second set of true leaves. As a home hybridizer, be assiduous in your care of the seedlings: The soil mix should be moist but not too wet. Damping-off is a real threat at this stage, and you won't want to lose any of your possibilities. Unlike the professionals, you won't have 100,000 seedlings from which to choose.

First blossoms can occur within a few months. Those plants that are obviously losers are tossed, but true flower and plant quality often is not apparent until the plant has been growing a year or more. Like the pros, you should give the roselings that kind of time to prove themselves.

The David Austin rose 'English Garden' resembles a gallica. Its rosettes open flat and possess a light tea-rose scent. Growing to only 3 feet tall, it's well suited to a small garden.

Mile after mile of roses in the fields of Wasco, California, attest to this being the rose capital of the United States. Between 70 and 75 percent of all roses produced in America are grown here.

## Producing the plants

Unless the rose is to be grown on its own roots, as most miniatures are, it must be budded onto a rootstock. Of thousands of seedlings, perhaps five will get to this stage.

Budding is done in the field; it is an art—and not a terribly comfortable one at that. The propagator rides almost upside down at the back of a machine; as he passes each rootstock plant (rooted in the field from cuttings the previous fall or early winter), he makes a cut into the rootstock's main cane and inserts a bud (eye) cut from the rose being propagated. The graft is then bound above and below the bud to keep the bud in contact with the cane.

Hundreds of grafts are done each day. The rootstock canes are allowed to grow along with the canes of the budded rose, because strength and vigor are desired at this stage, not beauty.

When the budded roses are growing strongly, they are scrutinized and evaluated over many seasons. If not discarded for any of a number of reasons, they eventually will be named and then mass-produced by the same budding process. Grown in fields for two years, the roses are finally dug and shipped for distribution to garden centers and nurseries.

# Selecting the perfect rose

'Midas Touch,' a 1994 All-America Rose Selections winner, has a medium musk fragrance.

Consider the characteristics that may define a perfect rose. Perfection, like beauty, is in the eye—and, where roses are concerned, the nose—of the beholder.

## Fragrance

Although probably the single most common trait people identify with a perfect rose, fragrance can be elusive. It can be the light scent of 'Peace,' the heady aroma of a musk or hybrid musk, the lasting sweet scent of *Rosa gallica officinalis,* the exquisite fragrances of the old damask 'Mme. Hardy' and the new 'Mary Rose,' the old myrrh scent of the David Austin English rose 'Constance Spry,' or the evocative tea perfume of his 'Graham Thomas.'

Breeding for fragrance was put on the back burner for years in favor of increased disease resistance, but hybridizers have come to recognize that the scent of a rose is a major factor in its appeal. They are working now with the older fragrant plants to breed for scent as well as form, hardiness, and disease resistance.

## Disease resistance

The bane of all rose growers, diseases such as black spot and powdery mildew are the top priorities of most breeders. Selecting roses that will continue to look good through an entire season of growth and bloom without dependence on chemical sprays and dusts is essential, they know, if home gardeners are to continue their love affair with roses. Yellow roses, for example, have been notorious for being weaker and less disease resistant than other roses, but newer varieties, such as 'Midas Touch,' a 1994 AARS hybrid tea winner, and 'Topaz Jewel,' a reblooming rugosa, are said to be very disease resistant. For the home gardener, the American Rose Society's (ARS) Annual is an excellent guide to vigorous roses. Because its test gardeners live across a wide range of climates, and special problems in various regions are highlighted, you can be forewarned about a specific rose before trying it at home. The ARS list of roses also includes information about many old-timers as well as newcomers.

## Color

Color definitely is a personal preference. One person's red rose may be anathema to another's preference for yellow or white blooms in the garden. Gradations of color, bicolors, petal reverse colors, a flower's ability to retain or attractively change hue as it ages—these are all considerations when searching for a perfect rose. 'Mister Lincoln' is said to be the best red rose ever; 'Pascali,' the best white; 'Queen Elizabeth,' the best pink; and 'Rainbow's End,' charming for bicolor miniatures. The list of possibilities is nearly endless, because only you can judge "best" for your garden. Perfect does not mean best, and best does not mean perfect, if it doesn't suit your plans.

## Size and shape

Size of the plant and the bloom, especially compact size, is an important quality in a perfect rose for today's gardens. The perfect size depends first and foremost on where and how the rose will be used. So does the perfect shape. A low mound or a stately sprawl—floribunda versus alba—either may be perfect if it fits in your landscape. Size and shape of bloom matter most to rosarians who want show-quality roses.

Fragrance, disease resistance, color, and size and shape are all characteristics of the perfect
rose, but, thankfully, pretty does not have to be perfect.

# an encyclopedia of roses

Thousands of different roses exist, some wild and others hybridized. The benchmark for sorting them out is 1867, the year 'La France' was introduced. Roses known before are officially "old"; those since are "modern."

Jean-Baptiste Guillot first noticed the rose with "something different" about it among seedlings at his nursery in Lyons, France. It was upright and tidier than most mid-19th-century hybrid perpetuals. Moreover, the buds ballooned with promise before they opened into high-centered blossoms resembling those of the day's many-petaled tea roses. Guillot concluded that a cross had somehow occurred between a hybrid perpetual and a tea, yielding what could rightfully be called the first hybrid tea. It took several years, however, before 'La France' was accepted officially in its homeland and yet another generation before it was recognized by the British National Rose Society.

The importance of 'La France' might never have been recognized except for the work of a single English connoisseur, Henry Bennett, who between 1879 and 1890 produced several impressive new roses from a breeding program designed to mate certain teas with selected hybrid perpetuals. In retrospect, it can be seen that some of the beautiful new roses Bennett created were merely hybrid perpetuals, 'Captain Hayward' and 'Mrs. John Laing,' to name two. Many were the real McCoy, however, proving that the design of new roses was not limited to the French. Although 'La France' was essentially sterile, Bennett's 'Lady Mary Fitzwilliam' was an outstanding stud, so fertile that breeders on both sides of the English channel used it, thereby honoring Bennett as Lord of the Hybrid Teas. Later in this chapter you'll discover that like any war won, this one has lately been lost, or, at the very least, victory superseded by new terminology for such roses. Henceforth, they are large-flowered hybrids.

The more you know about the cast of rose characters, the better you can choose for your own garden. Because you are almost certain to fall in love with more roses than you can grow, your knowledge will take you into others' gardens better prepared to appreciate their rose choices. In this chapter, you'll take a walk through rose history, beginning with the wild or species roses—those found in nature—and ending with the very latest in self-cleaning landscape roses, ground-cover roses, care-free shrub roses, and new roses that look exactly like old roses.

# Wild or species roses

*Rosa xanthina spontanea 'Canary Bird'*

Many wild rose look-alikes have other names. The cinquefoil, for example, is a member of the rose family that belongs to the genus *Potentilla.* Another familiar blossom that resembles a single white wild rose is that of the strawberry, genus *Fragaria,* itself a member of the rose family, along with apples, pears, apricots, and plums, to name but a few of the rose's delectable relatives. To the casual observer, the snowy blossoms of mock-orange might be mistaken for those of a wild rose. Yet close inspection reveals blossoms comprised of four petals and four sepals, making this often-scented flowering shrub, the *Philadelphus,* a member of the *Saxifrage* family, which is closer botanically to the hydrangea and lilac than to the rose.

Some gardeners are taken with wildflowers or those that seem wild, such as a simple rose with five petals. Others find these flowers to be charming along a roadside or by an old barn in the country but want only modern, large-flowered hybrids in their more formal gardens at home, as if these were of an innately superior race.

Not every rose that looks wild, presumably a delicate-appearing single or five-petaled blossom that smells like a rose, is actually a wild or true species belonging to the genus *Rosa*. Single-flowered modern roses that appear cursorily to be wildings exist in every type of pleasing configuration. A lovely case in point is 'Canary Bird,' known botanically as *Rosa xanthina spontanea,* but thought to have originated from a cross of *Rosa hugonis* x *Rosa xanthina,* introduced into the West from China around 1908. The single blossoms are, indeed, the color of a canary, with prominent stamens in the center and a light rose scent. Although primarily spring blooming, as are species roses in general, 'Canary Bird' also flowers intermittently in the fall. It is given to an angular habit that adapts well to training on a wall. If an otherwise healthy 'Canary Bird' suffers dieback, simply remove the deadwood and it will likely return.

## Roses for beauty and health

The word *Rosa,* when capitalized in italics, takes on a certain presence, as though it represented a kingdom or at least a princess. And indeed it does. The rose has been known historically as the queen of flowers. Scientifically, the genus is genetically rich, endowed with many distinct species that occur in widely differing climates over the Northern Hemisphere. Through their vitamin C content, the seed hips of wild roses were saving lives and improving the health of those who ate or drank them as tea long before the vitamin itself was discovered, named, and its benefits recognized.

Students of *Rosa* count up to 200 different species around the world, with a preponderance in central Asia and China, but also occurring in the contiguous United States, in Alaska, and, to some extent, in Europe. As roses evolved over 60 million years, they have adapted to a range of temperatures, from arctic cold to the intense heat of India, parts of Mexico, North Africa, and the Philippines. It is noteworthy that the largest chapter of the American Rose Society is in Houston, where there is a protracted season with nights consistently above 80°F and considerably hotter by day. In any climate resembling that from which came the species rose, it is almost certain to thrive without any special attentions such as spraying or fertilizing. An advantage to the species roses, in general, is that they bloom early in the season, before the arrival of troublesome predators such as Japanese beetles and leaf diseases that seem inevitable on modern hybrids. They also grow on their own roots, which means that any offshoots arising from the ground around a species will be identical in leaf and flower. In cold climates, where grafted roses are subject to winterkill, these always return true from their roots—which also facilitates propagation.

## Species roses are care-free

As cultivated plants, the species roses excel as large, care-free shrubs, perfect for spacious yards and gardens. They need little pruning, only to remove deadwood, to thin out excessive crowding, or to restrain a specimen that has extended beyond its welcome. This can be undertaken at any convenient time, but ideally in winter because some bloom on both old and new wood and because that's also when the branches can be seen clearly. Besides blooming earliest in the rose season, the species often produces seed hips that are colorful from the time they ripen in late summer to early winter, or until birds have consumed them. Some also have foliage that turns an attractive yellow, orange, or scarlet in autumn. It is especially pleasing in the company of tall, hardy asters and blue monkshood.

The first species rose to leaf out in early spring is among the last to bloom: It is the eglantine or sweetbrier, *Rosa eglanteria* (known formerly as *Rosa rubiginosa*), immortalized by Shakespeare in "A Midsummer-Night's Dream" for its medium-pink flowers, singly or in clusters, white centered, and intoxicatingly fragrant. Native to England and Europe, it has become naturalized in eastern North America and is possibly one of the most garden-worthy of the species. A nearly irresistible aspect of the eglantine is that from the time its leaves unfurl at the dawn of a new season until they have been frosted at the end, there emanates from them a tantalizing aroma reminiscent of ripe apples and pie spices. When brushed in the garden or handled while making a flower arrangement, the fragrant oils transfer to your hands. Envision the eglantine and its hybrids as bounteous arching shrubs, which can grow to 10 feet in height and as wide.

*Rosa eglanteria*, **the eglantine or sweetbrier rose**

# Wild or species roses

Considering the desirable traits of *Rosa eglanteria*, it's not surprising that breeders would think to cross it with other roses. This was done most notably by Lord Penzance in England at the end of the 19th century. The Penzance hybrids, as they are called, were developed by crossing hybrid perpetuals, bourbons, or other species with the eglantine. In almost all cases, the seedlings carried the trait of scented foliage. Characters in the novels of Sir Walter Scott inspired many of the names given by Penzance to his hybrids. He was also a judge, which could explain why he named the exceptionally beautiful 'Meg Merrilies' rose for a very human Meg Merrilies, who lavished her time and money helping down-and-outs in London's Soho.

## Earliest species to flower

Soon after the eglantine leafs out, the Carolina or pasture rose, *Rosa carolina*, becomes covered with single, soft pink, fragrant roses about 2 inches across. This North American native, from Nova Scotia to Texas, was designated the official flower of Iowa in 1897. In the wild, the bushes stay about hip high, but under intense cultivation they can grow to twice this size. They do not bear significant hips so a shearing back after spring flowering is all that is needed to keep them orderly and bounteous in flower. Removing oldest wood in winter, when it can be most clearly discerned, is a way to encourage vigorous new shoots the ensuing season. Be forewarned, however: If you plant the

**Rosa x hibernica,**
**opposite and above**

Carolina rose in your enriched perennial and shrubbery border, it almost surely will send up invasive suckers that must be dug out in order to maintain floral order.

Arriving in bloom almost simultaneously with the Carolina is 'Father Hugo's Rose,' *Rosa hugonis*. Known also as the golden rose of China, it was found there in 1899 and introduced to American gardeners by the Arnold Arboretum, in Jamaica Plain, Massachusetts. Single, dark yellow flowers with little scent are generously borne on arching branches that can reach 8 feet tall but often much less. Because it is ironclad hardy, 'Father Hugo's Rose' succeeds just about universally. *Rosa hugonis* is in all likelihood a parent of 'Canary Bird.'

The dog rose, *Rosa canina*, originally from Europe, western Asia, and North Africa, and long naturalized in North America, is another inherently strong species. It grows from waist high to as much as 10 feet tall, with arching branches aggressively set with curved or hooked prickles. The two- or three-paired leaflets have a bluish appearance on the undersides, more noticeable when riffled by a breeze. The single, sweet-scented flowers vary from pink to white on long pedicels, solitary or in clusters to four. The ½-inch-long hips turn scarlet when ripe and have long been used medicinally for their high content of vitamin C.

Considering that *Rosa canina* is today the most common wild rose in Britain and Europe, it seems inevitable that insects or the wind would eventually mate it with other roses. Such is the case of *Rosa* x *hibernica*, thought to be the offspring of a chance mating between *Rosa canina* and *Rosa pimpinellifolia*, the Scottish rose. One source speculates that *Rosa* x *hibernica* is the wild Irish rose discovered near Belfast in 1802. Another says it was introduced in Ireland 37 years before. In any event, this child of nature appealingly retains its sepals like *Rosa pimpinellifolia* and displays colorful, showy hips like those of *Rosa canina*. The medium-size, single, pink flowers are fragrant, silvery white at the petal bases, topped by a generous ring of beguiling stamens laden with yellow pollen. This charming variety can grow to 10 feet tall, its barbed branches a definite liability if they swing across a garden path. This can be remedied by tying them to a trellis or by cutting them back to any reasonable size, in late winter or when convenient.

# Wild or species roses

One of the first wild or species roses encountered by all budding gardeners, if not rosarians, at least in much of North America, is *Rosa multiflora*. This answer to all landscaping problems, the "living fence" featured in advertising too dubious to mention, arrived in the West from eastern Asia around 200 years ago and is said to have entered U.S. gardens in 1875. The relatively thornless and gracefully arching stems form explosions of clustered single, lightly scented, creamy white blossoms for one brief moment in spring.

Through summer the pale green leaves of *Rosa multiflora* seem unusually prone to mildew and spider mites, yet the hips ripening red in autumn are always a welcome sight, and not for birds only. If you have a large property and want a multiflora rose hedge, be aware there is also a spiny form that is more effective if a barrier is required. Set the rooted plants a foot apart so they'll fill in rapidly. *Rosa multiflora* is easy to start from both seeds and cuttings. It has often been used as an understock. If the part grafted on top dies for any reason, the *Rosa multiflora* roots may send up strong shoots. These look promising, but they will not flower unless they are left without pruning until the following spring. It is at this point when the neophyte learns, providing the right question is asked of the right person, that "rosarianspeak" for top growth sprouting directly from the understock is "sucker." Usually suckers are removed as soon as they are identified as such.

Perhaps the multiflora rose has been exploited and even maligned unfairly. Hardly any wildflower can equal the beauty of a successful multiflora hedging beside the highway, gracing a country roadside ditch or possibly a single bush spilling over the bricked wall behind a municipal parking lot in Natchez, Mississippi, which is where the photograph on the opposite page was taken in mid-spring.

Although *Rosa multiflora* may itself have something of a vulgar reputation, the species has several notable varieties, and its genes have contributed immeasurably to a host of roses we treasure, including the hybrid musks, multiflora ramblers, modern shrubs, polyanthas, floribundas, and modern climbers.

A famous cultivar is the fabled Seven Sisters rose, introduced from China in 1816 and officially named *Rosa multiflora* 'Platyphylla.' It became popular in Victorian times and has continued to have its champions. This is understandable considering the big trusses of spring flowers in which seven different colors are discernible at one precise moment. There are several shades of pink from dark to soft, lilac, and occasionally dark red. There is another Seven Sisters rose, a cultivar of *Rosa sempervirens* named 'Felicite et Perpetue.'

## A "living fence" that climbs

Although you may be aware of multiflora roses at the instant they are in peak bloom, you may see them only as large, billowing shrubs. If two or more are planted together, they become impenetrable. Should this occur on a small lot, complete eviction of an overgrown multiflora can be daunting to say the least. So much for the down side. An advantage is that a well-placed multiflora can be easily coaxed up into a tree, where it will be spectacular in bloom. This is something the English do very well, encouraging or just permitting one plant to scramble over another, and you can do it to similar breathtaking effect. In fact, it's not unusual to see an escaped multiflora tumbling down a bank or twined up a tree's trunk and branches until it has topped out in the sky, a true sun worshipper.

You might think a rose named *Rosa pendulina* would have gracefully hanging stems or pendulous clusters of flowers. In this case, the reference is to pendent, bright red hips. Also known as the alpine rose, *Rosa pendulina* grows to 4 feet high and as wide, forming an attractive small shrub that is nearly thornless. The reddish-purple stems arch so as to display advantageously the spring flowers, to 1½ inches across, singly or in clusters of up to five. They are single, dark pink to rose, with showy stamens. Considering that it was found originally around 1700, growing at higher elevations in Europe, cold-hardiness to below 0°F makes this a reliable rose in cultivated gardens through Zone 6. It is grown primarily in scientific collections such as at the Brooklyn Botanic Garden in its Cranford Rose Garden.

*Rosa multiflora*

# Wild or species roses

## *Rosa rugosa* from China and Japan

The rugosas are unique among rose species. Their disease-resistant foliage has a pebbled or wrinkled quilting rarely seen in other species. The early summer until end-of-season flowers, often redolent of old-fashioned roses, are typically large and single or semidouble. *Rosa rugosa*, introduced into the West from Japan and western Asia around 1796, has mated rather freely with other roses, so there are those having double flowers and mixed parentage. Two notables are 'Blanc Double de Coubert,' introduced by Cochet-Cochet in France in 1892 (almost fully double, pure white, from a cross of *Rosa rugosa* x 'Sombreuil,' a tea), and 'Agnes,' introduced by Saunders Central Experimental Farms in Canada in 1922 (fully double, amber yellow paling to white, from a cross of *Rosa rugosa* x *Rosa foetida persiana*).

Some rugosa roses bear large and showy fruit. If cheery fall color is important to you, choose one of these: *Rosa rugosa* (the type) or *Rosa rugosa* 'Alba,' *Rosa rugosa* 'Rubra,' 'Belle Poitevine' (magenta-pink, almost double flowers), 'Calocarpa' (also called 'Andre,' single, rose-pink), 'Frau Dagmar Hartopp' (also sold as 'Frau' and 'Hastrup'; single, silver-pink; recommended especially as a producer of high-quality flowers in autumn), 'Jens Munk' (semidouble lilac-pink), 'Moje Hammarberg' (double, purplish red), 'Nyveldt's White' (large, single, white), 'Schneezwerg' (semidouble, pure white) and 'Vanguard' (semidouble, salmon-bronze).

Another attribute of the rugosas is that the healthy foliage can be retained into autumn until cool nights and warm, sunny days bring outstanding fall color—yellow in some, red to burgundy in others. Strong in this category are the species and its varieties. Virtually all rugosa hybrids have showy hips as well. For fall foliage color, consider: 'Roseraie de l'Hay' (semi-double, crimson-purple; always in bloom, rarely sets fruit), 'Scabrosa' (single, silver-cerise; recommended for hedging), 'Sir Thomas Lipton' (double, white, staggeringly sweet-scented) and 'Will Alderman' (double, clear pink; introduced by American breeder Skinner in 1954; exceptional hardiness to cold).

## Rugosas are ideal landscape roses

Clove scent and hardiness under difficult conditions such as high winds and salt spray have made these roses a favorite for planting in public places, such as Jones Beach on Long Island, New York. The bushes grow strongly, stand on their own, and are well armed with prickles. They inevitably give a spectacular flowering at the beginning of the rose season and then will appear continuously or intermittently. 'Linda Cambell,' from American breeder Ralph Moore and introduced in 1991 by Wayside Gardens, gives up to seven flushes of double blooms a year, saturated crimson, in clusters of five to 15. Another Moore hybrid, 'Topaz Jewel,' from the class of 1988, is considered the first reblooming yellow rugosa. Not only is it always flowering, this scented rose lightly sheds old petals, casting them to breezes and making the bushes self-cleaning. In the right place, it can grow to 5 feet tall by 7 feet wide. 'Max Graf,' by contrast, a cross of *Rosa rugosa* and *Rosa wichuraiana*, has a trailing habit that makes it an ideal ground cover.

Another rugosa hybrid that is worth considering is 'Sarah Van Fleet,' a choice introduction in 1926 from Van Fleet himself. The semidouble flowers are rose-pink and open but cupped in an attractive way. The young foliage is tinted with bronze. In some areas, rust can mar the otherwise dark green leaves on stems so densely prickled they seem indestructible. Prune hard in late winter or early spring to encourage strong new shoots and protracted bloom.

The canes sent up by a rugosa rose this season will yield next year's blooms. As a rule of thumb you can prune out the oldest wood at the beginning of a rugosa's fourth growing season. Continue this practice each succeeding year, and you will have vigorous rugosas and lots of blooms. They are also amenable to the usual pruning done to keep any rosebush healthfully open toward the center and free of any dead growth. It is fortunate that the rugosas are so naturally resistant to pests and diseases, because the usual sprays used on other roses will seriously disfigure their leaves.

*Rosa pendulina*, the alpine rose (opposite)
*Rosa rugosa* 'Rubra' (opposite, inset)

# Gallica roses

*Rosa x francofortana*, also known as 'Empress Josephine'

The French or gallica rose, *Rosa gallica*, represents a group of roses with showy flowers in colors and conformations that are in complete harmony with what many gardeners expect in a true old garden rose. It is also the parent of many modern hybrid roses and the only rose of the four most historic whose lineage can be traced to a single ancestor. Oldest of the old garden roses,

gallicas date back more than 3,000 years to a wild European rose. There are no white cultivars, but the palette by which they are known and revered—crimson, lavender, pink, and purple—is something of a standard by which to judge these colors in all other roses. Owing to bluish undertones, these shrubs look well with lavender, rosemary, and catmint.

# Gallicas ideal for cutting

The typical gallica becomes a compact shrub around waist high and as wide, densely stemmed but having next to no thorns. The foliage is dark green, and the flowers are nicely displayed above it. Late spring to early summer is the time of concentrated bloom, and hardly any flowers that can be cut and brought into the house are as beautiful or smell so divinely. Aromatic glands on the flower stalks transfer a long-lasting fragrance to the hands of any person who works with them.

As a group, the gallicas are considered fair game in Zones 4–9, suggesting cold-hardiness to minus 30°F. They are a success also in much milder climates, where killing freezes are a distinct possibility but not an inevitability in winter. Texas Rose Rustler Margaret Sharpe, one of Houston's most knowledgeable growers and a consulting rosarian in the American Rose Society, laments, "They are just about a lost cause for us." She means along the Gulf Coast, where summers are beastly hot and humid. In almost any more temperate climate, however, the gallicas have a reputation for thriving, even tolerating poor soils.

One of the most famous of all roses is *Rosa gallica officinalis*, the Apothecary's Rose of Provins, also the Red Rose of Lancaster. It is said to have been brought to France and England by the Crusaders from Damascus and has been grown widely since the 13th century. A special trait is that the light crimson petals retain their fragrance even when dried and powdered, which explains their historic use for fragrance and as a conserve. The semi-double flowers in late spring or early summer open to reveal golden stamens in the center. They appear in unusual abundance on erect bushes to 4 feet tall and wide.

'Empress Josephine,' also known as *Rosa* x *francofortana*, has been known since 1820 and was presumably named for her at or near the time of the great rose gardens she maintained at Malmaison, approximately 1798 to 1814. The rose is considered to be a cross of *Rosa gallica* x *Rosa pendulina*. Although lightly scented, these loose, wavy-petaled blossoms are well worth examining closely for they are a subtle blending of dark pink with pronounced veins and highlights of pale pink and lavender. The only flowering is at the beginning of summer, but you can use the sturdy bushes, 3 to 5 feet tall and sprawling nearly as wide, for hedging and in mixed shrubbery borders.

## Graceful and fragrant by nature

'Belle de Crecy,' known since before 1848, is an especially fragrant flower that opens dark pink with cerise flashes, then melds into a soft Parma-violet color with a distinctive button eye. The nearly thornless canes arch gracefully, all the better to display the dark green leaves, on shrubs about waist high and wide.

'Duc de Guiche,' introduced in 1835, opens large, fully double flowers that are crimson at first, then give way to veinings and blushings of purple. It is exceptionally fragrant on bushes to 4 feet tall. The color and form of these blossoms are without peer in the class, lovely in the warm-climate garden and memorable in any bouquet.

'Camaieux'

# Gallica roses

*Rosa gallica 'Rosa Mundi'*

the florist trade can compare with the presence of a 'Rosa Mundi' in an arrangement or alone in a bedside bud vase. Because it is by nature a sport or mutation, don't be surprised if a branch reverts to *Rosa gallica officinalis* while the rest of the bush blooms 'Rosa Mundi.'

## Propagate gallicas from offshoots

It is fair to ask how a rose such as this could survive through the centuries and still be rated by one expert as "widely available." In writings dating from 300 B.C., Theophrastus suggested observing how the "torch of life" is passed from plant to plant through the medium of small cuttings. In the case of 'Rosa Mundi' and gallica roses in general, they do not propagate readily from cuttings but rather from offshoots that grow from roots spreading underground. The ideal time to remove one of these is in early spring, with some moist earth held about the roots and immediate transplanting to the new site. Rooted offshoots also can be set in pots and even transferred successfully to a distant garden.

Among the old European roses, none has quite the cachet as 'Rosa Mundi.' It is a rose of antiquity that is known also as *Rosa gallica* 'Versicolor,' a sport or offspring of *Rosa gallica officinalis*, the 'Apothecary Rose,' not to be confused with *Rosa damascena* 'Versicolor,' the York-and-Lancaster rose. 'Rosa Mundi' is set apart by the colorings that stripe through the flowers, light crimson and white. It was reportedly named for Henry II's mistress, Fair Rosamund. Not even today's long-stemmed, large-flowered, French-grown roses that command premium prices in

The gallicas need little pruning except thinning out the oldest canes immediately following the current year's flowering. Otherwise, they become too dense, a condition that favors their susceptibility to powdery mildew. Little or no pruning may be needed in the first couple of seasons after planting. Should you inherit an old, neglected gallica, prune it back sharply to size in late winter or spring; this will revitalize the bush.

Although 'Rosa Mundi' is the most famous French rose with striped petals, other cultivars that display this remarkable trait include these:

**'Camaieux,'** introduced in France in 1830, has double, very fragrant flowers that are pale pink—almost white—and purplish crimson aging to lavender and purple. The leaves are gray-green on gracefully arching but relatively short stems.

**'Georges Vibert,'** introduced in France in 1853, combines carmine and purple, many-petaled flowers on a tidy plant that you can accommodate readily in a small garden.

**'Nanette'** is also small and compact, a bush that can be grown in a patio pot for double flowers with purple-striped crimson petals and a green eye at the center when fully open.

**'Oeillet Flamand,'** introduced in France in 1845, is vigorous and emphatically erect. The double flowers are pink-and-white striped with dark pink to near magenta.

**'Tricolore de Flandre,'** introduced in Belgium in 1846, has pale pink, purple-striped, almost fully double flowers that have an exceptionally beautiful shape. The compact bush has lots of dark green foliage and makes a pleasing specimen for potting.

Although the more precise origins of the gallicas are lost to history, the gallicas contributed to the gene pool of modern roses through crosses made with both European and Asian species beginning in the late 18th century, providing most notably color, scent, and hardiness.

## Gallicas can be own-root or grafted

When you obtain a gallica rose for your garden, determine if it is growing on its own roots or if it has been budded onto a different rootstock. The good news is that own-root gallicas seem less prone to mildew-blighted foliage. The bad news is that own-root gallicas can colonize beyond the point of welcome in a garden having limited space. In any event, these roses are ideally sited where there is free circulation of fresh air.

Because the gallicas bloom only once a year, they need remarkably little attention and may even be said to thrive on benign neglect. Following the annual pruning to remove dead and bloomed-out canes, apply a balanced rose fertilizer in early spring. An alternative to a synthetic is to side-dress in late fall or winter with well-rotted cow manure or compost.

Owing to the outcrossing with other roses, the gallicas vary considerably in growth habit. Not all of them colonize aggressively. Some remain essentially small and comparatively thorn free. Some stay where they are planted, grow canes 6 or 7 feet tall, or have pronounced thorns. Any gallica that grows long canes can be trained either of two ways, as an espalier or pegged down for shaping and bloom encouragement.

Espalier suggests a plant having height and width but not much depth. This method of training is used on a trellis or wire framework, usually set about 8 inches out from a building or garden wall. Another possibility, keeping in mind the gallicas' need for freely moving air, is to train the long canes on wires between fence posts set about 6 feet apart. Bending the canes into a horizontal position encourages lots of lateral growth and an abundant flowering the following season.

## Pegging suits the gallicas

A training method that works with exceptionally satisfying results for the taller gallicas is to peg down the growing tips. Fall is the preferred time. Use a galvanized wire hoop or brushwood cut into a "V" that when inverted and pushed or driven into the ground holds the cane tip in place. In this horizontal position, the same as when espaliered, the laterals are favored and a heavier flowering results. Because you dispense with all of the canes one by one and peg them into place, you can create a shapely mound that also makes an ideal ground cover. 'Cardinal de Richelieu' produces tall canes that are limber enough to facilitate pegging down, to better show off its purple blossoms. 'Scarlet Fire' with smooth, brownish-purple stems is another.

# Damask roses

The damask roses were first cultivated by the Romans and cherished for the habit of some to bloom in both the spring and the fall. There is no true species *Rosa damascena.* Yet among the old European roses the class is distinct, perhaps most noteworthy for the abundant production of the fragrance associated with attar of roses. As a group, the damasks are inclined to foliage that is downy in spring and light green, canes that are quite thorny, up to 6 feet tall, and delicate flower stems in generous clusters. It is speculated that all of the roses loosely classified as belonging to *Rosa damascena* are, in fact, combinations of *Rosa gallica, Rosa canina,* and *Rosa phoenicia,* the last a climbing wild rose from Asia Minor. The Empress Josephine is said to have grown nine different damasks at Malmaison, a fact that no doubt gave them certain favor among 19th-century French rose breeders. They saw great potential in the autumn damasks for introducing repeat flowering into almost any other rose known before the introduction of remontancy (reblooming) from the China roses.

Possibly oldest of the damasks still in cultivation is the fabled 'York and Lancaster,' also known as *Rosa* x *damascena* 'Versicolor,' whose flowers vary from entirely blush pink to pure white and all stages in-between, sometimes within the same cluster. Known prior to 1551, this probable sport of the summer damask was named, according to legend, following England's War of the Roses, 1455 to 1485, in recognition of the union between the House of York, whose badge was a white rose, and the House of Lancaster, whose badge was a red rose.

## The source for attar of roses

Another very old damask that remains in cultivation is 'Kazanlik' or *Rosa damascena* 'Trigintipetala' (having 30 petals). It is said to have originated in the Bulgarian fields where attar of roses is a traditional crop. 'Kazanlik' has pink, double, shaggy flowers that give off superb fragrance. They are ideal for making potpourri, a practice that removes the petals for drying before the aging blossoms turn moldy on the bush. If they are not harvested for potpourri, these blooms need to be promptly deadheaded.

'Blush Damask' is also of ancient origins, dating at least from 1759. Not to be confused with 'Old Blush,' one of the stud roses from China, 'Blush Damask' is vigorous and tall, with double flowers of medium size, dark pink at the center, paling toward the edges, fetchingly cupped and intensely fragrant. Their time in the garden, however, is fleeting, and wet weather rapidly spoils them.

The damask roses are, in general, white or some shade of pink. The flowers may be double or semidouble, sometimes loose or shaggy, but not necessarily. They are likely to grow taller than the gallicas and to display a generous amount of both glandular bristles and hooked prickles. Any that repeat, such as the autumn damasks, need pruning in winter or earliest spring to remove all deadwood, and to thin out the oldest, the weakest, and the lesser of crossing canes. For the damasks that bloom once yearly at the magical moment between spring and summer, wait to do major pruning until after they have flowered. It is safe to remove most of the flowered shoots and canes. This encourages strong, young growths from the base. These, in turn, can be shortened in winter, but only parts extending beyond the shrub's desired bulk. If you have a damask that develops long, pliable canes, it will probably benefit from pegging. This tends to boost lateral growths, on which the flowers are borne.

The *Rosa* species name *damascena* refers to the Damascus region of Syria, where this type of rose is thought to have originated. Damask has several definitions, one being a color—deep pink or rose—and another, a silk or linen reversible fabric often woven into familiar tablecloth twill. These words are likely to conjure something on the order of a joyous Sunday dinner at home, and nothing could be prettier for the centerpiece one or two weeks out of the year—up to four if there are some autumn damasks—than a bouquet of these truly old roses. 'Celsiana,' for example, has been gracing gardens and tables for nearly 250 years with once-yearly sprays of semidouble, soft shell pink roses in clusters of generous-size blooms, to 4 inches across. When fully open, each rose reveals a center halo of golden yellow stamens. 'Celsiana' forms a graceful shrub to 5 feet high and nearly as wide, with gray-green foliage. It has an appeal in the garden, to painters, and for making potpourri that is apparently timeless. Most notably, it was one of the Empress Josephine's roses that was painted by Redouté.

*Rosa damascena* 'Blush Damask'

# Damask roses

## Younger but mostly "old" damasks

Even the younger damask roses are technically "old," with some exceptions. 'Jacques Cartier' was introduced in 1868, a year after the introduction of the first hybrid tea, so technically it is a modern rose. Some rosarians place it in a damask subclass for Portland roses; others say the Portlands are a definable class. 'Jacques Cartier,' also known as 'Marquise Boccella,' produces clear, light pink, fragrant roses that open to resemble fluffy peonies on a compact, 4-foot-tall plant.

Another Portland found among the damasks is 'Rose de Rescht,' also tagged autumn damask. Dates regarding this short, bushy plant with rosette blooms more than 2 inches across and fuchsia-red with purple tints are scarce. It is claimed to have been carried from Persia or France to England by a Miss Nancy Lindsay. Because it grows to a compact 3 feet tall with a similar girth, and an extended or second flowering, 'Rose de Rescht' is often planted in shrubbery or perennial borders for its all-round landscape capabilities.

**'Comte de Chambord,'** also technically a Portland, was introduced in France in 1860. It is an autumn damask as well, one that yields the true attar of roses scent. The flowers are full, flattened and quartered, and bright pink with tints of lilac. In the garden on tidy plants to waist high and not quite as wide, or cut for bouquets, these blossoms are the embodiment of one's most romantic notions about beautiful roses.

**'La Ville de Bruxelles,'** introduced in France in 1849, is a true damask. It has very large and generously scented flowers, possibly the largest of any of this type in cultivation. They are a saturated pink, flattened and quartered, with incurved centers. If the plant can be sited so as to maximize the effect of the arching branches, so much the better, for they will bend down to exceptional effect with the weight of the blooms.

**'Madame Hardy,'** introduced in 1832, has been recently blessed by Graham Stuart Thomas as, "A thing of rare beauty—it has no peer." The man Hardy, who bred the rose he named for his wife, began the century as rosarian to the Empress Josephine's collection at Malmaison. He must have had exceptional taste, for 'Madame Hardy' is today more admired than ever. The double flowers are blush pink as they begin to open,

then become pure white with green button eyes. The form begins cupped, but the aging outer petals turn backward, all the better to emphasize the incurving central ones. Educated rose noses will not be surprised that the delightful scent of the 'Madame Hardy' rose has a light lemony character. The plant itself is strong, growing vigorously 4 to 6 feet tall.

*Rosa damescena 'Jacques Cartier'*

# Alba roses

Because alba means white, it often comes as a surprise that as a class the alba roses include, besides white, blossoms that are blush or pink. There is no rose species identified as *Rosa alba*, but botanists do recognize *Rosa* x *alba*, the "x" indicating a natural hybrid, in this case between *Rosa canina*, the dog rose, and *Rosa damascena*, the damask. The latter is the source of the pink tinting.

The albas date at least as far back as the Middle Ages, and for centuries they have given extreme pleasure to the gardeners who have grown and perpetuated them. Today, the albas are considered to be both refined and exceptionally strong, disease free, and tolerant of poor soil and trying weather conditions. The canes are sturdy but bear only a few stout prickles. The silvery-green leaves on bushes with an upright, vigorous habit add to the appeal of the albas in Zones 4–9. They are outstanding in their tolerance of partial shade.

As a class, the albas are noted for attar of roses fragrance and for blooming a fortnight or longer in early summer. Excepting semidoubles such as *Rosa* x *alba* 'Semi Plena,' the flowers are of the full cabbage type that is expected of any true old rose. Prune initially after flowering to boost new shoots from the base. Any of these that outshine the bulk of the shrub in winter can be shortened so that they conform.

**'Konigin von Danemarck'** ('Queen of Denmark'), introduced in 1826, opens dark pink buds into soft rose-pink flowers up to 4 inches across. These are exquisitely quartered, generously produced, and followed by a long-lasting display of large scarlet hips in fall and winter.

***Rosa* x *alba* 'Semi Plena,'** also known as the White Rose of York, is perhaps the oldest alba cultivated. It bears clusters of large, flat, semidouble, white flowers that are set off by a central crown of golden stamens. 'Semi Plena' is one of the roses grown in Bulgaria for the production of attar of roses. Under garden conditions, this alba reaches to 6 feet high by nearly as wide and yields a generous crop of red hips through late summer and fall.

Three other popular albas are:

**'Félicité Parmentier,'** which dates from 1834 and produces very double, fragrant flowers that are soft pink edged with cream. They are highly perfumed and reflex with maturity into a shapely globe.

**'Madame Legras de St. Germain,'** which dates from at least 1846, is cherished for camellialike blossoms that contain many creamy white petals. Its canes are nearly thornless, to 6 feet high by 4 feet wide.

**'Celestial' (or 'Celeste'),** which is very old, is strong and tidy in habit. Its blossoms are luminescent shell pink, semidouble, highlighted by yellow stamens, and sometimes strongly resembling a tuberous begonia.

'Konigin von Danemarck' ('Queen of Denmark')

# Centifolia roses

The centifolia roses have a complex gene pool, possibly having originated from a mating of the autumn damask with an alba. This could have occurred in the eastern Mediterranean region or southern Europe. Its further dissemination was facilitated by Dutch traders, for the centifolias were immortalized to such an extent by the Flemish painters that another accepted popular name is the Holland rose. Occasionally you'll find these referred to as the Provence roses, for the region in southern France where they were widely cultivated early in gardening history. This reference tends to confuse them with the gallica known as Rose of Provins, however. Josephine grew 27 different centifolias at Malmaison, so they were among the roses painted by Redouté.

The name *Rosa centifolia* is recognized, or at least tolerated, in some botanical circles, for its implication that there is a true species. The grouping is likely *Rosa* x *centifolia,* the "x" indicating the probability of hybrid origins. *Centifolia,* meaning "having a hundred leaves," is used to indicate that the flowers have this many petals, which they probably do not, but at least the word conveys their plenty. It also preserves a common misconception about what to call the various parts of a plant, particularly the precise difference between a petal (part of a flower) and a leaf (all the leaves on one plant constituting its foliage). Finally, centifolia roses as a class are known as the cabbage roses, for the petal-packed, sphere-shaped buds and blossoms.

## Centifolias improve with age

It is true that the centifolias resemble the gallicas, but as a class they are taller and thornier. The large cabbagelike blossoms are also heavy, so they have a charming habit of nodding. It's the sort of behavior that couldn't be tolerated in a long-stemmed, large-flowered bush rose, but which is considered excellent form in a centifolia. One of their strongest points is that the centifolias get better with age, becoming serviceable shrubs in the landscape that, in return for a little pruning, produce an annual show of flowers that is nothing short of glorious. Siting in full sun in the open garden, where the air moves freely, will produce the most vigorous centifolias with the least amount of black spot and powdery mildew on the leaves. Deadheading will keep aged blossoms from rotting on the bush, especially if the weather turns cloudy and wet. These prodigiously petaled roses rarely set hips, but the fall foliage color is worth noting.

After planting a centifolia, give it a couple of years to settle in before doing any serious pruning. In general, the most blooms come on the older wood. Cutting out the oldest and weakest immediately following the annual flowering in early summer will result in strong new shoots from the base. These generally grow more up than out in their first season, but in the next, with the weight of the flowers, they arch gracefully. The tallest centifolias can sometimes be accommodated in the smallest of gardens by training them as pillars.

*Rosa x centifolia*

# A miniature centifolia

One of the most unusual centifolias is 'De Meaux,' which looks and acts like a miniature but is not officially classed as such. Other names for it are 'Rose de Meaux' and pompon rose. The bush is an erect, twiggy dwarf shrub, clothed in tiny light green leaves. In season it is set all over with very full, very small, petal-packed light rose-pink flowers. Under the most encouraging conditions, it attains hardly more than the mass of a bushel. Similar in size but with larger, rose-pink flowers is another Lilliputian-size centifolia, 'Petite de Hollande,' also suited to a small plot, where its shape and habit can be controlled by pegging.

**'Tour de Malakoff,'** introduced in 1856, is an old rose that will respond with great vigor if situated in highly fertile soil. The large blossoms have a profusion of loose, papery petals that are purplish crimson to Parma violet with magenta overtones set off by prominent veining. As the blossom opens fully, the yellow stamens at the center can be glimpsed. 'Tour de Malakoff' needs some means of support, making it an ideal rose for training on a tripod of stout stakes at least 8 feet high, spaced 18 to 24 inches apart at the bottom, and tied together toward the top. As this year's new canes are tied diagonally upward on the tripod, numerous laterals will be encouraged, the result being a full flowering the next season. To complete the effect, plant a tidy flowering vine such as *Clematis viticella* with it.

*Rosa* **'Bullata,'** also known as lettuce-leaved rose, has unusually large leaves that look and feel crinkly. The foliage is dense and the thorns are few; otherwise, this variety is very similar to *Rosa* x *centifolia*.

**'Fantin Latour'** is something of a mystery because no date of introduction is known. Beales notes that its perfume is ". . .rather more albalike than centifolia." The form of the soft, delicate pink flowers is definitely that of a centifolia, and so is the category where most rosarians place this shrub rose with its smooth, rounded, dark green leaves and thinly thorned canes to 5 feet high.

**'The Bishop'** is an unusual centifolia whose large rosette-style flowers mix cerise, magenta, and purple. It flowers earlier than others of the class, growing nicely upright to 4 feet tall and 3 feet across.

*Rosa centifolia* 'Paul Ricault'

**'Village Maid,'** which is quite different but at least bicolored, has slightly off-white petals striped with pink. It blooms a bit later than the others and is reputedly one of the most generous. When the bush is exceptionally well-sited, an occasional flower may appear in late summer or early fall.

**'White Provence,'** also known as *Rosa* x *centifolia* 'Alba,' 'Unique Blanche,' and 'Vierge de Clery,' is possibly the most beautiful white rose in all the world. It was first discovered in the United Kingdom in 1775 and is thought to have sported from another centifolia. The very fragrant and very double flowers have the appearance of fine silk.

# China roses

Because the arrival in the West of the Chinese stud roses coincided with the Empress Josephine's planting of the grandest rose gardens of all time at Malmaison, it is no wonder that breeders pounced on these new roses as priceless studs. In retrospect, it can be seen that while the China roses brought the genes for different colors, it was remontancy, the ability to flower continuously all season on both old and new growth, that made them irresistible. As a rule, their flowers were neither large nor overly endowed with scent, but these traits could be gotten from a Western parent. A flurry of hybridizing soon resulted in new classes that now are recognized by such familiar names as bourbon, damask perpetual, hybrid musk, hybrid perpetual, and noisette.

## Pruning the China roses

The primary object in pruning a China rose is to keep the bush thinned and open at the center, and to develop an overall size and habit that is pleasing. Where winter cold is sufficient to defoliate them, it is safe to remove in winter or earliest spring about a third of the growth, or an amount that seems advantageous for the individual bush and its site. Prompt deadheading preempts certain diseases and assures that no seed hips will form, a factor in promoting flower production over the longest period possible. The China roses vary in habit from bushy to climbing. In colder regions where they are grown, a small, bushy shrub is likely, while in the Deep South they can become large shrubs or climbers that are virtually care-free.

## Small rose, surprising capabilities

A wonderful example of how Eastern and Western roses came together to parent a permanent new entity in the rose repertoire can be seen in 'Cecile Brunner,' introduced by Pernet-Ducher in France in 1881. It is the progeny of an unknown polyantha (The first were introduced by Guillot in the 1870s, from crossing a dwarf China rose with *Rosa multiflora*.) crossed with 'Madame de Tartas,' a tea rose introduced in 1859 and soon appropriated by the Victorians as a prodigious stud. Although 'Cecile Brun-

*Rosa chinensis* 'Serratipetala'

ner,' also known as 'The Sweetheart Rose,' 'Mignon,' and 'Maltese Rose,' produces a continuous supply of shell-pink flowers of perfect size and on a stalk the right length to be employed as a boutonniere, the bush itself is inclined to lack both vigor and foliage. Neither trait seems to diminish flower production, however, and little 'Cecile Brunner' continues to win a place in contemporary rose collections.

Coincidentally, 'Climbing Cecile Brunner' is about as vigorous as a rose can be, clothed with dark green leaves and able to establish in most soils. It was first seen in the United States and identified as a sport of 'Cecile Brunner' in 1904 and is today considered excellent for running up a tree or over an outbuilding that would be ugly without it. The only drawback, if it can be called that, is that 'Climbing Cecile Brunner' blooms once yearly, in late spring to early summer.

'Parson's Pink China' ('Old Blush')

# Tea roses

The tea roses, thought to have originated in China many civilizations ago from a cross of *Rosa chinensis* with *Rosa gigantea*, (the latter evergreen and from Burma and China) were favored in Europe from 1850 on. By the turn of the century or in the early 1900s, they were eclipsed by the modern roses. Some are extinct, but some of the loveliest, and possibly the strongest, have survived.

Think of the tea roses in today's terms as landscape shrubs in the South, not as cold hardy as the Chinas. In coldest regions, the tea roses are for coddling, maybe growing in large pots or tubs, so when severe cold threatens they can be conveniently wheeled to warmth. If adequate sunlight is available, they will continue growing and flowering. Placing the bushes directly under fluorescent grow lights is another method for coaxing containerized tea roses through inclement outdoor weather.

Hardly any other class of roses transcends the appeal of the tea rose for cutting. Even in the stems and leaves there is a grace that sets them apart. Then there are the delicate colors and a wonderful fragrance that may or may not fulfill the prophecy of what they were called originally: tea-scented China roses. Conjecture has it that they were so-called because the blossoms smelled of tea leaves, or because the bushes themselves smelled of the tea crates in which they arrived in England from Asia in the early part of the 19th century. You may decide for yourself which interpretation you prefer, using what your nose tells you upon visiting a dewy tea rose some sunny, mild morning.

Another attribute of the tea rose that appeals to some gardeners is that little pruning is needed. Yes, remove any wood that is dead or inconvenient. No, there is not a ritual annual pruning as for most cultivated roses. The climbing tea roses really need no pruning, except possibly after three years establishment on one site, then removing to the base some of the oldest or flowered-out canes, in late winter or earliest spring. Excepting the spring-only 'Dean Hole,' all of the tea roses remaining under cultivation are at least recurrent flowering; most are continuous or remontant.

## A rose for a President's lapel

Although it was first introduced in France in 1857, 'Duchesse de Brabant' was to become one of America's favorite cultivars when it became the blossom of choice worn daily in the lapel of President Theodore Roosevelt, 1901–1909. The exquisite buds furl together at least 40 soft pink petals; these open 2 to 3 inches across and then reveal an inner glow verging on orange. Perhaps a truism of the tea rose, and this one in particular, is that warm climates favor more profuse flowering.

'Mrs. Dudley Cross,' introduced in 1907, has a reputation for being among the hardiest of the teas. It is often associated with San Antonio, Texas, but, despite this and its yellow coloring, this is not the definitive Yellow Rose of Texas. In fact, there isn't one, except for the original woman who inspired the song lyrics. Another rose often taken to be the official Yellow Rose of Texas is *Rosa x harisonii,* or 'Harison's Yellow,' which actually sprang up in a New York City farm garden around 1830, from a cross that could have involved *Rosa spinosissima, Rosa hugonis,* or *Rosa foetida persiana.* 'Harison's Yellow' is an entirely reliable spring-blooming old shrub rose that can get on without any pruning, spraying, or fussing of any sort. It spreads by underground roots and will benefit from an occasional thinning of the oldest canes following spring bloom.

'Mrs. Dudley Cross' is a tea rose more to be favored in drier climates than damp ones, owing to the petals' resistance to opening in moisture-saturated conditions. Each next-to-thornless stem produces two or three fragrant, many-petaled flowers, the latter blushed pink in cool weather.

When the American Rose Society asked each member of its Old Garden Roses Committee to nominate a favorite, G. Michael Shoup, owner of the Antique Rose Emporium, Brenham, Texas, responded, "in favor of the 'Unknown Tea,' like the Unknown Soldier, for its symbolism of what the class has achieved: longevity, disease resistance, tolerance to heat and drought, proven by survival. Handsome bushy form. Often the commercial name will have been long forgotten and the 'Unknown Tea' will be referred to fondly as 'Grandma's Rose,' or, in some cases, 'Grandpa's Rose.' Whenever I encounter this mysterious 'Unknown Tea,' I know that its flowers can be pink or yellow, cream or crimson, fragrance guaranteed, and they will be continuously produced. Here in the South you can count on a tea rose. Any old tea rose!"

*Rosa* 'Duchesse de Brabant'

## Tea roses under fluorescent lights

An efficient fluorescent-light garden can be put together for growing tea roses (and others) by installing a commercial reflector or shop-light fixture that can be adjusted to be 8 to 15 inches directly above the roses. The light fixture can be raised or lowered by means of a pulley, and the heights of the roses themselves can be adjusted from below by standing the pots on boosters advantageous to each bush. Use a minimum of two 40-watt tubes, one each of generic cool-white and warm-white, in each reflector, for a growing area of 2 by 4 feet. Burn the tubes 16 to 18 hours out of every 24, preferably on a timer so as to keep days and nights of uniform duration. Situate the light unit in a space where air circulation is free and temperatures are moder-

ate, 55° to 72°F. Under these conditions, the roses can continue growing and flowering during times of the year when the outdoor garden is at rest. This also means that even in the midst of winter, with snow outdoors and frigid temperatures, a toasty-warm, fluorescent-light garden indoors will need regular watering and fertilizing.

Another way to protect tea roses too tender to live outdoors in winter is to bring the pots to a heated sunporch, conservatory, or old-fashioned, sun-heated pit greenhouse, an idea that never goes out of style. (A trench is dug 3 to 5 feet in the ground, then a roof is added, half of which is window glass or translucent plastic and half of which is insulated against the cold. Supplemental heat from thermostatically controlled portable electric units can be applied in times of extreme cold or sunlessness.) Tea roses

# Tea roses

discussed here are hardy outdoors as far north as New York City, but even in warmer regions it may be appealing to grow some indoors through the coldest days of the year. In all cases, the more sunlight the better, with temperatures ranging from cool to moderate, 50° to 72°F, and active air movement, possibly with some help from an oscillating electric fan.

Under these conditions, spider mites can be especially troublesome. They can be managed by spraying weekly with insecticidal soap and water and by watering the roots adequately so the rose does not become too dry or soggy to the exclusion of oxygen from the roots.

Hardiest of the white tea roses is the 1850 French introduction 'Sombreuil,' also among the most redolent. It is the habit of the bush to climb, so this is an old garden rose that lends itself to realizing the dreams of every new generation of rose growers, romantic visions of garden pillars and lattice structures woven with roses. Another way to manage 'Sombreuil' is to train the canes along a low wall or trellis. This horizontal procedure maximizes the production of laterals, from which are borne the large, flat, creamy white blossoms that when fully open reveal a faint blush from the center. 'Sombreuil' flowers recurrently, so its appearances in several flushes of bloom each season are always refreshing and welcome.

One of the oldest tea roses still extant is 'Bon Silene,' known prior to 1837. The fragrant, loose, double flowers open from a classic long-pointed bud, dark rose-pink on a vigorous bush that yields blooms off and on in all growing seasons. No wonder it has remained a favorite for many generations.

A tea rose with a fascinating story is 'Safrano,' which was first introduced in 1839. Rosarian Roy Shepherd describes it as ". . .the result of the first successful attempt to control parentage by hand pollination," thus beginning a new age of rose breeding. The flower is double, fragrant, and bright fawn unfurling from a long-pointed bud. New foliage shoots are a shade of plum that is particularly flattering to the color of the flowers.

That paragon of gardens and garden writings past, Gertrude Jekyll, included 'Souvenir d'Elise Vardon,' introduced in 1855, on her list of best roses, also recommending it for exhibition. At a height and spread of 3 to 4 feet, this rates as compact among teas and a logical choice where space is limited.

One of the favorites of acknowledged tea-rose lover Michael Shoup is 'Perle des Jardins' in the climbing form, first introduced in 1890. The sport of what was once the most important yellow greenhouse rose grown for the florist trade, this one excels in the garden by producing the same full, canary yellow flowers, generously perfumed and set above dark, waxy foliage.

'Monsieur Tillier,' introduced in 1891, produces large, very double and flat blossoms that are a bodacious combination of pale rose, salmon, and purple. When fully open, there may be seen both quartering and imbrication, the latter describing petals that overlap like shingles on a roof.

## A tea rose for high humidity

'Archiduc Joseph,' introduced in 1892, has fewer petals than 'Monsieur Tillier' but is no less dramatic. It combines pink, purple, and orange in the petals, with centers of paler pink. In areas given to high humidity, the low petal count gives this tea an advantage because it opens well despite dampness.

A tea introduced in 1893 as 'Maman Cochet' epitomizes the classic long-budded rose. The shape of the blossom, the strength of the stems, and the production of true orris fragrance has made this a perennial favorite in gardens of the South and West. Expect thrifty bushes about thigh high, set with only a few thorns and clothed with leathery, dark green foliage.

An example of a "found" tea that is in cultivation and available in commerce, but whose true identity is not presently known, is one offered as 'Odee Pink.' Ideal for cutting, it bears loosely formed, pale pink, double flowers on bushes 4 or 5 feet tall. Stock being distributed under this stopgap name came from the Brenham, Texas, private garden of a Mrs. Odee.

*Rosa 'Sombreuil'*

# Bourbon roses

The bourbon roses originated in 1817 east of Madagascar in the Indian Ocean on the Ile de Bourbon (later renamed Reunion), where hedges of 'Old Blush' and the rose they called 'Rose des Quatre Saisons' (autumn damask) were commonplace. Scientifically, the bourbons arose from a chance crossing of *Rosa chinensis* or one of its own hybrids and *Rosa damascena bifera,* the

'Zephirine Drouhin' with foxgloves

autumn damask. Because of their extraordinary beauty and easy disposition in cultural matters, these roses were among the most loved of the 19th century. The roseling that started it all, *Rosa* x *borboniana,* may be extinct, or it may be alive and well as 'Rose Edward.' If of true stock, the color would be dark red, with a major flowering in spring and another, somewhat lesser, flowering in autumn on a strong bush about chest high.

Count on the bourbons as strong, vigorous shrubs, hardy to around 0°F. Most are remontant, giving a big show in spring and fewer but larger flowers later. The flowers are typically cupped, quartered, and fragrant. In areas where black spot is a problem, these roses will benefit from fungicidal treatments. If the pegging technique appeals to you, look to the bourbons for some of the best material with which to work, specifically 'Madame Isaac Pereire' (1881; fat flowers like cabbages, intense rose-pink), 'Madame Ernest Calvat' (1888; pale pink), and 'Georges de Cadonel' (1904; round, petal-packed, luminescent pink).

Bourbons also are ideally suited for training as pillars. 'Zephirine Drouhin' (1868; cerise-pink, classic high-centered) is by nature a climber to 12 feet. Because the canes are thornless, this rose is ideal in the company of small children at play and can be trained around the columns of a porch. Other bourbons for pillars, a wall, or trellis training include 'Souvenir de la Malmaison Climbing' (1893; pale pink) and 'Madame Ernest Calvat' and 'Honorine de Brabant' (date of introduction unknown; soft pink with streaks of violet and mauve).

## Bourbons as self-reliant shrubs

Many bourbons make acceptable, self-reliant garden shrubs without any special training. These include 'Louise Odier' (1851; warm pink and lilac), 'Boule de Neige' (1867; crimson-tinged buds open snow white), 'Reine Victoria' (1872; rose-madder), 'Madame Pierre Oger' (1878; pale pink), and 'Reine des Violettes' (1860; lilac-purple; also effective trained against a wall or lattice construction). All of the bourbons can be coaxed to bloom more by shortening any shoot after it has flowered. In late winter or early spring, remove from the base some of the oldest canes that have previously flowered.

# Noisette roses

When Charleston, South Carolina, rice planter John Champneys crossed *Rosa chinensis* 'Old Blush' x *Rosa moschata*, the musk rose, he got a notably promising seedling bearing clusters of small, light pink, double roses, incredibly sweet-smelling at the peak of the annual spring flowering season. Cuttings shared in the early 1800s with Philippe Noisette, a Charleston nurseryman, were called 'Champneys Pink Cluster,' the name by which it is known today. Noisette, in turn, sent cuttings and seeds to his brother in Paris, who introduced as well 'Blush Noisette' (1817; an open-pollinated seedling of 'Champneys' Pink Cluster'; pink buds open into clusters of small white roses recurrently through an extended rose season) and 'Rosier de Philippe Noisette,' later known as 'Noisette' and now apparently no longer in cultivation.

The early noisettes tended to be smaller flowered and hardier than the later ones, with larger flowers and more genes from the tea roses. They are rated for growing to Zone 7, or hardy to about 10°F.

Although the French embraced the noisettes as their own, these roses are perhaps at their best in the southern United States and in New Zealand. Besides 'Blush Noisette,' also recommended are:

**'Aimee Vibert'** (1828) is the progeny of a mating between 'Champneys Pink Cluster' and a hybrid of *Rosa sempervirens*. The plant is nearly thornless, with a climbing nature that makes it ideal for training in almost any home garden. The small, white, double flowers appear in clusters beginning in late spring and continuing to frost.

**'Bouquet d'Or'** (1872), introduced by French breeder Ducher and a cross of the tea rose 'Gloire de Dijon' x an unknown seedling, grows vigorously to 10 feet high and two-thirds as wide. The large, double, quartered flowers combine coppery salmon and yellow.

**'Reve d'Or'** (1869; also 'Ducher') is French for "dream of gold," which suits perfectly this large, loosely double rose that combines buff-yellow color with the very epitome of noisette scent. The season-long producer is often at its best in the fall.

**'Madame Alfred Carriere'** (1879) can be vigorous to the extreme, with canes capable of reaching 15 to 20 feet tall. It produces large, full, double flowers that open pink but soon pale to creamy white. In the right place, few shrubs can surpass this one,

'Champneys Pink Cluster'

often blooming in the Deep South in the dead of winter when all other roses are resting.

**'Marechal Niel'** (1864; French breeder Pradel; a noisette 'Cloth of Gold' seedling) requires extra shelter in all but the mildest climates, but its devotees will not mind catering to any special needs. The shapely, pointed buds furl into exceptionally large, double, glowing yellow flowers with a generous scent. Vigorous canes arch to 15 feet long by half as wide and bloom recurrently.

# Hybrid perpetual roses

The hybrid perpetuals emerged as a distinct class in the 1830s, and the term was soon to become synonymous with Victorian roses. The first such rose came from a French breeder named Jules Laffay, only one of whose cultivars is still cultivated: 'La Reine,' also known as 'Reine des Français,' was introduced in 1842. High-centered buds open into fat, cupped blooms of silvery rose-pink with a dusting of lilac. It flowers continuously on a well-behaved upright shrub only 3 feet tall. 'La Reine' is considered early in terms of hybrid perpetual development, and its influence can be traced even to some of today's roses.

Hybrid perpetuals as a class are a complex mixture that involves the Chinas, bourbons, Portlands, noisettes, and, later, the teas. In many instances, perpetual has proven more hopeful than accurate in describing the flowering capabilities. If not perpetually in bloom, at least they are remontant. For a while there was intense competition between the bourbons and the hybrid perpetuals, but the latter won out and came to be linked inextricably with the reign of Queen Victoria, 1837–1901. Actually, she exceeded them for by the beginning of the 20th century the hybrid teas had completely eclipsed the hybrid perpetuals. Nearly half of the 1,000 roses listed in the 1882 book "The Rose" by H.B. Ellwanger were hybrid perpetuals.

## The ultimate 19th-century roses

In the heyday of these roses, when nearly 4,000 were on the market, they were looked upon as the ultimate creations that humankind might labor to develop and bring to utter and complete perfection, to be pit, one beauty against another, in popular exhibitions and competitions. Unlike the more nodding China forebears, these blossoms stood regally erect on long stems that could be cut without thought of weakening the large bushes that were by nature thrifty. It is worth noting that the hybrid perpetuals are still first-rate roses that are able to survive tough growing conditions found over much of America.

## Pruning hybrid perpetuals

Keep in mind that it is natural for the hybrid perpetuals to produce a large blossom at the apex of the cane. Late winter to early spring is the time to thin and take out some of the oldest canes, then to cut back those remaining by two-thirds of their length. After the first flowering, repeat this cutting back. If the canes of a hybrid perpetual are trained horizontally, wrapped upward on a pillar, or pegged, laterals will be induced to develop on which many more flowers can be produced. After the laterals flower, shorten each one by two-thirds. During dormancy the following winter, shorten all laterals again by two-thirds, repeating the procedure after flowering, and so on. Perpetualness can be encouraged by providing ample irrigation in times of drought and adequate nutrients from a side-dressing of an organic fertilizer such as well-rotted cow manure.

**'Baronne Prevost,'** introduced in 1842 by the French breeder Desprez, produces an intermittent showing of intense rose-pink flowers that are fragrant, flat, and quartered, opening from globular buds that are packed with petals. By any measure this is a sturdy shrub rose, to 5 feet tall and similar width, that can also be managed by pegging. Although considered a bit coarse where gardening space is extremely limited, 'Baronne Prevost' makes a splendid addition in a spacious mixed shrubbery border or alone as impenetrable thorny hedging.

## First long-stemmed florist rose

**'General Jacqueminot,'** introduced in 1853, is a prototypical hybrid perpetual. It was the first long-stemmed rose of the florist trade, possessed of beauty, shapely, very fragrant, and dark red, with an occasional flashing of white on the petal reverses. The bush grows strongly erect, 4 to 6 feet tall.

**'American Beauty,'** an introduction from 1875 that came across the Atlantic as 'Madame Ferdinand Jamin,' was to become synonymous with bunches of long-stemmed beauties sent and received by lovers at all the auspicious moments of life. Spherical buds unfurl into large, cupped flowers, intense, glowing pink, and fragrant. Most flowers occur in the spring and fall, but some appear on an occasional basis in-between. Originally, this proved not such a trouper in the garden but a dependable producer of high-quality cut flowers under greenhouse conditions. Planted in the garden, this bush needs time to become established, but eventually there will be vigorous, upright canes.

**'Climbing American Beauty'** is not a sport but rather the result of a series of crosses between its shrub form, *Rosa wichuraiana* and a hybrid tea. It is not quite a hybrid perpetual, but

'Frau Karl Druschki'

commercial name 'White American Beauty,' something synonymous with long-stemmed beauty and all that could be divined as elegant and stylish for the times it graced.

'Hugh Dickson' was not introduced until 1905, yet it continues to this day as a rose considered worth growing by enough connoisseurs for it to be in catalogs and gardens. This is the quintessential high-centered, perfect, fragrant, red rose, each containing 35 petals. There are lots of blooms at the beginning of summer, then again in the fall. It can be maintained as a shrub, to 5 or 6 feet tall, but pegging is the preferred training technique.

'Paul Neyron,' a French cultivar from 1869, is another good one for pegging, for it has long canes. This hybrid perpetual also gets high marks for repeat bloom, for being one of the largest of all rose flowers, and for giving generous scent. The lilac-pink blooms when fully open greatly resemble

the blossoms look exactly like those of the shrub form, while the other parents gave it the vigor to climb and large, fragrant flowers, dark pink and cupped, mostly at the beginning of the rose season, but some rebloom can occur.

'Frau Karl Druschki' was not introduced until 1901, when the craze for hybrid perpetuals had passed. Yet this cultivar is legendary for its admirers in every new generation of rosarians. Although without scent, this large, globe-shaped white rose that opens from high-pointed buds, became its own classic under the

those of an herbaceous peony, except they recur throughout the long rose season.

'Magna Charta,' introduced in 1876 in the United Kingdom, is an example of a hybrid perpetual that is susceptible to both powdery mildew and black spot, yet manages to rise above them. Recurrent flowers are double, cupped, bright pink with carmine shadings, on a tidy bush to 3 feet tall.

Although hybrid perpetuals were at their most popular in the second half of the 19th century, their garden worthiness is

# Hybrid perpetual roses

particularly significant today, at a time when gardeners are being encouraged to diversify and to seek out plants that are self-reliant in times of drought or other weather extremes. If to adore the beauty of one of these roses is to worship life's abundance, then the hybrid perpetuals will surely go on being grown by each succeeding generation. Besides those recommended on the preceding pages, here are additional hybrid perpetuals currently sold in catalogs and nurseries where old garden roses are carried, arranged in the order of their introductions:

**'Marquise Boccella'** (1842) has at times in the past been sold as 'Jacques Cartier.' It blooms more or less continuously and well deserves to be associated with the term "perpetual." The flowers are flat when open, packed with pale pink petals, sweet-scented, and set on erect canes. Hardly anything in life could be nicer than to find one of these in a vase by your dining spot or bed.

**'Anna de Disebach'** (1858) has flowers that are cupped in profile but fairly flat when fully open. The profusion of dark rose-pink petals contained within have a fragrant bouquet. Flowering is constant for what was once known as 'Gloire de Paris.'

**'Maurice Bernardin'** (1861) is a cultivar of 'General Jacqueminot,' having clusters of bright crimson, fragrant flowers. Another name for it is 'Ferdinand de Lesseps.' Allow a space 4 to 6 feet tall and two-thirds as wide for this rose.

**'Alfred Colomb'** (1865), another 'General Jacqueminot' descendent, yields large, full, rounded flowers packed with bright crimson petals that have reverses of purple or dark carmine. They are generously scented on a healthy bush that grows 3 to 6 feet tall.

**'Gloire Lyonnaise'** (1885) contains up to 84 petals in a very large, double, pure-white flower that reveals a touch of yellow at the center. It is reminiscent of 'Frau Karl Druschki,' but is more fragrant and more compact.

**'Ards Rover'** (1898) is a hybrid perpetual climber. Michael Shoup reports it has been Texas-proven for vigor, heat tolerance, and keeping a modicum of leaves through the most intense heat. Flowers are dark red, high-centered, and fragrant, with a remarkable form and a recurrent appearance.

**'Granny Grimmetts'** (date unknown), introduced by the Antique Rose Emporium from a Swedish nursery, is decidedly remontant, producing an abundance of velvety-crimson double flowers that open out to reveal a crown of golden stamens. There is a spiciness in the way these smell that sets them apart from the others.

## Hybrid perpetuals have hardiness

One distinct advantage of the hybrid perpetuals is that they are hardy just about everywhere in the United States. The bushes may need some extra attention until they become established, usually by the second or third season. Thereafter, their production of ungainly, sparsely foliaged, long canes is more likely to be a problem. The problem is easily solved by cutting back in late winter or early spring so that all canes conform to the overall outline of the shrub, and again, lightly, immediately following the first flowering period of the season, which is when the majority of the year's blossoms will appear. If you are applying the pegging technique to a hybrid perpetual, make sure only the tip of each cane is touching the ground. Support and lift the cane at intervals of 10 to 12 inches using pieces of twigwood cut into a "Y" configuration and long enough—perhaps 12 to 18 inches—to anchor each support in the ground under the cane it is to lift.

'Baronne Prevost'

# Large-flowered bush roses

Although 'La France,' the first rose recognized as a hybrid tea, was introduced in 1867, it was not until early in the 20th century that this new class drew the attentions of the rose world away from the hybrid perpetuals. By 1918, the end of World War I, the hybrid tea had taken center stage in the gardens of rose growers on both sides of the Atlantic. It was seen as something of a super race, one that combined the flower form of the hybrid perpetuals with the long, straight stems of the teas. Such a large number of growers favored the hybrid teas that all the roses preceding them were for a time neglected.

**'Queen Elizabeth'**

Now, near the end of the 20th century, the hybrid tea as it was is something of an endangered species. Already the name has been changed in official nomenclature to large-flowered bush rose, a category that also embraces what we have been calling grandiflora roses, the first of which, 'Queen Elizabeth,' was introduced in 1954. Surely as long as there are rosarians there will be roses identified as hybrid tea or grandiflora. Here they will be considered as individuals as well as members of a single class renown for high performance standards, particularly well suited to formal beds, and often framed by low hedging such as boxwood, Japanese littleleaf holly, or English lavender. They are roses suited to rose gardens but usually not gardens in general, which is where the species and old garden roses shine.

If the hybrid tea represented perfection of the long-stemmed rose, then the grandiflora took this a step further, to the production on one long stem of an entire bouquet of large roses. 'Queen Elizabeth,' on being named an All-America Rose Selections (AARS) winner in 1955, was hailed as the perfect bedding plant, one that would go on producing masses of flowers after most roses had lapsed into quiescence. All of this was more or less true, or 'Queen Elizabeth' would not have become a perennial favorite. It is the habit of grandiflora roses to grow around 6 feet tall, however, so they have proved useful for background color as well as for cutting.

## Roses you can pamper

If you want care-free roses, look elsewhere. If you are a budding or at least hopeful rosarian who thinks nothing could be nicer than pampering a rosebush, large-flowered bush roses offer a welcome challenge. These roses flower on new growth. The more you prune back, the more vigorous the new shoot. If these bushes are not disciplined in this way, they will grow taller and taller, gradually thinning out and producing uncharacteristically small flowers. It is also necessary to administer a major pruning annually, at the very dawn of the new growing season, cutting the main living canes to 5 or 6 inches and removing all others. Further, it is always the goal with each bush to keep it open toward the center, with new growth outward bound. Prompt deadheading promotes better health and quicker rebloom. Cut back to a five-leaflet with a bud that is pointed out from the center of the bush.

**'Olympiad,'** a hybrid tea honored by the AARS in 1984, is typical of the class and an outstanding red rose. A seedling from a cross between 'Red Planet' x 'Pharaoh,' it came from New Zealand breeder Patrick McGredy, who earlier lived in Ireland, where the family name has long been associated with roses. The bright true-red color holds from the high, pointed bud stage through the fully open double flower. The plant is vigorous, medium tall, and upright, with strong stems for cutting and distinctive medium green leaves. There is a luminous quality about the large, full blossoms and a light fruity fragrance.

'Olympiad'

# Large-flowered bush roses

'Arizona'

Since 1867, and possibly 1859, the debut year for a new rose called 'Victor Verdier' that may have been the first hybrid tea, thousands of new hybrid teas have been introduced. They are named for all kinds of reasons; personal, romantic, business, political, descriptive, even commercial appeal. Below are some of the large-flowered bush roses that have made their mark and become standard bearers as well as some recent arrivals.

**'Abracadabra,'** a 1993 hybrid tea from Jackson & Perkins, grows to 5 feet tall with glossy, dark green foliage. Each 14- to 18-inch stem displays a large bloom to 5 inches in diameter that combines pink, purple, tan, cream, and shades in-between, a blend of colors that some gardeners love and others will dislike or ignore. There is a light tea-rose fragrance.

**'Alabama'** suggests one premise for naming a rose: a state's need to be immortalized in an earthy way, not as the official state flower, but as the official state rose. 'Alabama' has big, dark pink buds that open into blossoms with white reverses. They give a sweet tea fragrance.

**'American Pride'** was 1979 Rose of the Year, a forthrightly commercial distinction made by its seller and promoter, the Jackson & Perkins Company. Because the Jackson & Perkins name has been associated with roses for more than 100 years, it is doubtless in the best interest of the company that any rose sold as Rose of the Year be worthy. This fragrant, bright red flower that darkens to near black at the outer petal edges, has blooms to more than 5 inches across.

**'Arizona,'** a grandiflora, is named for the 48th state, and joins the thorns of the official state flower, saguaro or giant cactus, and the official state tree, the paloverde. It was bred in California by Weeks and introduced by the Conard-Pyle Company in 1975. The flowers are a blend of colors evocative of the dry Southwest: yellow, red, and coppery orange. In regions given to high humidity and muggy weather, the foliage of 'Arizona' may prove susceptible to diseases. In dry climates such as that of its namesake, it is outstanding.

**'Audrey Hepburn'** honors the beloved actress and rose gardener for whom it was named in 1991, a hybrid tea with apple-blossom pink and fragrant flowers 4 inches across, on disease-resistant plants to 3 or 4 feet tall.

**'Baccara,'** a 1954 hybrid tea from the French family of Meilland—only nine years after it had given the world a rose called 'Peace'—is a reliable producer of bright red, long-stemmed cut flowers when it is grown under greenhouse conditions. After several decades, 'Baccara' is still considered to be as fine as any other florist rose, despite having little scent.

**'Barbara Bush,'** a hybrid tea from Jackson & Perkins, is a perfect example of a rose named to honor the spouse of an American president. In this case it is all the more appropriate because

# The myth about fragrance

There was a period when rose breeders seemed more interested in color and form than in vigor, disease resistance, or fragrance. This time coincided with the introduction of 'Baccara.' In the early 1970s, however, *House Beautiful* magazine conducted a survey of fragrant roses and found that for the previous 100 years each crop of new roses contained some with abundant fragrance, some with a hint, and some with none at all. Those having no appreciable scent seemed least likely to survive the test of time, thus supporting the notion that all the old roses were fragrant.

the real Barbara Bush is a gardener and a garden club member. The rose honoring Mrs. Bush is a pink and white blend, to 5 inches in diameter, with 30 to 35 petals on tall stems to 22 inches. There is a light fragrance.

**'Bewitched,'** a hybrid tea that won AARS honors in 1967, was named for a television sitcom popular at the time. It has large buds that open into big double blooms of cotton-candy pink, richly perfumed, and set on strong, stiff stems. The bush is unusually vigorous, clothed with large, apple-green leaves.

**'Blue Moon,'** a hybrid tea introduced in 1964 by German breeder Tantau, is known variously in other countries as 'Blue Monday,' 'Mainzer Fastnacht,' and 'Sissi.' It is a seedling from 'Sterling Silver' that continues to be ranked as one of the best of the so-called "blue" roses. 'Blue Moon' produces a large, perfectly formed flower that is generously scented.

**'Brandy'** is a hybrid tea that earned AARS honors in 1982. It has long, curved buds that unfurl into classically formed roses of golden apricot, slightly deeper on the petal reverses. There is a strong tea scent. 'Brandy' has quickly become a favorite in its class, a medium-height plant to 4 or 5 feet with 12- to 18-inch stems supporting large blooms to 6 inches across.

'Blue Moon'

# Large-flowered bush roses

'**Brigadoon**' is a hybrid tea honored by the AARS in 1992. Large, pointed buds open to velvety cream blushed coral-pink and strawberry, the result being a display that is constantly melding into different color combinations. The naturally vigorous plant produces shapely, colorful blossoms, one to each dark green foliaged stem, that are ideal for cutting.

'**Buccaneer**' resulted from the breeding work of American Herbert Swim in 1952. A grandiflora that is still considered one of the best yellows, 'Buccaneer' is a model for this class as it was originally defined. It grows tall and upright, producing on each stem a bouquet of large, almost shaggy blooms with a light scent.

'**Caroline de Monaco**' has strong, densely foliaged bushes lifting up countless blossoms, each in its own way the most beautiful: creamy white, lightly edged with pink, and nicely fragrant.

'Caroline de Monaco'

## Famous people as roses

There are almost as many ways to meet and become acquainted with a rose as there are roses and people. A spring flower show is one ideal place to look. 'Cary Grant,' for example, appeared at the New York Flower Show in 1987, the year it was introduced by the French House of Meilland. 'Caroline de Monaco' became the toast of the 1990 Philadelphia Flower Show. The real Princess Caroline selected the rose from the Meilland trial gardens. 'Caroline de Monaco' was also one of the season's outstanding performers at the 1992 AmeriFlora held in Columbus, Ohio.

## Automobiles as roses

Beginning with the introduction of 'Chrysler Imperial,' an All-America Rose Selections honoree in 1953, it became fashionable to name new roses for products, in this case an apparently successful marriage because both the auto and the rose are still in business.

'**Cary Grant**' is a hybrid tea, a commendable example of the exhibition rose, one with exceptionally strong canes that display huge blooms, bright burning orange with red overtones. The blossoms are also shapely, have a spicy fragrance, and take an enticingly long time to open fully.

'**Century Two**' is a hybrid tea noted for fast turnaround from one bloom cycle to the next. The bush is medium tall with clear, dark pink buds that open into exhibition-shaped flowers.

'**Charlotte Armstrong**,' a hybrid tea, was given AARS standing in 1941 and by now has become a modern classic. Very long pointed buds open into large, dark pink flowers that are moderately fragrant. Old rosarians know it fondly as an easy-to-grow plant.

'**Chicago Peace**' is a 1962 sport of 'Peace,' an exact copy of the world's most-loved rose, but in darker colors, more vivid yellow to a paler shade, more intense blushing of pink from the edges inward. The plant has the large glossy leaves of 'Peace' as well as the upright bushy habit. The flowers have a slight fruity fragrance, and few hybrid teas could give more pleasure cut, alone, or in a bouquet.

'**Christian Dior**' is Meilland's answer to a perfect long-stemmed, high-centered red hybrid tea rose. It is highly rated for cutting and is immune to turning "blue" as it ages. There is also a soft, spicy fragrance. 'Christian Dior' made AARS in 1962, the immediate descendant of three impressive parents: 'Independence,' 'Happiness,' and 'Peace.'

'**Christopher Columbus**' was named by Meilland to honor the 500th anniversary of the explorer's arrival in America. The rose itself could suggest what may be seen increasingly: a self-reliant, disease-resistant bush that stays continuously in bloom but whose individual flowers are smaller, up to 3½ inches across. The peppery orange-red color offers high and warm visibility in the landscape.

'**Chrysler Imperial**' is a hybrid tea possessed of classic buds that open into large, shapely flowers on strong, straight stems. The compact plant has strong foliage and is the roseling of a cross between 'Charlotte Armstrong' x 'Mirandy.' One nose proclaims "strong damask rose fragrance"; another seemingly scoffs "fair scent."

'**Color Magic**,' a hybrid tea that was an AARS winner in 1978, has continued to be popular as the sort of rose that has the ability to look different each day. Creamy apricot-pink buds open to ivory-pink in the center, with shadings of darker shrimp pink, finishing scarlet pink. It is a medium-tall upright plant.

'**Dainty Bess**' was introduced in 1925 as "a hybrid tea whose flowers are produced in well-spaced clusters." That makes it sound like a grandiflora, the first of which, 'Queen Elizabeth,' was not introduced until 1954. 'Dainty Bess' is also a true single

'Chicago Peace'

rose, delicate pink with slightly darker reverse and ruby stamens. It is a medium-tall, upright plant, sturdy, and blessed with tough, disease-resistant foliage. Free-flowering and moderately tea-scented, this rose by any class will go on earning high marks.

'**Dolly Parton**' is everything a modern hybrid tea rose could be, somehow exactly like the woman herself. The rose, introduced in 1983 by American breeder Winchel, is from a cross between two popular parents, 'Fragrant Cloud' x 'Oklahoma,' from whom it inherited beautifully shaped buds and large, recurving exhibition flowers, with the color a blend of dark copper and orange-red. The fragrance is strong, of rose and clove.

'**Double Delight**,' a 1977 AARS hybrid tea from American breeders Swim and Ellis, has creamy white buds with ruby-red petal edging. As the bloom opens, the red spreads into the white parts. These last long on the bush as well as when cut, and the rose fragrance is notably strong and spicy.

145

# Large-flowered bush roses

'**Duet**' is a 1960 hybrid tea from Swim, the result of a cross between 'Fandango' x 'Roundelay.' Large, shapely, high-centered blooms are pale pink with darker colored reverses and a slight fragrance. The foliage is medium green, and the rose holds up well as a cut blossom.

'**Duke of Windsor,**' introduced by German breeder Tantau in 1969, has beautiful flowers on bushes that are almost too stiffly upright and formal. The Duke himself was a passionate gardener and in the later years was often accompanied by Russell Page, leading garden designer and author of the classic book "The Education of a Gardener."

'**Dynasty**' is a hybrid tea that was named 1991 Rose of the Year. It grows to 5 feet tall and has nearly thornless stems crowned by orange-and-yellow flowers to 5 inches across that have high visual impact in the garden as well as when they are cut for bouquets alone or with other flowers.

'**Eclipse**' came from American breeder Nicolas in 1935, an example of a relatively old modern rose that continues in commerce. The long, slender buds open to large, high-centered, golden yellow flowers that are still among the finest in this class and color. The vigorous plants grow in a bushy, upright habit, to 3 or 4 feet tall.

'**Elizabeth Scholtz,**' a 1989 grandiflora, honors the director emeritus of the Brooklyn Botanic Garden, who has said that in more than 30 years of work there nothing has given more pleasure than walking almost daily through the Garden's Cranford Rose Garden, an acre of roses in beds framed by white trellises and focused upon a lattice viewing pavilion. The rose was developed by J. Benjamin Williams of Silver Spring, Maryland, from a cross of the roses ['Granada' x 'Oregold'] x ['Arizona' x 'Sunblest']. It is a strong, upright bush with waxy foliage and perfectly formed large flowers that blend orange-red and gold.

'**Eternity**' is a 1993 grandiflora with large individual flowers, to over 4 inches across, that are a showy combination of orange-red and cream-white. The bushes grow 5 to 6 feet high, to half as

wide, and yield a long-running show of long-stemmed flowers. These flower-covered bushes have considerable visual impact in the garden, and the clusters of large blooms on a single sturdy stem are nothing short of perfection in a modern cutting rose.

'**First Prize**' won honors as a 1970 All-America Roses Selections hybrid tea. It is the quintessential show rose, a standard for high-centered classical form. The large rose-pink buds spiral into immense flowers in a less vivid pink. They have a mild tea scent and appear atop sturdy stems on a medium-tall bush.

'**Flaming Peace**' is yet another offspring of that greatest of all large-flowered bush roses, 'Peace.' 'Flaming Peace' has the same impressive strength associated with the family name and pro-

'Elizabeth Scholtz'

'Flaming Peace'

**'Fragrant Memory'** is another modern hybrid tea that is blessed with the true perfume of an old damask rose. The slender, graceful buds become large blossoms that are medium pink with a trace of lavender. The disease-resistant bush is upright, 3 to 5 feet tall. It is exceptional for cutting and one of the best for scenting the air, indoors and out.

**'Friendship'** is an award-winning hybrid tea with sweetly scented, large flowers that display a tantalizing range of colors, from dark coral to blush pink, with a blushing of salmon-red at the petal extremities. The plants grow to 4 feet tall and produce heavily, notably in hot weather.

**'Gail Borden'** came from German breeder Kordes in 1956. Although it has only a slight scent, the strength of the bush and the beauty of the rose-pink and cream-white flowers have made it a long-running commercial success. The individual blossoms are large and tend to cup appealingly when they are fully open.

duces a steady show of vividly colored blossoms that have considerable impact in the garden as well as when cut.

**'Folklore'** is a hybrid tea with pale orange petals that are orange-yellow on the reverse side. These appear on an upright spreading plant that has glossy disease-resistant foliage. It is both fragrant and excellent for cutting.

**'Fragrant Cloud'** hybrid tea has dark red buds that become high-centered flowers in an enticing coral-red. The fragrance is extraordinary, a redolence of old-fashioned true rose and spicy clove. These appear above glossy green leaves on a medium-tall bush. If any modern rose can dispel the notion that only old roses are fragrant, 'Fragrant Cloud' is it.

**'Garden Party'** won AARS distinction in 1960, a hybrid tea bred by Swim and introduced by the Armstrong Nursery of California, noted for ivory-white petals blushed with faint apple-blossom pink. Sometimes it is known by the unofficial but descriptive name "White Peace." The strong plant grows 4 to 6 feet tall and sports leathery, dark green leaves. The flowers yield a light tea fragrance.

**'Georgia'** is a hybrid tea with large, very double flowers that blend peach, apricot, and hints of lemon, with a moderate tea fragrance. The bush has glossy, dark green leaves and grows in an upright habit.

147

# Large-flowered bush roses

'Gold Medal'

'Gina Lollobrigida' came from Meilland in 1991. It is the epitome of a perfect intense yellow hybrid tea that is also endowed with a heady perfume. The relatively small flowers, to 3 inches across, are packed with 60 petals. They appear on a bush to 4 or 5 feet tall and 3 feet wide, in great abundance over the longest rose season imaginable.

'Glory Days' is a hybrid tea noted for large, fragrant flowers in a rose-and-pink blend. The bush has exceptional vigor, to 6 feet tall, and is a generous producer of blossoms.

'Gold Crown,' also known as 'Corona de Oro,' 'Couronne d'Or,' and 'Goldkrone' (depending on the country where it is being marketed), came from German breeder Kordes in 1960. It is a hybrid tea borne out of a cross between 'Peace' x 'Spek's Yellow.' Although it is a large, dark yellow, mildly scented rose, the occasional splashing of the outer petals with red makes this an unusual cultivar. The glossy leaves are set on dark cordovan stems.

'Golden Melody,' also known as 'Irene Churruca,' is a hybrid tea introduced by breeder La Florida in the United States in 1934. Its family tree is 'Madame Butterfly' x ['Lady Hillingdon' x 'Souvenir de Claudius Pernet']. Some experts consider this to be one of the finest roses of its time. The large, high-centered blossoms are an elusive blend of pale yellowish buff and hints of pink, darker toward the center. The stems are sparsely thorned and tend to an angular growth that may not be best but is certainly tolerable considering the exceptional beauty and scent of the blooms.

'Golden Times' is a hybrid tea from United Kingdom breeder Cocker, introduced in 1970. It is from a cross of 'Fragrant Cloud' x 'Golden Splendor,' and the large, loosely formed flowers have a clear, lemon-yellow color that is easily accommodated in a variety of garden and flower-arrangement color schemes. Although the flowers carry only a slight fragrance, they appear in generous numbers and over a long season on an upright, compact bush to 3 or 4 feet tall and as wide.

## A favorite yellow rose

'Gold Medal' resulted from the breeding work of J.E. Christensen and was introduced by Armstrong Nurseries in 1982. In addition to its other qualities, 'Gold Medal' has a rich color that does not fade even in hottest weather. The plants are extra hardy and inclined to hold their foliage in good health beyond the time when other roses have defoliated. The cultivar has an impressive record of outstanding performance wherever roses are grown. It has been honored by the New Zealand Star of the Pacific Award.

'Gold Medal' grandiflora is a consistent yielder of high-centered, golden yellow roses that have a hint of orange. Sometimes these appear singly; at others they are clustered on one sturdy stem. It is the habit of the bush to grow very tall, upright, with canes that are sparsely set with thorns. The leaves are disease resistant. 'Gold Medal' has earned a permanent place among the world's favorite yellow roses, because it is almost always in bloom and looks well in the garden as well as in a vase, alone or mixed with other flowers.

'Granada' was a 1964 AARS honoree as a hybrid tea. It has medium-size flowers that blend reds, oranges, and yellows in a semidouble form. Sometimes these are borne one to a stem; at others, in a cluster. They have a pronounced spice-and-rose scent. The bush grows tall and spreading, with new growth that is an appealing reddish color.

'Grandpa Dickson,' also known as 'Irish Gold,' is a large-flowered hybrid tea from United Kingdom breeder Patrick Dickson in 1966. The family tree includes ['Perfecta' x 'Governador Braga da Cruz'] x 'Piccadilly.' The unusually large blossoms are pale yellow, occasionally blushed ever so faintly with pink. The bushes grow strongly upright and come outfitted with a very large number of thorns.

# Large-flowered bush roses

**'Great Century,'** a hybrid tea, is a pale pink exhibition type on an exceptionally vigorous bush. These always appear one to a stem on a plant noted for dark green, leathery leaves. There seems to be a built-in resistance to the usual foliar diseases. Although the blooms are only lightly scented, they appear in exceptionally large numbers considering the large size of the rose.

**'Hallmark'** is a medium red hybrid tea that was introduced in 1966 by American breeder Dennison Morey for Jackson & Perkins. 'Hallmark' came from a cross of 'Independence' x 'Chrysler Imperial.' The fragrant flowers contain 25 to 30 petals. 'Independence' figures in the parentage of another outstanding bright red rose, 'Scarlet Knight,' which was introduced by the Meilland firm in 1967. It is also in the background of 'Swarth-more,' a dark pink cultivar that frequently wins top honors in competitions.

Meanwhile, the other parent of 'Hallmark,' 'Chrysler Imperial,' figures in that great dark red rose 'Oklahoma,' which was introduced in 1964. With parents like these, it is no wonder that 'Hallmark' is an outstanding red hybrid tea that has a reputation for producing large numbers of exquisitely formed blossoms, from the beginning of the season until the very last roses at winter freeze.

**'Harry G. Hastings'** is a hybrid tea introduced by Von Abrams in 1965 from a cross of 'Mark Hatfield' x 'Helene Schoen.' It is an exceptionally fine red rose named to honor the 90th birthday of a noted southern seedsman and horticulturist. The large flowers are semidouble in a strong dark red. They are intensely fragrant and hold a desirable form for an extended period on the bush. The petals have the helpful habit of quickly withering and disappearing, the effect being a bush that is always in flower and self-cleaning. They appear on a vigorous, upright bush 3 to 4 feet tall, with leathery dark green leaves that are noticeably disease resistant and handsome in the garden.

**'Harry Wheatcroft,'** also known as 'Caribia,' was introduced by the world-renown eccentric and English rosarian Harry Wheatcroft in 1972. It is a hybrid tea sport from 'Piccadilly,' with orange-red blooms that are striped with radiant yellow. There is only slight fragrance, but the blooms are among the most unusual to be found in this class of modern roses.

**'Hawaii'** is a 1960s hybrid tea with orange-coral flowers that have a slight fragrance. The rich coloration is perhaps best appreciated early in the morning or late in the afternoon. The 'Hawaii' bush grows upright, to 3 or 4 feet, and has excellent foliage. A more recent introduction involving this cultivar is 'Faint Heart,' from breeder Mike Pavlick in 1980. It came from a cross of 'Hawaii' x an unnamed seedling and produces creamy flowers that are blushed pink from the petal edges inward. It is in the mold of the finest exhibition roses, with long, strong, nearly thornless stems and a tea scent.

## Pages from my notebook

Some years ago, some little rosebushes were distributed as a gift to children in a certain city school. One little girl who received one was the daughter of a wealthy man. Intrinsically, the rosebush was nothing to him or her, for it was worth only a few cents. Yet—"That little rose cost me $50,000," said the father to a friend of mine not long ago. "We didn't have a place to plant it except between flagstones in the courtyard of our city home. So to get a suitable place, I bought a whole block of land farther out, built a new house, and since you can't landscape with one rose, I had to buy other roses and trees and evergreens and shrubs.

"Why, that rosebush changed our whole life. We never knew how to live before. We used to think we enjoyed life, with parties, theaters, and sun. Now we know that it was just excitement. The enjoyment comes from working with these living, growing plants."

—Writings of the Plain Dirt Gardener

# Large-flowered bush roses

'Headliner'

'**Headliner'** is a hybrid tea from American breeder William Warriner, introduced by Jackson & Perkins in 1985. It is from a cross of 'Love' x 'Color Magic' and the vigorous producer of exhibition-style blooms that have creamy white petals edged with cerise. It is lightly scented.

'**Helmut Schmidt,'** a large-flowered hybrid tea, has shapely yellow buds that open into flowers that hold their color even in hot weather. It flowers nonstop above large gray-green leaves and gives a sweet, tea scent.

'**John F. Kennedy'** is a hybrid tea with long buds that are tinted green, but as they progress, the petals become snow-white, furling into blooms 6 inches across. They give off a light licorice or anise scent above leathery, disease-resistant foliage on resolutely upright plants.

'**Just Joey'** is a hybrid tea with classically shaped buds that blend buff-orange to soft apricot, then open into large, ruffled, apricot flowers that yield a strong, fruity scent. The plant is medium size and rounded.

'**Kardinal'** is a hybrid tea popular among florists and is also a satisfactory performer in home gardens. The bright red flowers, to over 4 inches across, have a slight fragrance, but the color never fades and there is a delightful profusion of blooms over a long season.

'**King's Ransom'** garnered AARS honors in 1962 and continues to be one of the most popular yellow roses, with strong fragrance and big blooms supported by long, strong, straight stems. The plants grow to 5 feet tall.

'**Lagerfeld'** is a grandiflora named to honor renowned French fashion designer Karl Lagerfeld. It exudes a sweet scent and the rare, coveted silvery-lavender color that some rose lovers prefer above all others.

'**Legend'** is a hybrid tea introduced as the 1993 Rose of the Year. It has a moderate fragrance in a bright red flower that opens from a long, ovoid bud on 18-inch stems, making it ideal for cutting.

'**Louisiana'** is a creamy to ivory-white hybrid tea that opens to a classic exhibition form in a fully double blossom and has a light scent. The stems are strong, long, and straight, with dark green leaves on a vigorous bush that is tall, upright, and slightly spreading—impressive in the garden.

'Love'

'Love' is a 1980 AARS grandiflora that has classic shapely blooms combining scarlet-red surfaces with white reverses and a slight rose scent. It blooms generously above dark green, disease-resistant foliage, which is reddish at first.

'Lucille Ball' is a 1993 hybrid tea with moderate fragrance in a 5-inch bloom that is an exquisite pale apricot. The strong bush supports plenty of matte-green leaves and lots of 2-inch buds that are almost as exciting to watch perform as Lucy herself.

'Medallion' is a 1973 AARS hybrid tea winner. Its long, pointed buds are golden apricot at first, then they become extremely large, creamy pastel apricot flowers with plenty of rose fragrance. The plant is vigorous with leathery, dark green, disease-resistant leaves.

'Mint Julep' is a unique hybrid tea with apple-green flowers that carry a hint of pink tinting at the petal edges. The bush blooms generously in the garden, and the flowers last well when cut. They are fragrant as well.

'Mirandy' is a 1945 AARS winner that continues to be a favorite of today's rosarians. It has large garnet-red buds that turn into double flowers with the bounteous scent of the finest damask rose. The medium-size bush is strong.

'Miss All-American Beauty' won 1968 AARS honors. It is dark, vivid pink with large, promising buds and full, open blooms that yield a strong rose scent. The medium-size bush supports vigorous leathery foliage.

'Mister Lincoln,' a hybrid tea, was honored by AARS in 1965 and continues to be one of the most widely planted long-stemmed red roses. There is a decided damask fragrance on a tall, upright, strong plant with dark green leaves. 'Mister Lincoln' is reputed to have won more honors at the show table than any other large red rose.

'Lucille Ball'

'Mister Lincoln'

# Large-flowered bush roses

'Paradise'

'Peace'

**'Oklahoma'** is known as the best of the black-red hybrid teas. Generous buds become large but graceful flowers that give off pronounced rose perfume. The foliage is large, a dark shade of green on a bushy plant.

**'Oregold'** won AARS honors in 1975 and continues to be a favorite among many rosarians for its large, pointed buds that early on reveal the dark yellow seen in the beautifully formed blossoms; they give a hint of fruitiness. These are produced one per stem, hybrid-tea–style on a medium-size bush that has impressive vigor.

**'Paradise,'** a hybrid tea, was an AARS winner in 1979, for its abundant production of lavender flowers that have ruby-red petal edges, all the more pronounced by the spiraled form. The plant is bushy and vigorous; its fragrance suggests fruit.

**'Party Time,'** a hybrid tea, is cherished as a large rose that blooms with exceptional generosity. It is also of the exhibition type, dark yellow with dark rose blending inward from the petal edges. The blooms smell of anise or licorice and stand alone on strong canes.

**'Pascali'** won AARS distinction in 1969 and continues to be one of the loveliest of the pure-white hybrid teas; there is a light tea scent. It blooms freely on a strong plant with leathery, dark green leaves. Although classed as a hybrid tea, 'Pascali' is actually from a cross of the original grandiflora 'Queen Elizabeth' x the hybrid tea 'White Butterfly.'

**'Peace,'** a hybrid tea, was a 1946 AARS winner, and almost ever since has been considered the world's favorite rose. The pink-tinged, pale yellow flowers may defy description, but they have come also to define the modern, large-flowered bush rose. There is also a mild fruity scent.

**'Peach Beauty,'** a hybrid tea, is favored by those who must grow roses in hot weather. Large, peach-pink flowers with high-centered form, appear freely, and last in the garden or cut.

'**Perfect Moment**' is a 1991 AARS winner that is known for large, classically shaped buds that become sizable yellow flowers edged with bright red. They have a light fruity fragrance and appear on a plant that is compact and bushy with large, dark green, disease-resistant foliage.

'**Perfume Delight**' is a modern hybrid tea (AARS, 1974) that is endowed with a strong damask rose scent. The beautifully shaped buds and blooms are dark rose-pink on a strong, upright plant clothed in dark green.

'**Princesse de Monaco**' was named by Meilland to honor Princess Grace of Monaco. The blossom is large and beautifully sculpted, somehow recalling both 'Peace' and the American beauty for whom it was named. It is a hybrid tea that is white with pink blushing from the petal edges inward and has a distinct fruity fragrance.

'**Pristine**,' a hybrid tea, has ivory buds that are tinged with pink, foretelling the large white blooms with pink-blushed petal edges and a touch of fragrance. The plant is medium tall, strong, and the producer of leathery, disease-resistant foliage, itself notably garden-worthy.

'**Queen Elizabeth**,' a 1955 AARS winner, is said to be the first classified as a grandiflora. The large, clear pink flowers may appear singly on a stem or sometimes in a cluster. The plant is much admired for growing tall and vigorously and producing lots of flowers that are ideal for cutting. They have a tea fragrance.

'**Royal Highness**,' a hybrid tea (AARS, 1963), is one of the most classically beautiful, pastel pink roses ever created. It was developed by American breeders Swim and Weeks and first introduced by Conard-Pyle in 1962. The light fragrance, together with the strong plant that has healthy, dark green leaves and exquisite flowers, makes this rose all but irresistible.

'Perfect Moment'

'Princesse de Monaco'

# Large-flowered bush roses

'Royal Velvet'

'Sheer Bliss'

**'Royal Velvet,'** a hybrid tea (Meilland, 1986), is a lightly scented dark red, a dream of a long-stemmed red rose that rises constantly from a bush of medium size.

**'Seashell,'** a hybrid tea (AARS, 1976), has pale orange buds that open to a blend of golden peach and salmon-pink. Strong canes form a medium, upright bush that is both vigorous and floriferous. Dark, disease-resistant leaves offer a pleasant foil for blossoms that smell mildly fruity.

**'Sheer Bliss,'** a hybrid tea (AARS, 1987), is a lightly tea-scented blush to palest pink rose created by American breeder William Warriner. As might be expected of a rose from this period, 'Sheer Bliss' is exceptionally disease resistant.

**'Sheer Elegance,'** a hybrid tea (AARS, 1991), delightfully fulfills the promise of its name. Buds in classic form become exhibition blossoms combining soft, pale pink and cream. Strong stems support these, making them stand regally in the garden or

as well in a bouquet. The dark green leaves are highly disease resistant, on medium-upright growth. Add a light tea scent, and it is no wonder this has risen to stardom among rosarians.

**'Shining Hour,'** a grandiflora (AARS, 1991), is the ideal large-flowered, gleaming yellow bush rose, when well grown. The rounded, medium-size bush has disease-resistant foliage, something that has come to be required of the roses being introduced in these post-dangerous-pesticide, pro-environmental times. 'Shining Hour' blooms over a long season and smells fruity.

**'Solitude,'** a grandiflora (AARS, 1993), is orange-pink on the petal surfaces, yellow on the reverses. The medium-tall bush has lots of dark green foliage and a hint of spiciness in the blossoms.

**'Speaker Sam,'** a hybrid tea named after Texas Congressman Sam Rayburn, is a vigorous sport of 'Peace.' It has a dark pink picotee edging on creamy yellow petals in a large, classically formed flower with at least a hint of rose fragrance.

'Sunbright'

'Tiffany'

**'Summer Sunshine,'** a hybrid tea, is another perfect large-flowered yellow bush rose. Long-pointed buds reveal the clear dark yellow that is ultimately seen in the large exhibition flowers. The bush is medium-size, clothed with many large, dark green leaves. If you stoop to smell one of these on a mild, sunny morning, you will enjoy a distinct mild fruity fragrance.

**'Sunbright,'** a hybrid tea (Warriner, 1984), has big, bright yellow blossoms, a light scent, and a floriferous habit that makes the bush highly productive.

**'Swarthmore,'** a hybrid tea, is a large, fully double rose of dark pink with a smokiness spreading from the petal edges inward. These are borne atop strong, long stems on a tall, upright bush with plenty of dark green leaves. There is a mild spicy fragrance.

**'Sweet Surrender,'** a hybrid tea (AARS, 1983), is one of those glistening silvery pinks that many find hard to resist in the garden and cut. There is an abundant tea rose fragrance from the

large, many-petaled flowers on a bush that is medium-size, upright, and vigorous. The dark green leaves can be an asset in the garden, and the long stems are just right for bouquets.

**'Tiffany,'** a hybrid tea (AARS, 1955), has long, pointed buds of phlox pink with yellow shading from the base that furl into large flowers with many petals. Not only is this rose exceptionally easy to grow, it also has been endowed with a generous sweet fragrance and an all-around pleasant disposition. Perhaps it will make you think of Audrey Hepburn, Truman Capote, and "Breakfast at Tiffany's."

**'Touch of Class,'** a hybrid tea (AARS, 1986), is well named for a classic exhibition rose whose spiraled buds furl into large flowers that are warm pink shaded coral and cream. These appear on long, strong stems that favor them for cutting. There is also a light tea scent. The bush is notably vigorous.

# Large-flowered bush roses

'**Tournament of Roses,**' a grandiflora (AARS, 1989), produces large, very double flowers in two shades of pink, reminiscent of the floats in the parade for which it is named. The bushy plant grows vigorously upright with plenty of glossy green leaves that are remarkably resistant to diseases. This cultivar has a reputation for being easy to grow; the light, spicy scent is a bonus.

'**Tropicana,**' a hybrid tea (AARS, 1963), with its clear orange coloring, was a sensation at the time of introduction, and the cultivar's standing among other vivid oranges continues at the top. The plump, pointed buds open slowly into large double flowers that last unusually long in the garden as well as when cut. They have a sweet fruity fragrance, perhaps suggesting the taste of raspberries plucked from the bush. The 'Tropicana' bush is vigorous, well branched, and inclined to plenty of healthy leaves. Also called 'Super Star,' it came from German breeder Tantau and represents a complex family tree: [Seedling x 'Peace'] x [Seedling x 'Alpine Glow']. First introduced in Europe in 1960, this rose was a landmark for its color and habit. Soon it was being cultivated by code number in America and praised universally as a superior cultivar.

'**Uncle Joe,**' a hybrid tea, has large, pointed buds that open into dark, dusky red flowers. They stand on long, straight stems and have a light rose scent. The plant is tall and upright, with leathery dark green foliage.

'**Unforgettable,**' a hybrid tea (Rose of the Year, 1992), recalls the ballad immortalized by singer Nat "King" Cole. Long, pointed buds become large flowers, to over 5 inches across, that are dark to clear silvery pink and smell lightly of rose. The long, straight stems are just right for cutting, and the flowers seem to last longer cut than they do in the garden.

'**Voodoo,**' a hybrid tea (AARS, 1986), is a yellow, peach, and orange blend with scarlet blushes. The classic form on a tall, upright plant gives this rose an exhibition quality even if the blossoms are left in the garden. The dark green leaves are disease resistant. A rich fruity fragrance makes 'Voodoo' an exceptional modern rose.

'**Whisky Mac,**' a hybrid tea, blends tangerine and orange with yellow in large flowers carrying a heady, fruity fragrance. The plant is low and bushy, freely blooming, and clothed in dark green leaves.

'Tournament of Roses'

**'White Christmas,'** a hybrid tea, is a large, fragrant, pure-white rose that is produced in great abundance over a long season. The plants are upright and compact, to 4 feet tall, and carry leathery, light green leaves. 'White Christmas' is descended from 'Sleigh Bells' and is one of today's loveliest white roses.

**'White Delight,'** a hybrid tea (Rose of the Year, 1990), blooms in rapid cycles with large, tapered buds and exhibition flowers that are ivory-white shading to soft pink at the centers. They have a light scent, and the bush is strongly active with an upright habit and dark, glossy, leathery foliage. Few modern roses are more beautiful than one of these in a bud vase or mixed with other flowers in an artful arrangement.

**'White Masterpiece,'** a hybrid tea (1969), resulted from the impressive work of Jackson & Perkins breeder Eugene Boerner. It has high-centered exhibition flowers that are pure white and lightly fragrant. The bushes grow upright and produce tall, strong stems that are ideal for cutting. The mid-green foliage looks good in the garden.

**'White Wings,'** a hybrid tea (1947), came from American breeder Krebs, who got it by crossing 'Dainty Bess' x seedling. The result is a large, single white rose with scintillating reddish-brown stamens. The foliage has a leathery or matte finish, medium green, and excellent disease resistance.

**'Yankee Doodle,'** a hybrid tea (AARS, 1976), is a cultivar from German breeder Wilhelm Kordes that was introduced in America by Armstrong Nurseries of California. Rosarian Stephen Scanniello, the gardener responsible for the Cranford Rose Garden at the Brooklyn Botanic Garden, Brooklyn, New York, has singled out 'Yankee Doodle' as one of the best roses for the beginning gardener. It is the producer of exceptionally large buds that become huge cupped flowers with more than 70 petals and a luscious coloring of yellow-orange centered by apricot-pink. They are also endowed with fragrance.

A beginning rose breeder might well grow several bushes of 'Yankee Doodle' in order to study them for what a desirable modern large-flowered bush rose can be. First there is the vig-

'Yankee Doodle'

orous plant itself, which grows tall and self-reliant. The foliage is extraordinarily resistant to disease, a factor that no doubt figures in the habit of the bush to produce constantly over a season as long as any other rose in the class.

**'Yves Piaget,'** a hybrid tea from Meilland, honors the Swiss jeweler who designed the gold rose awarded to the Geneva New Rose Competition winner. 'Yves Piaget' rose is deliciously pink and when fully open resembles a peony blossom. It possesses tremendous rose fragrance, and the medium-size bush blooms abundantly—each blossom has about 80 petals. There is great disease resistance, as well. This rose has received numerous honors, including the Gold Medal at Geneva, the City of Geneva Award, and the Fragrance Award—Golden Rose 1982.

# Cluster-flowered bush roses

**'Apricot Nectar'**

Floribunda roses, now classified as cluster-flowered bush roses, are the result of crosses between the polyanthas and hybrid teas. In general, the class has moved toward a shorter, more compact habit, with variously doubled flowers and forms, some like perfect high-centered exhibition hybrid teas, but smaller. Recent developments have favored disease resistance and fragrance.

The floribundas need less pruning than most roses. Take them back by about one-third in the early spring. Thin any crowded canes, also those that are dead or twiggy. Aim for a bush that is open at the center, so always cut just above a new bud that is headed outward. After each wave of bloom, trim back lightly, but not as severely as might be done for a hybrid tea. The goal here is tidiness and a small nudge from the rosarian that will keep the bushes constantly blooming.

The 1939 World's Fair in New York City marked the first official appearance on these shores of what was to become known as the floribunda, a vigorous, shrubby rose that produced clusters of flowers and gave an outstanding performance as a bedding plant. That first floribunda was called 'World's Fair.' Although introduced in America by Jackson & Perkins, it came originally from Germany under the name 'Minna Kordes,' for a family member of rose breeder Wilhelm Kordes.

The floribunda as a class originated earlier in Scandinavia at the hands of Danish breeder D.T. Poulsen. It was his aim to produce new roses that could survive harsh winters and also recover quickly at the onset of a dishearteningly short growing season. 'Rodhatte,' introduced by Poulsen in 1912, was probably the original floribunda, to be followed by numerous others that were subsequently developed by his sons, Dines and Svend.

**'Betty Prior'**

**'Angel Face'** (AARS, 1969) is still judged "best lavender yet." Classic Grecian urn buds open to ruffled flowers of dark lavender blushed ruby-red. There is spicy old-rose scent on an all-round superior bush.

**'Apricot Nectar'** (AARS, 1966) came from Jackson & Perkins breeder Eugene Boerner and yields 5-inch flowers that are apricot colored and tea scented. They appear singly or in clusters and in a nearly nonstop show.

**'Betty Prior'** (1938) has no appreciable fragrance, yet it has been one of the world's favorite roses for many generations. It yields clusters of single (five-petaled) flowers that are vivid carmine-pink. The bush grows tall and wide, harbors no diseases, and is ironclad hardy. Add the curiously attractive, bristly, long red peduncles surrounding each of up to 10 flowers in a cluster and a propensity for never being out of bloom, and 'Betty Prior' always comes out smelling like a rose, at least figuratively speaking.

# Cluster-flowered bush roses

'Columbus'

few thorns that has been the treasure of Southern gardens for more than 100 years. 'Cecile Brunner' figures in the parentage of numerous miniature roses.

'Cecile Brunner,' also known as "sweetheart rose," 'Mignon,' and 'Maltese Rose,' doesn't always look thrifty, but it has a longstanding reputation for ending nearly every rose season as one of the winning performers. The lightly caned bushes can be easily accommodated in small quarters, even in pots, for winter greenhouse flowers.

**'Cecile Brunner White'** (France, 1909) is a sport with white flowers that also contain tints of peach and yellow. This cultivar is now rare, but if you like the original 'Cecile Brunner,' this one will also delight.

**'Charisma'** (AARS, 1976) produces petal-packed double flowers, usually in clusters, that are in a kaleidoscope of changing colors—yellow, orange, and red. They appear in such prodigious numbers the glossy, dark green leaves on a compact, bushy plant are almost obliterated. It also cuts well.

**'Cherish'** (American breeder Warriner, 1980) is from a cross of 'Bridal Pink' x 'Matador.' It is noteworthy for clusters of very double, classically formed high-centered flowers that are coral-pink and lightly scented. The plant has a compact, bushy habit and plenty of dark green, disease-resistant leaves.

**'China Doll'** is favored as a dwarf, compact, bushy plant for the formation of low hedging and borders. It is the dependable producer of large clusters of feathery pure-pink flowers that are held attractively above the bright green leaves.

**'Cecile Brunner'** first appeared in 1881, and it is the true old-fashioned sweetheart rose. Peter Beales casts it with the China roses, but because 'Cecile Brunner' is the result of French breeder Pernet-Ducher's crossing an unknown polyantha x 'Madame de Tartas,' it is listed here with the other modern cluster-flowered bush roses. The bushy plant is of medium size and the producer of small pastel-pink blossoms in loose clusters. There is a modest amount of tea rose fragrance from this rose of

'Circus' is an American-bred floribunda introduced by Herbert Swim in 1956 that dependably produces a never-ending display of clustered small roses that constantly change colors, one cluster often containing flowers variously colored orange, buff, or pink. The bush is upright and spreading, to 3 feet tall and about as wide. 'Circus' came out of a cross between 'Fandango' x 'Pinocchio.'

'City of Birmingham' was introduced by German breeder Kordes at the 1989 world horticultural exposition held in Birmingham, England. It is the producer of huge trusses of scarlet-crimson flowers, each packed with petals until it is fully double. The leaves are vibrant dark green on a bush that is uniformly compact. The rose is not scented, but it is hard to imagine a cultivar better suited to civic plantings that need to look attractive at all times yet require little or no grooming.

## Polyantha roses

The breeder who reportedly gave the world its first hybrid tea also generated another class of roses that were introduced between 1870 and 1880: Jean-Baptiste Guillot. He got them by crossing *Rosa multiflora* and a dwarf China rose. Polyantha, meaning "many-flowered," seemed appropriate for these new small and compact roses that were knee-high as a rule and perfect for bedding-out and low hedges. They are hardy in general and constantly in bloom. Their form and habit cannot be faulted, but they don't have much perfume among them.

The polyanthas need only one main pruning at the beginning of each growing season, usually back by one-third, occasionally more if the bush has gotten out of bounds for its particular site. The rules are essentially the same as for other bush roses: Remove the dead, diseased, or twiggy inner parts, then prune back so as to leave the uppermost bud on each remaining cane pointed outward from the center of the bush. When any polyantha rose is promptly deadheaded, it will spring back into bloom production more quickly than if the old flowers are left to wither away on their own.

'Clotilde Soupert' was introduced by French breeders Soupert & Notting in 1890. It is from a mating of 'Mignonette' x

'Madame Damaizin.' The round buds in clusters are kissed with red, and the petal-packed, flat flowers open white with blush to dark pink suffusing the centers. On the plus side, the flowers are intensely fragrant. On the minus, they won't open properly when the weather turns cool or wet. Few modern roses look lovelier in a mixed bouquet.

'Columbus,' a floribunda (1992) created to honor the Ameri-Flora Horticultural Exposition in Columbus, Ohio, is by description of its creator, Weeks Roses breeder Tom Carruth, ". . .old-rose pink, large flowers, and lots of them, mostly in clusters." The well-formed bush becomes a globe-shaped shrub about 3 feet tall and as wide. There is no appreciable fragrance, but the cultivar is constantly in bloom, disease resistant, and the producer of roses that are perfect in the garden or cut.

'Clotilde Soupert'

163

# Cluster-flowered bush roses

'**Corsage,**' a floribunda (1965), is the result of a cross between 'Blanche Mallerin' x 'White Swan.' The bush is encouragingly tall and spreading, the generous clusters of 2-inch pink-blushed white flowers are highly scented and constantly produced. The cultivar is blessed with disease resistance. Few roses could be nicer for making bouquets. Despite all this, 'Corsage' is one of the difficult-to-find modern roses still in cultivation. You're unlikely to locate it without contacts in the inner world of rose collectors and propagators.

'**Daily Sketch,**' a floribunda, is named for a newspaper; in this case one based in London. It's also in keeping with the Fleet Street tradition of promoting the Chelsea Flower Show, held the third week in May. Not only do the newspapers actively publicize the Chelsea, they also sponsor exhibitions filled with practical garden ideas—and new roses bearing the newspaper's name. 'Daily Sketch' was introduced by McGredy, then of the United Kingdom, in 1961, the offspring of 'Ma Perkins' x 'Grand Gala.' The flowers, which resemble a hybrid tea are pink with silvery edging of the petals, large, but in clusters, on a vigorously upright plant.

'**Dainty Maid,**' a floribunda, came from a breeder named Edward LeGrice, of the United Kingdom (UK) in 1940. A cross between 'D.T. Poulsen' x unknown produced this lovely rose with large, single (five-petaled) flowers. They are that romantic silvery-pink color associated with roses, but rarely any other flower. The petal reverses are a darker shade of pink; the central crown of stamens in the fully open rose is golden yellow.

'**Dame of Sark,**' a floribunda, came from UK breeder Jack Harkness in 1976. From a cross involving ['Pink Parfait' x 'Masquerade'] x 'Tablers Choice,' it has a maverick flower by comparison to most other roses. The double flowers in big clusters combine orange and yellow with red spots.

'**Dame Wendy,**' a floribunda, came from UK breeder Cants in 1990. A cross between 'English Miss' x 'Memento' yielded this truly spectacular salmon-pink rose with hints of yellow from the outer petal bases.

'**Dearest,**' a floribunda, came from UK breeder Dickson in 1960, from a cross of a seedling x 'Spartan.' The semidouble, salmon-pink flowers are large and exceptionally fragrant, on tidy bushes to 2 feet tall.

'**Dick Koster,**' a polyantha, is a sport of 'Anneke Koster,' introduced by the Dutch breeder of the same name in 1931. Its generous clusters of small, globe-shaped, dark orange-pink flowers above a plant clothed in shiny medium-green leaves, together hardly knee-high, set this cultivar apart from almost all other roses save its own sport, 'Margo Koster,' which has the same globe shape but salmon blooms.

The Koster roses bloom initially in a burst at Easter or in April in gardens of the Deep South. They seem especially at home in Natchez, Mississippi, where they often bloom at the same time as amaryllis (hippeastrum) planted in the ground. Later, the dark green straplike leaves of the amaryllis contrast boldly with the diminutive roses and may even give them a little shade against the intense summer sun. The Koster roses bloom constantly, and they are even suited to greenhouse potting. In fact, some admirers may know these as Easter, or Mother's Day roses, for the long-standing tradition of potting and forcing them as florist gift plants.

Although normally offered as small bushes or shrublets, the Kosters are seen occasionally as patio-size, tree-form standards, or about 24 inches tall. If such a plant is desired and cannot be found from a nursery source, it is possible to train one from a bush or rooted cutting in a season's time. The idea is to encourage one strong cane to grow straight up until the height is reached where the head of the tree will be formed, usually around 15 to 18 inches. All other growth and shoots are removed. When the cane chosen to become the tree's trunk has reached the desired height, there will likely be a cluster of flowers. When these finish, cut just below where they originated. Now encourage every new shoot to develop, and when it has two or three sets of leaves, cut or nip out the tip.

'Dick Koster'

164

# Cluster-flowered bush roses

'**Elizabeth of Glamis,**' a floribunda, is also known as 'Irish Beauty.' It came in 1964 from breeder McGredy, then of the United Kingdom, now residing in New Zealand. 'Elizabeth of Glamis' came from a cross between 'Spartan' x 'Highlight.' The fragrant, classically formed exhibition flowers are vivid salmon-pink in generous clusters. This is not the hardiest of floribundas in terms of cold tolerance, but elsewhere it is a superb rose, one worth coddling with extra protection if needed.

'**Europeana,**' a floribunda (AARS, 1968), is one of the all-time commercial successes in the modern rose world. It is the constant producer of enormous clusters, also called trusses, of dark red, semidouble flowers. There is a light tea scent. The plants are bushy, compact, medium tall, and wide. The new cane tips are bronzy red, then they mature to dark green. The plant has a high disease resistance. 'Europeana' makes a fine garden rose, solo, as hedging, or in mixed plantings. It is also a superb container plant for patios and decks.

'**Eyepaint,**' also known as 'Tapis Persan,' is a floribunda that came from New Zealand breeder McGredy in 1975. It is striking in the garden and a knockout when placed in a bouquet, alone or mixed. The medium-size single blooms (five-petaled) are vivid scarlet with white at the center, in large clusters. The bush tends to be tall and vigorous, never ungainly, but useful where it will have room to spread freely and make a great show from spring until the very last roses of any given season.

'**First Edition,**' a floribunda (AARS, 1977), starts with clusters of small, delicately pointed buds that go on to become classically formed rose blossoms in a glowing coral-orange that just won't stop. The color has high visibility in the landscape, and the bushes themselves are remarkably disease free. The freshly opened flowers have a light tea scent, especially midmorning on a sunny day. They are ideal for cutting, never lovelier in a bouquet than when accompanied by blue, such as larkspur or delphinium.

'**French Lace,**' a floribunda from American breeder William Warriner in 1981, is from a cross between 'Dr. A.J. Verhage' x 'Bridal Pink.' Large clusters containing many buds open into

'Elizabeth of Glamis'

fully double roses that are ivory with apricot highlights, then aging to white. This makes an excellent rose for containers, either for planting outdoors in the normal rose season or for placing in a greenhouse or other controlled environment for bloom production in cold weather.

'**Garnette,**' a floribunda, came from German breeder Tantau in 1951. It is the result of a cross involving ['Rosenelfe' x 'Eva'] x 'Heros' and the producer of garnet-red roses that are pleasingly cupped, doubled, and clustered. The bushes grow upright. 'Garnette' is rarely a garden rose, but it is a time-honored rose for the florist trade, sold as a cut flower and as a potted plant in bloom.

'**Great Ormond Street,**' a floribunda, came from the work of English rosarian and author Peter Beales in 1991. It is from the cross of a seedling x ['Arthur Bell' x 'Allgold'] and produces clusters of soft, glowing yellow semidouble roses that age to a pale, creamy yellow. These are beautiful in the garden and superb for cutting, the subtle color changes adding to the life and interest of almost any mixed bouquet. When fully open, there are golden brown anthers of notice in the center of each blossom, and a good nose will detect a slight rose scent. 'Great Ormond Street' has large, dark, strong foliage that grows on an exceptionally compact, knee-high bush.

'Iceberg,' a floribunda, is one of the most widely planted white landscape roses. Penelope Hobhouse has pointed out that its shade of white is "laundry white," not, for example, the creamy white of 'Class Act' or any number of the more ivory-white roses. Nevertheless, 'Iceberg,' like 'Europeana,' makes a good impression, whether planted in a public park or in a very special con-

tainer in a tiny city garden where every plant must be chosen with the utmost restraint. The 'Iceberg' bush is notably hardy, rarely succumbing to any disease or other blight. The buds are long and pointed, opening into semidouble flowers that are mildly scented. They appear in delightful profusion above bushy, mounding plants clad in medium green leaves.

'Ivory Fashion,' a floribunda, came from American breeder Eugene Boerner in 1958. It is from a cross between 'Sonata' x 'Fashion,' and the result is a lovely rose that is cupped, semidouble, ivory, fragrant, and in great clusters.

'Judy Garland,' a floribunda, has multicolored medium-size loose flowers comprised of yellows, oranges, and reds. These are generously and constantly produced above a medium-size, rounded bush. The leaves are a pleasing glossy green, and the fragrance is excellent, a rich blend evocative of both roses and apples.

'Little Darling,' a floribunda, produces clusters of small semidouble flowers that begin as classically shaped buds, pastel pink brushed with gold and apricot. The plant is vigorous, upright, and the possessor of disease-resistant, dark green leaves. It has a light scent.

'Ma Perkins,' a floribunda, was introduced by American Breeder Eugene Boerner in 1952, from a cross between 'Red Radiance' x 'Fashion.' The large, many-petaled flowers combine salmon, shell pink, and cream, with a light fragrance. The clusters are large and generous, atop vigorous, upright plants. This modern rose is now relatively "old," which means it is hard to find in commerce, but it will always be cherished by collectors. Tomorrow's rose breeders may well use it again as a parent.

'Iceberg'

# Cluster-flowered bush roses

'**Masquerade,**' a floribunda, is another of Boerner's early and trend-setting roses in this class, a 1949 introduction from a mating between 'Goldilocks' x 'Holiday.' It was a precursor of many more recent roses with the fascinating habit of changing from glowing yellow to pink to orange to dark red. This is a fertile cultivar that freely sets hips; prompt deadheading will keep 'Masquerade' blooming instead of going into the seed production business.

'**Montana,**' a floribunda, is a 1974 introduction from German breeder Tantau, the result of a cross between 'Walzertraum' x 'Europeana.' The large clusters of lightly scented flowers are a glow-in-the-dark orange-red, and they keep going even when the weather turns miserably hot. This is an outstanding rose for bedding and low hedging.

'**Nearly Wild,**' a floribunda, is a recently introduced rose that is desirable in every respect. The mid-pink single flowers appear constantly in such profusion as to practically hide the strong, supportive bush. This makes a superb hedge, as lovely and self-reliant in a public park as at home. The show begins with the first major blooming of all roses in late spring to early summer and continues until killing frost or the once-annual serious pruning.

'**Neon Lights,**' a floribunda, is among the newer cultivars described here, a hot pink that is strongly fragrant, also compact, free blooming, vigorous, and disease resistant. In retrospect, it would seem that this rose has finally achieved all the desirable characteristics that were originally set forth as goals for the floribunda class.

'**Orange Triumph,**' a polyantha, came from German breeder Kordes in 1937. As it is known today, this rose seems more a clear red than an orange, but it is no less garden-worthy. The small, cupped, petal-packed flowers appear in great clusters above a dark leaved, sturdy plant.

'Nearly Wild'

'Pinocchio'

'**Perle d'Or,**' a polyantha, was introduced in France in 1884, one of the sweetheart roses and reminiscent of 'Cecile Brunner.' The button-eyed, coppery apricot flowers appear in delightful clusters, abundantly scented. Like the polyanthas in general, 'Perle d'Or' adapts well to container culture and greenhouse forcing.

'**Pink Parfait,**' a floribunda, came from American breeder Swim in 1960, from a cross between 'First Love' x 'Pinocchio.' The large, semidouble blooms comprise several shades of pink, and they appear in big clusters, showy in the garden and excellent for cutting. They have a light scent. The bush gets high marks for leathery, shiny foliage and a self-reliant, upright habit.

'**Pinocchio,**' a floribunda, is a 1940 introduction from German breeder Kordes that by name and its own superior performance has become a modern classic. The parentage is 'Eva' x 'Golden Rapture,' yielding a small rose having cupped blossoms that appear in a sort of tattered profusion, salmon-pink with a glow of yellow at the base and a hint of fragrance.

'**Pleasure,**' a floribunda (AARS, 1990), has a slight fragrance but high marks in everything else: coral-pink, ovoid buds, 4-inch blooms of 30 to 35 petals, ruffled and abundant on a disease-resistant upright bush. It blooms constantly over a long season.

169

# Cluster-flowered bush roses

'Showbiz'

'**Purple Tiger,**' a floribunda, has dark purplish-red-and-white striped and splashed flowers to 4 inches across that appear in clusters on a perfect stem for cutting, about 12 inches long. There is medium damask rose fragrance. The bush grows compactly to 4 feet tall.

'**Regensberg,**' a floribunda, is ideal as a low hedge and in containers, for it is a notably compact bush. The semidouble, hot-pink flowers almost completely hide the glossy dark green leaves.

'**Rosenelfe,**' a floribunda, produces small double flowers that are clear pink and in generous clusters. It is an exceptional little rose for cutting, and the bush is a constant and vigorous bloom machine. 'Rosenelfe' was introduced by German breeder Kordes in 1939.

'**Sexy Rexy,**' a floribunda, came from New Zealand breeder McGredy in 1984. Its petal-packed double flowers open out flat in a mixture of pink and pale salmon. There is a light fragrance. The bushy plant with glossy, bright green leaves gets high marks for consistent satisfying performance in the garden.

'**Showbiz,**' a floribunda (AARS, 1985), is possibly one of the best garden performers ever to come from this type of modern rose. Cluster after cluster of many round buds become scarlet-red blooms, flat with wavy petals and a glimpse of golden anthers in the fully open blossoms. There is also a light, sweet fragrance.

'**Sue Lawley,**' also known as 'Spanish Shawl,' is a floribunda that came from New Zealand's McGredy in 1980. Its semi-double flowers are unique, carmine-red with white to pale pink edges. The family tree is remarkably complex: [('Little Darling' x 'Goldilocks')] x ['Evelyn Fison' x ('Coryana' x 'Tantau's Triumph')] x [('John's Church' x 'Elizabeth of Glamis') x ['Evelyn Fison' x ('Orange Sweetheart' x 'Fruhlingsmorgen')].

'**Summer Fashion,**' a floribunda, is a pink-yellow blend in classic spiral, high-centered form. The blooms can be 5 inches across with 35 to 40 petals. They are fragrant and because with age the yellow pales to cream and the pink darkens to rose, the subtle differences create an enticing and constantly changing show in the garden or in a bouquet.

'**Summer Snow,**' a floribunda, has a light tea scent from bounteous clusters of buds that unfurl into snow-white roses in a non-stop display. The leaves are glossy light green on a medium-low, bushy plant. This is an ideal rose for massing in beds and as a compact hedge.

'**Sun Flare,**' a floribunda (AARS, 1983), is the perfect, high-centered, exhibition yellow rose in the cluster-flowered bush format. The flowers appear in generous clusters and freely on a vigorous bush that is disease resistant and exceptionally hardy. There is a light anise or licorice scent.

'**Sweet Inspiration,**' a floribunda (AARS, 1993), is a clear-pink semidouble with so many clusters of flowers the bushes themselves are nearly obliterated. The leaves are light green and disease resistant on a naturally mound-forming plant that is great at the front of any planting or alone as a low flowering hedge.

'**The Doctor,**' a floribunda, was introduced by American breeder F.H. Howard in 1936. The buds in classic spiral form unfurl to become large, high-centered, silvery pink flowers that are abundantly fragrant. This old favorite is a repeat bloomer, not as constant as the new roses but reliable and disease resistant.

'**The Fairy,**' a floribunda, is one of the most popular modern roses and could well be on the list for every beginning gardener. The small double pale or soft pink flowers appear in huge clusters that by their sheer mass and weight often display a cascading habit from the medium rounded bush. The leaves are small, glossy green, and remarkably resistant to diseases. The fragrance is light, suggesting the smell of a ripe apple. 'The Fairy' is usually marketed in the bush form, but it is also available on occasion as a patio or medium-size tree-form standard. This cultivar has many uses in the landscape, from bedding, to mixing in a cottage garden border, to growing in containers. You also can find it offered on its own roots, not that of a grafted stock.

# Modern shrub roses

When a modern shrub rose called 'Bonica' captured All-America Rose Selections honors in 1987, it was the first such rose of its type to be given this distinction. Leading up to the late 1980s, there was a growing demand by the rose community at large for new roses that would be more self-reliant, not dependent on routine treatments too costly to maintain or politically incorrect. In the same time frame, garden and landscape designers began to use more of the species and old shrub roses and to ask for a greater selection from which to draw.

It is perhaps no accident that 'Bonica' was to be a benchmark rose, for it came from the French House of Meilland, the birthplace of 'Peace,' the hybrid tea by which all others have been judged since its dazzling arrival in the years immediately following World War II. 'Bonica' is one of a whole class of new cultivars known generically as "Meidiland" (pronounced may-deh-land) and generally as hybrid everblooming shrub roses. Not every cultivar discussed here is from the Meidiland family, but the performance standards set by 'Bonica' and its classmates are what is expected from the modern shrub rose:

- All-season color in the landscape
- Minimum maintenance
- Traffic control hedges (planted on 2-foot centers)
- Hardiness
- Fall and winter appeal
- Quick ground coverage
- Erosion control
- Mass planting economy, planted on 4-foot centers

The modern shrub roses grow on their own roots, so they can return from the ground even following a sub-zero winter that kills the canes. Such a plant will be blooming on new growth with amazing speed. Another advantage of modern shrub roses is that little pruning is needed other than to remove dead tips. Overall shaping can be done with hedge shears—electric, gas, or hand operated. All of these cultivars are worth considering for almost any private or public garden.

'**Alba Meidiland**' is pure white with petal-packed flowers up to 4 inches across in abundant clusters. Early summer or June brings the first wave of bloom, which will be succeeded by others until the end of the season. The canes are up to 30 inches tall with a spread to 60 inches and are clad in glossy, dark green leaves. This makes a superb ground cover that requires no pruning, although deadheading does tend to quicken the return of another major blooming.

'**All That Jazz**' (AARS, 1992) produces large, semidouble flowers in a bright, coral-salmon blend. The dark green leaves have the necessary disease resistance to qualify for low maintenance, and the clusters of blooms have beautiful presence in the garden or when cut.

'**Bonica**' (AARS, 1987) yields impressive numbers of medium-size, shell-pink flowers in clusters of three to five. The upright stems grow to 4 feet tall, thus assuring a rose that is impressive in the garden and ideal for cutting. There are lots of colorful hips for fall and winter color.

'**Carefree Beauty**' is a low-upkeep plant that blooms all season. It is semidouble and coral-pink. For autumn and winter interest, there are plenty of orange-red seed hips.

'**Carefree Wonder**' (AARS, 1991) has semidouble blooms in great waves over the longest rose season imaginable. These are a cheerful bold pink on the surface and creamy white on the petal reverses.

'**Copenhagen**' came from Danish breeder Poulsen in 1964. It is the result of a cross between a seedling x 'Ena Harkness' and the producer of double, intense scarlet flowers in clusters. The plant grows upright and has foliage that is bronzy red at first. This can be a bush or small climber to 8 feet tall and about half as wide.

'**Country Dancer**' is a 1973 introduction from American breeder Buck, the result of a mating of 'Prairie Princess' x 'Johannes Boettner.' The fully double roses are large, rosy red, and abundantly scented. The plant grows bushy, to 3 feet tall, and has lots of glossy foliage.

**'Bonica'**

# Modern shrub roses

**'Distant Drums'** is a modern shrub rose from the 1950s that has settled quietly into the realm of a collector's rose. The medium-size semidouble to fully petaled flowers are as close to being brown as a flower can be without appearing to be dead. This is not a criticism of 'Distant Drums,' for the flowers are truly exquisite, unique among roses if not the floral kingdom. Besides the suggestion of rich brown, there is an overall blue-pink suffusion or smokiness that gives these blossoms an air of mystery.

**'Dorothy Wheatcroft'** came from German breeder Tantau in 1960. The flowers are exceptionally large, semidouble, and a vivid velvety red. The inner petals cup distinctively, and when the blossoms are fully open, the central crown of golden anthers is quite showy against the red of the blooms. There is a hint of scent.

'Distant Drums'

**'Fred Loads'** was introduced in 1968 by the United Kingdom breeder Holmes, from a cross between 'Dorothy Wheatcroft' x 'Orange Sensation.' It makes a vigorous shrub, upright to 5 feet tall with a similar spread. The large blossoms are essentially single but in exceptionally big clusters and in a bright salmon-pink color that many gardeners find highly desirable in a rose.

**'Golden Wings,'** from American breeder Shepherd in 1956, shares with modern shrub roses, in general, a mixed parentage. In this case the involvement of *Rosa pimpinellifolia altaica* places this also with the Scottish roses and their descendants. The large, clear-yellow flowers of 'Golden Wings' are nearly sin-

gle, and the stamens surrounding the center are brown and gold and very showy. Flowering is continuous from early summer through fall, singly and in clusters, always lightly scented.

**'Grand Master'** is from the work of German breeder Kordes, introduced in 1954. Raised from a cross between 'Sangerhausen' x 'Sunmist,' 'Grand Master' has classically curved, pointed buds that open into impressively large semidouble flowers. The color is lemon shaded apricot-pink, and there is a light fragrance.

**'Heidelberg,'** also from Kordes, in 1958, is a notably vigorous modern shrub rose, to 6 feet high and nearly as wide. From a cross between 'World's Fair' x 'Floradora,' it yields exceptionally big clusters of petal-packed double roses that are crimson-scarlet splashed and flecked with dark orange. The dark green leaves are leathery, disease resistant, and entirely garden-worthy over a long season.

**'Hon. Lady Lindsay'** came from New Jersey breeder Hanson in 1938, out of a cross between 'New Dawn' x 'Rev. F. Page Roberts.' The double flowers have upper petal surfaces that are silvery or clear pink, while the reverses are a darker shade. The best performance occurs where the summer weather is likely to be both hot and sunny.

**'Jacqueline du Pre'** came from English breeder Harkness in 1989, from a cross between 'Radox Bouquet' x 'Maigold.' It is the constant producer of large, ivory-white roses that are nearly single and highlighted by a ring of bright golden red stamens in the center. There is also a generous portion of musk-rose fragrance. The shrub grows vigorously to 6 feet tall and a similar width.

**'John Franklin'** was introduced by the Department of Agriculture in Canada in 1980. It is the result of a cross of 'Lilli Marlene' x unnamed seedling. The medium-size double flowers are red, fragrant, and produced in small clusters. The upright plant grows to 4 or 5 feet tall and to a similar width, with rounded leaves that are medium to dark green. The plant has lots of yellowish thorns. At midmorning the blooms are moderately fragrant.

**'Kathleen Ferrier'** was originated by the Dutch breeder Buisman and introduced in 1952. Raised out of a seed hip from 'Gartenstolz' x 'Shot Silk,' 'Kathleen Ferrier' is a strong, productive plant with glossy, dark green foliage and sturdy canes to 4 or 5 feet tall and just as wide. The semidouble flowers are salmon-pink in small clusters. They have only a slight scent, but this modern shrub rose gets high marks for beauty and performance.

**'Joseph's Coat'** came from Americans Armstrong and Swim in 1964, out of a cross of 'Buccaneer' x 'Circus.' This modern shrub rose is classified also as a climber, but it performs possibly better as a self-reliant shrub or when confined to a pillar. There is moderate fragrance in the loose clusters of multicolored flowers that range and change over the life of each from yellow to salmon-pink to orange and finally to brick red.

**'Lafter'** was introduced by the American breeder Brownell in 1948, from a cross involving numerous parents: ['V for Victory' x ('General Jacqueminot' x 'Dr. W. Van Fleet')] x 'Pink Princess.' The well-behaved shrub grows to 5 feet tall and makes a bush to about 4 feet wide, clad in glossy, dark green leaves. The flowers are a salmon-pink and apricot blend with a center of strong yellow. There is a light fragrance.

'Golden Wings'

# Modern shrub roses

'**Pearl Meidiland**' is generally thought to be the most prolific bloomer of its class. The profusion of shell-pink buds opens to nearly white flowers more than 2 inches across. The plant is vigorous and broad, an effective earth cover with dark green foliage strong enough to smother weeds in the vicinity. 'Pearl Meidiland' looks beautiful from any angle, from a distance or as close as you like.

'**Pike's Peak**' was introduced by an American breeder named Gunter in 1940, selected from a cross involving *Rosa acicularis* x 'Hollywood.' The plant becomes a vigorous bush to 5 feet tall and about 3 feet wide. The semidouble flowers, light red with yellow centers, appear in clusters. The foliage is distinctively wrinkled and a light green that looks especially well in the landscape. Because *Rosa acicularis* is an American native, it is not surprising that rosarians in many regions give 'Pike's Peak' high marks as a modern shrub rose.

'**Pink Meidiland**' is recommended for landscape uses such as hedging or as part of a barrier planting to restrict and guide pedestrian as well as vehicular traffic. The season-long display is of single pink roses with a distinctive white center and bright stamens. In the fall, there also will be a generous show of red seed hips. The growth habit is upright and vigorous, with sturdy foliage, altogether an invaluable shrub.

'**Red Meidiland**' has a useful ground-covering habit with so many single red flowers the leaves are nearly invisible. The clustered roses are mostly single, red with a white center and a show of yellow stamens. This thoroughly modern shrub rose is probably at its best with the first flower show in late spring or early summer, but the flowering does continue with some generosity until fall, when the foliage drops and the orange-red seed hips take over for strong visual impact.

'**Scarlet Meidiland**' produces huge clusters of vivid scarlet, 1-inch, petal-packed double roses. The very strong, vigorous canes arch gracefully, almost weighted down with the great masses of flowers. Of all the Meidilands, this one is especially hardy.

'**Sea Foam**' is reminiscent of 'The Fairy' in that it occupies a unique place in rosedom. 'Sea Foam' produces long, trailing canes set with dark green foliage that is highly resistant to diseases. The bushes are covered and recovered all season with pure-white double flowers shaped like a small old-fashioned rose and lightly scented. The habit of the bushes is such that they are perfect for a situation that will allow them to spill over a wall or down an embankment. Another possibility is to encourage 'Sea Foam' to become a climber or pillar specimen.

'**Sevillana**' is an upright modern shrub rose introduced in 1993. It reaches to 4 feet and almost as wide, becoming covered over and over through the season with large, flower-filled trusses of fiery red, double roses. This makes a hedge that is never without blooms in spring and summer or showy red seed hips in fall and winter.

'**Summer Wind**' was introduced by Iowa State University in 1975, the creation of breeder Griffith Buck, who has concentrated on producing modern shrub roses that can breeze through Iowa's sometimes brutally cold winters, but also look wonderfully romantic and beautiful all summer. 'Summer Wind' has large carmine-pink flowers with eight to 10 petals and is sweetly fragrant. The more inner petals carry a distinctive white streak. This cultivar has notably strong, disease-resistant foliage and an everblooming habit.

'**White Meidiland**' is the most prostrate of the Meidiland family. The large, abundant, healthy leaves appear on heavy canes that flow along the garden surface, automatically forming an ideal carpet over banks and rocky places. The pure-white blooms grow up to 4 inches across and appear in such profusion as to imitate a large drift of snow. 'White Meidiland' may be adapted in some situations to serve as a climbing or pillar rose with the long canes tied in place in part horizontally so as to promote more blooms.

'Pike's Peak'

# Dwarf cluster-flowered bush roses

The official designation of the dwarf cluster-flowered bush rose was made by the World Federation of Rose Societies in 1987 to acknowledge an emerging new class that up until then had been called a patio rose. In practical terms, these are cluster-flowered roses that seem too small to be considered regular floribundas grouped as cluster-flowered bush roses and too large to be placed with the miniature roses. They are also called compact roses.

To date, the primary marketers and promoters of the narrowly defined roses in this class have been the Conard-Pyle Company of West Grove, Pennsylvania, the original introducers in America of the 'Peace' rose, and the Jackson & Perkins Company of Medford, Oregon. Conard-Pyle distributes Meilland roses in America, and they are often sold in the mail-order catalog from Wayside Gardens of Hodges, South Carolina. All of these firms have been leaders in American horticulture for several generations. Today they supply a great many of the rosebushes you'll find at local nurseries and garden centers.

The international nomenclature authority may suggest a class name that is descriptive, but it is also comprised of many words. Therefore, you can expect to continue seeing the single word "patio" or "compact" applied to such roses. In the often hurly-burly marketplace, a single descriptive term conveys almost instantaneously to consumer eyes a body of information about the merits of the roses at hand.

**'Amorette,'** seen here in a serene garden setting, is a prime example of what continues to be sold and grown as a patio rose. The cultivar seems by nature free blooming, a sort of flower factory that continuously opens clusters of 2-inch white blooms. When one of these is not quite fully open, it can be appreciated up close as a perfect, high-centered exhibition rose; when many of these are fully opened on the bush, at a glance they could be taken for white carnations. The bush grows from 2 to 4 feet tall, has a small multitude of green canes, and adapts to every use imaginable in a garden setting that is small and meant to be experienced in an intimate way.

**'Amorette'**

# Dwarf cluster-flowered bush roses

'Amber Flash' grows 16 to 24 inches high and wide with 1- to 2-inch blooms in a yellow-orange blend. Its buds are shapely, and the bush adapts well to forcing. This is the sort of rose that can be readily brought to full bloom in a gallon-size commercial plastic pot and sold at this stage. Providing it isn't subjected to too much stress, such as drying out, standing in water for several hours, freezing, or overheating, this container plant will proceed to adapt and keep right on flowering.

'Boy Crazy' grows 24 to 30 inches tall and makes a many-branched shrublet that is both vigorous and tidy, clad in glossy, dark green leaves. The flowers are a vibrant raspberry pink, about 2 inches across, in clusters on stems 8 to 10 inches long.

'Candy Sunblaze' is from the French House of Meilland. It grows from 16 to 24 inches tall and as wide, a floriferous bush clad with glossy, dark green foliage. The flowers, to about 2 inches across, are packed with hot-pink petals that are amazingly colorfast, in clusters that have high visibility in the landscape but that are also on stems long enough to make them favored as cutting material for a variety of bouquets and arrangements.

'Cherry Sunblaze,' another Meilland rose, is predictably free flowering, 16 to 24 inches tall, with perfect 2-inch roses of an unusually vivid, sparkling red. 'Cherry Sunblaze' is closely related to 'Debut,' and like it in all respects except the color.

'Classic Sunblaze,' yet another Meilland creation, grows 16 to 24 inches tall and blooms freely, constantly. The generous-sized buds open into petal-packed double flowers that are an intense bright pink. The vigorous bush is blessed with a large portion of handsome, glistening, dark green foliage.

'Debut,' from Meilland (AARS, 1989), is early, abundant, and continuously in flower. The self-supporting bushes grow 16 to 24 inches tall and about as wide, becoming covered over and over with vivid scarlet buds that open into cream and red roses. The young foliage is a dark mahogany color that stands out against the older leaves, which are a rich green and accentuate all the other attributes of 'Debut.'

'Lady Sunblaze' (Meilland) is the usual size for this type, 16 to 24 inches tall and similarly broad. Fat buds that curve to a point unfurl into symmetrical double roses comprised of many large petals. This little rose has beautiful foliage and gets high marks for planting in a pot to be enjoyed up close.

'Orange Sunblaze' (Meilland) was the first in this series, and some rosarians say it is the best. The bush sets the standard, 16 to 24 inches tall and as wide, and yields an unbelievable number of dazzling orange flowers that are both long lasting and colorfast. After each bloom has lasted about two weeks, the petals quickly wither and disappear. The result of this habit is that 'Orange Sunblaze' is a model for the self-cleaning, more completely self-reliant landscape rose. It is by nature a vigorously growing and orderly plant that is as delightful in gardens as when it is potted.

'Pink Pollyanna' grows 3 to 4 feet tall and freely produces 2-inch blooms in high-centered, classic hybrid tea or exhibition form. The foliage is an attractive dark green, vigorous and disease resistant.

'Red Rascal' grows 3 to 4 feet tall and becomes covered with small, bright red, hybrid-tea–form flowers not quite 2 inches across. The foliage resembles that of a miniature rose, and it is the habit of the twigs or small branches to grow densely together. This cultivar is notably resistant to powdery mildew and an all-around outstanding trouper for such landscape features as low hedging or massed in a bed or large container.

'Red Sunblaze' (Meilland) is among the more recent additions to this series, in a vivid red color that is uniquely suited to a hardy shrub that lends itself to practical application as a traffic control barrier. The plants are singularly vigorous, upright, and extensively branched. The foliage is medium green, semiglossy, and sufficient to cover most of each plant.

'Royal Sunblaze' (Meilland) stands 16 to 24 inches high and as broad at the top. It is perhaps the best bright yellow available in a dwarf cluster-flowered bush rose. The petal-packed double

**'Debut'**

plant has astounding strength, including tolerance of excessive heat, cold, and a variety of soil conditions that would be daunting to lesser roses.

**'Stardance'** (Conard-Pyle) has exceptional vigor and may reach 24 to 30 inches in an average growing season. It has perfectly formed small roses that are pristine white with a glow of yellow from the center. 'Stardance' makes a glorious appearance solo, but it also mixes well with roses that are vivid reds and oranges.

**'Sunny Sunblaze'** (Meilland) maintains the standard for its series, growing 16 to 24 inches high and to a similar width at the shoulders of the bush. The petal-packed double blooms, to 2 inches across, are a golden buff that unfurls from short, full buds. Not even extended summer heat will fade these exquisite but durable little roses. Although 'Sunny Sunblaze' is perfectly adapted to the usual garden and landscape situations, in the ground and in pots, it has subtle coloring that may fit as well in finely tuned cottage gardening themes, possibly in the company of such blue perennials as balloon flower, hardy aster, monkshood, and delphinium.

blooms are a clear medium yellow that is colorfast and long lasting in the garden. Under certain weather conditions, these small roses also will be touched with scarlet at the petal edges. 'Royal Sunblaze' is a proven forcer with high-quality bloom on a bushy, well-formed plant that gardeners find hard to resist. It is also ideal in every garden or landscape setting imaginable, in the ground as well as containers.

**'Scarlet Sunblaze'** (Meilland) stands the usual 16 to 24 inches tall and as wide, like the many other cultivars in its immediate family, and produces 2-inch roses that are dark scarlet and long lasting. The foliage is glossy, medium to dark green, and the

**'Sweet Sunblaze'** (Meilland) is the clearest pink in this series. The bush is vigorous and about 24 to 30 inches tall. The leaves are semiglossy medium green. Petal-packed double blooms grow to 2 inches in diameter and appear nonstop from the late spring or early summer until frost or an annual sharp pruning takes them out of bloom.

# Dwarf cluster-flowered bush roses

## Pruning for "patios" or "compacts"

The dwarf cluster-flowered bush roses, known also as patio or compact landscape roses, need little pruning. They can actually be managed in public park or other civic plantings by light shearing with hedge trimmers. This efficient method also works as well in home gardens. Once a year, usually at the very beginning of a new season of active growth, cut the bushes back by at least one-third. This stimulates them and prevents their growing tall and spindly. At this time, it is also sound policy to give one quick check of all the canes, to remove any that may have been killed or mechanically damaged. Otherwise, the serviceable roses in this class get along well with nothing more than pleasant temperatures, lots of sun, ample water, balanced nutrients, and a modicum of admiration.

**'Trumpeter'** is an example of a patio, compact, or dwarf cluster-flowered bush rose that is also something else: It is, commercially speaking, a "roseling," the single word used by Armstrong Roses of California for its bold experiment in tissue culturing the best of the best of an already outstanding rose cultivar and then bringing it to market on its own roots. 'Trumpeter' is pictured on the opposite page as it appeared on a recent early autumn afternoon in the Columbus, Ohio, Park of Roses, one of America's premiere rose showplaces. 'Trumpeter' came from New Zealand breeder McGredy in 1977 and originated from a cross of 'Satchmo' x seedling. The double roses are bright orange-red in good-sized clusters. The glossy, medium green foliage holds up well on a compact bush.

**'Yellow Jacket'** grows 24 to 30 inches tall to form a plant that is upright and bushy. The brilliant yellow flowers, to over 2 inches in diameter, have classic exhibition hybrid tea form, and they are lightly fragrant. The foliage is glossy, medium green, and disease resistant.

Other modern roses classified as floribundas or cluster-flowered bush roses that grow to only about 18 inches and may be used in pots or small space gardens include:
- 'Abundance' (double; medium pink)
- 'Dreamland' (double; peach-pink)
- 'Fergie' (double; blend of orange-buff, ginger, and shell pink)
- 'Great Ormond Street' (semidouble; golden to creamy yellow)
- 'Gruss an Aachen' (double; creamy to peachy)
- 'Irene Watts' (double; ivory with hints of pink and orange)
- 'Ivory Fashion' (semidouble; ivory white and nicely scented)
- 'Kim' (double; yellow with red suffusion)
- 'Lady Romsey' (double; white with pink and cream blushings)
- 'Lagoon' (single; lilac; fragrant)
- 'Marlena' (semidouble; red and crimson)
- 'Meteor' (double; orange-scarlet)
- 'Penelope Plummer' (semidouble; pink to salmon)
- 'Stargazer' (almost single; orange-red)
- 'Tip Top' (semidouble; rose-salmon)
- 'Topsi' (semidouble; orange-red to scarlet)

## "Patio" tree roses

A slightly different meaning for "patio" is seen in a series of 24-inch tree roses sold by Jackson & Perkins. These are available in numerous cultivars, mostly floribundas or cluster-flowered bush roses, such as 'French Lace,' 'Sun Flare,' and 'Angel Face.' These look especially handsome in a 20-inch-square planter box such as wood in the Versailles tub manner or a terra-cotta pot of similar size. They are not, technically speaking, the roses now classed as dwarf cluster-flowered bushes, however.

A current catalog also offers a tree rose that consists of 'Europeana' grafted as the head on a rooted trunk stock 27 inches high. Such a specimen would mesh perfectly into a garden featuring the "patio" and "compact" roses discussed here, although it is, strictly speaking, a floribunda grafted onto a suitable stock for a tree rose of this size and stature.

'Trumpeter'

# Miniature roses

Petite and charming, miniature roses are winning the hearts of gardeners and rose growers around the world. They're relatively new, compared to the lengthy history of the entire rose family. In fact, miniatures were not widely known before the late 1930s, and none of the modern miniatures existed before that time. Some of the first available in this country appeared in 1937, when Californian Ralph Moore offered three miniature roses by mail order from his Sequoia Nursery in Visalia, California.

## Tracking the miniature factor

An original thinker, Moore had begun working with miniature roses as a teenager, eventually developing his own theory about the cause of miniatures. He suspected that the miniature factors in breeding act as the dominant element, perhaps because of an inhibitor action at work during plant development. After cross-breeding hundreds of thousands of plants in subsequent years at his own nursery, Moore confirmed his suspicions, and today his theory of miniaturization in roses is generally accepted.

Now, with more than 250 miniature hybrids to his credit, Moore is considered one of the world's foremost breeders of miniature roses. The parentage of about 70 percent of today's miniature roses can be traced to Moore's work in the 1950s, when he crossed 'Oakington Ruby' (one of the China group) with the Japanese *Rosa wichuraiana* (a wild species and the parent of the old rambling rose) and later crossed that progeny with 'Floradora' (a tall-growing, orange-red floribunda).

The parentage of the remaining 30 percent of the world's miniatures can be traced to *Rosa roulettii,* which was popular with European miniature rose breeders. (In the early 1930s, one of the first commercially successful miniatures was a hybrid of *Rosa roulettii* called 'Tom Thumb.')

After World War II, the popularity of miniature roses grew with their increased availability. Amateur growers collected and hybridized them, and gardeners continued to be charmed by their versatility.

Aptly described sometimes as micro-mini, mid-size mini, and macro-mini, these diminutive plants vary in flower size and bush height. Depending on the hybrid, flowers can be as small as a dime or as large as 2 inches in diameter. The micro-mini bush stays under 10 inches tall and can be as short as 6 inches. Mid-size bushes grow to about 18 to 20 inches tall, and macro-miniatures can grow as tall as 24 to 30 inches.

The definition of miniature rose refers to the size of the foliage as well as to the flower size.

## A plant of many uses

Miniatures do exceptionally well in containers. Some have a spreading habit, making them ideal for hanging baskets or ground covers. They're a boon for apartment dwellers whose gardening space is limited to containers on the balcony.

Almost all are everblooming, a trait that endears them to most gardeners. They make wonderful border plants in a sunny garden bed. Miniatures seem tailor-made for growing in front of taller floribunda roses, concealing the bare stems and severity of floribundas or hybrid tea roses. When climbing roses develop bare, unsightly branches, miniatures can hide those, too.

One rose enthusiast keeps a chain-link fence covered with climbing roses, then plants floribundas in front of the climbers and miniatures in front of those for a gracefully staggered effect. The same grower says, "Occasionally I get an empty aspirin bottle and fill it with cut flowers from a miniature rose and give it to someone who's having a tough day."

Miniature roses offer special advantages over their taller relatives in the garden. They're generally more disease resistant than their larger counterparts. They're also somewhat easier to tend: After the first year, miniatures don't need special care for wintering over in the garden. They're almost everblooming, providing lots of color in the garden all through the growing season.

Miniatures do exceptionally well in containers, where they can be moved about to provide color where needed. Many miniatures also have the lovely, delicate fragrance of old roses. The most intensely fragrant are those with lavender shades, as they are progeny of the floribunda 'Angel Face.'

Miniatures are available to suit almost any gardening need. Some are climbers, reaching 5 to 12 feet in height. One of the best is 'Jeanne Lajoie,' which grows to at least 6 feet tall and blooms with two-tone medium pink flowers. Another vigorous climber is 'Hurdy Gurdy,' blooming with red-and-white-striped

**Miniature roses, an American favorite**

184

# Miniature roses

flowers. 'Red Delight' and 'Red Cascade' both have red flowers. 'Angel Pink' blooms with coral-pink flowers. 'Golden Son' is dark yellow with orange highlights. 'Snowfall' grows to about 8 feet tall and blooms with white flowers.

Miniatures also thrive in hanging baskets, where they bring color to sunny patios or balconies. The best ones for hanging baskets are spreading varieties with long, pendent branches. Look for varieties such as pink 'Spring Song,' red-and-white 'Little Artist,' coral-and-gold 'Anita Charles,' medium apricot 'Apricot Charm,' and the unusual 'Andrea,' a dark pink with silver reverse on the back sides of the petals.

Micro-minis do well in very small containers such as strawberry jar pockets, as well as in diminutive garden spaces. These include the light pink 'Baby Betsy McCall,' white 'Cinderella,' magenta 'Elfin Gold,' orange-red 'Tiny Flame,' medium pink 'Bo-Peep,' light pink 'Willie Winkie,' and yellow 'Lynne Gold.'

The medium-size bush varieties of miniatures do well in almost any growing situation. In recent years, miniatures have earned high marks and been honored by the All-America Rose Selections committee. Several years ago, 'Starina,' an orange-red miniature, earned the rank of highest-rated rose and continues to be a favorite. More recently, 'Jean Kenneally,' an apricot miniature, garnered a similar ranking.

Other favorites in the bush-type miniatures include coral 'Millie Walters,' dark red 'Black Jade,' medium pink 'Cupcake,' yellow 'Rise 'n' Shine,' white 'Little Eskimo,' mauve 'Lavender Jewel,' lavender 'Dilly Dilly,' and 'Magic Carrousel, white with dark pink edging.'

## Winter care

Before a freeze, make sure all plants are watered well to help ensure their survival. This applies to container-grown miniatures as well as to those in garden beds. With the onset of freezing temperatures, container-grown miniature roses should be brought into a garage or other sheltered area.

Miniatures growing directly in the garden are surprisingly winter hardy. The first year after they are planted in the garden, miniatures should be given some protection, such as covering them with hay or oak leaves. This gives the root system enough time to become established. After the first year, however, they need no additional winter protection to survive, even thrive.

'Autumn Fire'

**Miniatures and containers, a perfect match**

# Miniature roses

## Cultivation

Miniatures are planted in a garden bed in the same manner as larger roses. They need a good, friable soil, such as one-third sharp sand, one-third soil, and one-third humus. Because miniatures grow low to the ground, it's a good idea to leave plenty of room around each plant for optimal air circulation.

Compared to taller roses, most miniatures have the added advantage of getting by with slightly fewer hours of sunlight. A minimum of four to five hours of full sunlight may suffice for a miniature; floribundas or hybrid teas need at least six hours of sunlight daily.

For container roses, use any good soil-less growing medium, such as Pro Mix. Plant in the same manner as in a garden bed.

## Fertilizing

Wharever type of fertilizer you use—liquid, granular, chemical, or organic—it's important with a miniature to use only one-fourth of the amount you would use for a full-size plant such as a hybrid tea. As with any plant, never fertilize a rose when the soil is dry. First soak the soil, then add fertilizer, then water in the fertilizer.

Container-grown miniatures should be fed only with a good water-soluble commercial fertilizer (such as 20-20-20) that's not specifically formulated for acid-loving plants. It's good to choose one with trace elements added.

All professional growers emphasize regularity in feeding as the key to successful nutrition for miniatures. They also warn against overfeeding miniatures. If the center of a plant turns bright green and the plant becomes heavily foliated, chances are you are overfeeding the plant.

Some growers prefer the convenience of a granular fertilizer such as timed-release Osmocote or Nitrophos 21-14-7 for miniatures growing directly in a garden bed. When using these fertilizers, however, it's too easy to over- or underfeed. In a very rainy season, the fertilizer can be applied too quickly because water triggers its release. In a dry season, water must be applied regularly to trigger the nutrient release. Nevertheless, many growers have success with timed-release fertilizers that are usually

applied about once a month through the growing season. Supplement every four to six weeks with organic food such as liquid fish emulsion, alfalfa pellets, or bat manure.

## Watering

Consistency in watering is also crucial. Try to water miniatures (especially those in containers) at the same time each day. Don't let a rose dry out to the point where it begins to wilt. Even if rain is predicted, it's a good idea to give the plants their daily watering at the accustomed time, and they'll reward you with continuous color.

Like their larger cousins, healthy miniatures require proper care and feeding.

system to determine where to cut through the plant crown. Using a light pruning saw, make the cut so there will be two or more roots remaining on each half. After the cut is made, prune the top growth to 1 or 2 inches and place each half in a pail of water. Plant them as two new bushes.

Professional grower and hybridizer Harmon Saville of Nor'East Miniature Roses in Massachusetts considers it far easier—and safer—to propagate miniatures by taking cuttings from healthy new growth. That way, there's no danger of destroying an entire plant, a strong possibility when the plant is cut in half.

'Mossy Gem': True miniature, true moss rose

## Pruning and dividing

Miniatures can be pruned the same way as their taller cousins, cutting stalks from the center of the plant to create the traditional urn shape. Because they grow on their own root stock, miniatures can be dug up every three years and divided by cutting through their root mass. The method is as follows:

First prepare the new planting holes with soil mix before dividing. Cut away half of the top growth on the plant to be divided. Carefully dig up the plant and wash away soil from the roots. Remove any broken or diseased roots and trim the ends of all other roots to stimulate feeder root growth. Examine the root

# Ground-cover roses

Most people regard the rose as splendid and stately or romantically charming, but another category of rose has emerged because certain varieties also excel as ground covers. These varieties cover the ground with color and greenery, solving problem areas that may be erosion prone, or too steep, too rocky, or otherwise unsuited to traditional lawns.

The category of "ground-cover" rose has been around for much of this century. In Europe, the type, also called "park roses," was grown for municipalities and parks. The German breeder Wilhelm Kordes continued to work with 'Max Graf,' a variety said to have been developed early in this century by James H. Bowdith of Connecticut. Kordes developed 'Max Graf' into one of the great forerunners of ground-cover roses. Today, ground-cover roses are becoming increasingly popular in the United States, as breeders continually work at bringing new varieties to the marketplace.

There are two types of ground-cover roses: One is by nature low growing and spreading; the other is shaped that way by arching down and pegging the branches of otherwise spare and leggy rose varieties.

The low-growing, spreading types have the added advantage of being quite hardy and more disease resistant than most modern roses. Some good examples are the recent (1992) introductions from the French House of Meilland: 'Pearl Meidiland,' with pearly white, medium double flowers, and 'Red Meidiland,' with red, medium single flowers.

Many miniature roses also double as excellent ground covers. Look for 'Ralph's Creeper' (red), Pink Carpet (medium pink with apple-green foliage), Royal Carpet (medium red), and Green Ice (white), which requires pegging.

Earlier in this century, breeder Sam McGredy developed 'Snow Carpet' from the small rose 'Temple Bells,' the work of California breeder Dennison Morey.

The second category of ground-cover roses, those that require pegging to cover the ground, employ a gardening technique only recently undergoing a revival. The result is often cascades of flowers on gracefully arching branches that form taller,

**'Red Meidiland'**

# Ground-cover roses

'Paul Neyron'

and ordinarily it moves up and down the stem in a vertical route. When the stems are changed from a vertical to a horizontal axis, as in pegging, gravity causes the hormones to encourage new sprouts at the buds. The result: many more branches and flowers.

## The right choices

Certain types of roses make the best candidates for pegging. Among the old roses, look for the bourbons and hyperperpetuals. These are good for pegging because they're not bushy; instead, they tend to be leggy with longer canes. Pegging not only improves the looks of these roses, it can create an effective ground cover, as well.

The technique can be used on any rose, but it's most effective on those with long, leggy canes. If a rose variety tends to grow in a compact manner and the goal is to create a ground cover, pegging is usually not a good idea.

Certain shrub roses, however, can be pegged with good results. A shrub rose planted in front of a fence, for example, can be fastened to the fence and trained horizontally. By changing the vertical growth habit to horizontal, a response is triggered to produce more blooms. Cutting back roses or pinching them back encourages new growth along the stem and causes bushier growth.

Shoup notes that while pegging is not for all roses, it actually improves the floral display of some. There's great drama, for example, in the cascades of magenta flowers of a pegged bourbon 'Madame Isaac Periere,' or the hyperperpetual 'Baronne Prevost' or 'Paul Neyron' (both true pinks), or 'Marquise Boccella' (soft pastel pink).

To achieve a fuller single bush, select a variety with a determinate growth pattern for pegging. For an effective ground cover, choose one with an indeterminate growth pattern. Shoup adds a cautionary note for roses that are extremely vigorous growers: They spread quickly and will require frequent pegging.

larger mounds than low-growing miniatures. Mike Shoup, of the Antique Rose Emporium in Brenham, Texas, considers pegging certain roses a good idea. "It's an old-fashioned practice that originated in England," says Shoup. "It nearly fell out of use, but we're glad people are becoming more interested in it."

In pegging, the canes are bent down to the ground, forming several graceful arches from each rose shrub. The canes are pinned to the ground, where they continue to flower more profusely than before. The result is a cascading effect, quite dramatic, with blossoms up and down the arching canes.

## Why pegging works

Shoup explains the reason for increased flowering: Pegging changes the way hormones move through the stem relative to gravity. The growth hormone is produced at the tip of the stem,

# Pegging roses

Pegging is done with a bent wire approximately 9 inches long. It's necessary to sink the wire deeply into the ground to hold the rose branch securely. Generally, with a taller bush, only the ends of the branches are pegged down, leaving the middle of the branch in a nice soft curve. To achieve a ground cover with lower-growing miniatures, each branch could be pegged to the ground in several places to encourage spreading.

In the North, pegging is done in February or March, just prior to the onset of spring growth. For repeating roses grown in northern gardens, pegging also can be done in July or August to encourage repeat blooms in September and October.

Another bonus comes with pegging: It acts as a form of propagation similar to layering. Additional rooted plants develop as the branches grow roots in the ground where they are pegged. If you don't want the plant to root, simply bury the tip of the branch in the ground.

**Pegging roses prompts increased flowering.**

To achieve an impressive floral display with pegging, remember these key points:

•Not all roses are good candidates. Choose varieties that are somewhat leggy and thin and tend to grow upright.

•Some of the best types are neither true climbers nor full shrubs, but those with long canes that produce one or two flowers at the end of each cane.

•Select 10 or 12 branches from a circular pattern around the base of the plant. Gently bend each branch down to the ground in a graceful arch and fasten it to the ground with a peg.

•When their floral display is over, the plants generally produce new growth from the canes that have been pegged down. This new growth, in turn, can be pegged down, spreading the ground-cover effect. Continue to thin out older wood in favor of the new canes that are constantly being produced.

The procedure should be done in the winter while the plant is still dormant. In the South, that means January or February. Where rose gardens are possible both in the spring and in the fall, pegging can be repeated in August to encourage another burst of flowering in the fall.

•Finally, if it sounds like too much work, remember that pegging increases the floral display of a plant by two or three times.

# Climbing and rambler roses

'American Pillar'

Not all roses that climb are climbers; some are technically ramblers, and vice versa. Pillar is another word applied to roses that by virtue of their vigorous long canes can be trained upright. In all cases, such roses climb by means of a combination of inherent super vigor or upward thrust and thorns that are pointed, hooked, or otherwise empowered to help the rose achieve new heights. Climbing roses are mostly sports from the large-flowered bush roses and the cluster-flowered bush roses. Ramblers are not sports of bush roses but rather a distinct class that yields clusters of small flowers once yearly, in late spring and early summer. The ramblers bloom on canes that grew the previous season. After flowering, remove them to their point of emergence at the base in order to encourage and make way for new shoots and lots of flowers next year.

Climbing roses may bloom once yearly, recurrently or constantly. Those that bloom only in late spring or early summer can be pruned as soon as convenient thereafter, the same as the ramblers. Those that bloom recurrently or constantly can be pruned more in the manner of a bush rose. Oldest canes that have flowered in a previous season can be removed at the annual main pruning in the beginning of spring. Shorten these to two or three bud eyes. Also remove any old, twiggy parts. As new canes are produced, arch them over to a horizontal position and tie to lattice trellising or fencing so as to encourage maximum production of the lateral branches on which many flowers will appear. Climbing forms of hybrid tea roses bloom mainly this year from the foundation formed by canes that grew last season. Unless trained, guided, tied, and thoughtfully pruned yearly, climbing and rambling roses will be liabilities in the yard or garden, not assets.

**'American Pillar'** came from American breeder Van Fleet in 1909, the result of a cross involving (*Rosa wichuraiana* x *R. setigera*) x 'Red Letter Day.' It has earned a place among modern-day classics for extreme vigor and huge trusses of single flowers that pale from reddish rose to dark pink highlighted by near white

'Angel Face'

centers. There is a hint of fragrance. The canes of this spring-blooming rose can reach 15 feet long by 10 feet wide.

**'Climbing Aloha'** is a pillar-size climbing hybrid tea with recurrent, blush-pink flowers in clusters atop long stems. It is recommended for cold-climate gardens.

**'Climbing America'** came from breeder Warriner in 1976, from a cross of 'Fragrant Cloud' x 'Tradition.' Coral, ovoid pointed buds open to silvery pink, fragrant flowers nearly 5 inches across. This generous climber blooms on new wood the first season.

**'Climbing Angel Face'** is a floribunda that in this form can reach to 12 feet, blooming profusely all season. The dark green foliage, leathery and glossy, is a handsome backdrop for the fragrant, mauve-lavender flowers.

**'Climbing Blaze'** is a sport of 'Paul's Scarlet Climber,' introduced by Jackson & Perkins in 1932. Bright scarlet, semidouble flowers, 2 to 3 inches across and lightly scented, appear in large clusters at the beginning of the main rose season and then recurrently through summer and fall. An 'Improved Blaze' also is offered, purportedly the producer of a more constant flower show. Both types grow to a height of about 15 feet.

**'Climbing Cecile Brunner'** yields two main flower shows yearly, in spring and again in fall. This form of the 1894 polyantha from French breeder Mignon grows canes to 20 feet long. The small blooms are bright pink with enough yellow at the petal bases to give the blooms an inner glow. This cultivar is especially suited to large trellises, for covering entire walls and arbors.

**'Climbing Don Juan'** yields very large, dark, velvety red flowers on a pillar-type climbing plant that flowers on new wood the first spring and continues all season.

# Climbing and rambler roses

'Etain'

Armstrong' x 'Captain Thomas.' Marketed as a vigorous pillar or climber, the canes reach 6 to 10 feet long and have fewer thorns than most such roses. The plant can be guided handily into a self-supporting tall bush or pillar habit. 'Climbing Golden Showers' flowers abundantly on new wood and repeats recurrently all season. Long, pointed buds open into large flowers to 4 inches across with up to 35 petals in a rose that is high centered at first but flattens as it opens. The color is daffodil yellow, and there is a pronounced fragrance. This rose flowers singly and in clusters.

**'Etain,'** a rambler, has survived from the 19th-century repertoire of old roses. It has medium-size pale pink flowers composed of many rounded petals in a flower formation resembling an informal double camellia. This rose has a light fragrance and grows 10 to 15 feet tall.

**'Excelsa,'** a rambler, is also known as 'Red Dorothy Perkins.' It came from American breeder Walsh in 1909. The main flowering occurs in late spring to early summer, but the generous trusses of crimson roses last for an exceptionally long time. They are borne on sturdy but pliable canes that lend themselves to a variety of training situations, such as arbors, archways, or pillars or as festoons. They grow to a height of 15 feet and to a similar width.

**'Climbing Golden Showers'** is the most popular of all large-flowered yellow climbers. It was bred by Walter Lammerts and introduced by Germain's in 1956, from a cross of 'Charlotte

'Excelsa'

'**Climbing Joseph's Coat**' was bred by D. L. Armstrong and Herbert Swim, by crossing 'Buccaneer' x 'Circus.' It was introduced in 1964. The large multicolor roses are yellow and red, to 3 inches across, and have a light, fruity scent. They appear in clusters, first as nicely shaped buds that open yellow, dissolve to orange, then to pink, and finally red. 'Joseph's Coat, Climbing' is a strong, pillar-type climber, 10 to 12 feet high, that blooms on new wood all season.

'**Lady Banks**' (*Rosa banksiae alba plena*), the white Lady Banks rose, and *R. banksiae lutea,* the yellow Lady Banks rose, send up thornless canes to 20 feet. The leaves are a refreshing willow green. This rose is delightful in almost all gardens in warmer regions, Zones 8–11. The flowers are small, very double, and their once-yearly appearance in spring is one of the greatest shows known to the world of roses. The scent is that of true Parma violets, delicate and pervasive.

'Lady Banks' in the double white, *Rosa banksiae alba plena,* was introduced to the West from China in 1807. The 'Yellow Banksia,' *R. banksiae lutea,* arrived from China about 20 years later. Because of the pale creamy yellow color and extraordinary profusion, this is possibly the favored Lady Banks. In warm climates it is not unusual to see these roses planted at the base of a sizable dead tree. The long canes rapidly lace up through the branches, then cascade downward.

The Banks roses grow so abundantly in the Deep South that they are sometimes taken for granted, like so many ditch flowers. In colder regions, however, where they are likely to be severely frozen back if not killed, these roses are often afforded special coddling, such as wintering over in trenches with the canes coiled and deeply mulched in dried leaves or pine boughs.

'**Climbing Mermaid**' was introduced by United Kingdom (UK) breeder W. Paul in 1917 from a cross between *Rosa bracteata* x double yellow tea rose. It blooms continuously and has dark green foliage that can be nearly evergreen in relatively benign climates. The canes are cordovan or brown-maroon and are set with extremely assertive thorns. The single (five-petaled) flowers can grow up to 4 inches in diameter. The petals are darker yellow in the center, paling to creamy lemon at the tips. The stamens are prominent all through the life of each flower, reddish golden and fluffy as they ripen, then turning a darker golden brown that stands out attractively until the petals drop. In warmer climates, Zone 7 and up, it is not unusual for the canes of a healthy 'Mermaid' to reach 20 to 30 feet.

'Climbing Golden Showers'

# Climbing and rambler roses

'New Dawn'

**'New Dawn'** is a repeat-blooming form of the pale pink 'Dr. Van Fleet.' It is by nature a rank grower with shiny, dark green foliage. The profusion of blooms at the first flowering in spring is always impressive from this climber, and its continuous show until the end of the season has made 'New Dawn' a favorite cultivar since its introduction by the Somerset Rose Company of America in 1930. 'New Dawn' can grow by a leap of 10 feet in a single season, so it is probably not for a small-space garden. In other settings, few pale pink and fragrant flowers are as welcome as this one.

**'Climbing Paradise'** was the first lavender rose to be honored by All-America Rose Selections, in 1979. It was bred by Weeks from a cross of 'Swarthmore' x unnamed seedling. The long, pointed buds that open into large flowers, to over 4 inches across, have up to 30 petals in a silvery lavender color with ruby-red at the edges and an extravagant fragrance. The canes reach to 12 feet.

*Rosa multiflora platyphylla* is better known as the "Seven Sisters Rose," a pink blend introduced in 1816 or 1817 from China. The *R. sempervirens* hybrid 'Felicite et Perpetue' also travels on occasion by the passport of "Seven Sisters Rose." In both cases, the popular name romanticizes the presence of many roses in one enormous cluster that vary from pink so pale it is nearly white through various shades to dark pink, lilac, and even red. *R. multiflora platyphylla* is offered today as a rambler, to 10 or 12 feet tall or more.

**'Paul's Himalayan Musk Rambler'** was first introduced about 100 years ago by a rosarian in Cheshunt, England. The rosette flowers are blush-pink–lavender in delicate cascades from threadlike stems. There is a rich, rose fragrance when the blooms are out full force at the beginning of summer. The drooping foliage of this rose may indicate the *Rosa moschata* genes, but to many eyes this may appear more like *R. multiflora* or *R. sempervirens*. 'Paul's Himalayan Musk Rambler' is exceptionally hardy and is one of the best roses for giving an assist so that it will be able to climb into and thread up through a tree. The canes are long and readily bendable to a variety of training situations. They can attain 12 to 20 feet and come equipped with broad, hooked thorns by which their climbing is facilitated.

**'Climbing Paul's Scarlet,'** first introduced in the United Kingdom in 1916, was to become one of the most widely planted climbing roses until, as a once-yearly bright scarlet, it was replaced by the continuous-flowering 'Blaze,' introduced in America in 1932. 'Paul's Scarlet' has dark green leaves and stems, the latter nearly thornless. Its canes grow to about 10 feet.

**'Paul Transon'** is a large-flowered climber that was introduced in 1900. It has flowers of medium pink with salmon and copper tinting and came out of a cross by French breeder Barbier between *Rosa wichuraiana* x 'Mme. Charles Small.' In any site that favors this rose, it will give a second flowering in early fall. The leaves are coppery green at first.

**'Climbing Peace'** is a sport of the 'Peace' rose. It is predictably robust, producing unusually vigorous and thick canes set with large, glossy, leathery leaves. Some rosarians consider the climbing rose stronger than the bush and the better choice if you need an abundance of long-stemmed 'Peace' roses for cutting.

**'Pinata'** is a climber bred by Suzuki of Japan and introduced in America by Jackson & Perkins in 1978. Ovoid buds open into high-centered, double flowers of medium size, to 3 inches across, with up to 30 petals, orange-yellow, flushed red, and generously fragrant. The leaves are glossy on a shapely plant that can even be grown as a self-supporting pillar to 6 or 8 feet tall. 'Pinata' trains readily and, because it is not given to haphazard or sprawly habit, makes an ideal choice for any small garden where these colors are favored.

**'Climbing Queen Elizabeth'** is a sport of the first modern grandiflora cultivar, introduced in 1954. The rose is today one of the most popular pink climbing roses. This is understandable considering the masses of large, clear-pink, delicately scented flowers, produced both singly and in clusters, on sturdy stems 6 to 10 feet tall or long.

**'Red Fountain'** is a dark red climber introduced in 1975. It has double flowers to 3 inches across that are endowed with old-rose fragrance. The dark green, glossy, leathery foliage is disease resistant on thrifty canes that can reach 10 to 12 feet in a season.

'Pinata'

# Climbing and rambler roses

**'Reine des Violettes'** is an extraordinarily beautiful example of a rose in one official class that also earns high marks for performance in another. In this case, 'Reine des Violettes' is a hybrid perpetual and one of the best by any standards. It also grows rather insistently upright, and when set next to a wall or trellis and the main canes are bent into a more horizontal position, it will have many laterals on which a marvelous flowering can occur. It is the habit of these blooms to hide among the gray-green leaves. The color is violet-pink in a medium-size rose that is quartered, petal packed, and highly scented, appearing continuously from the late spring. The individual flowers are not long lasting, but they have the helpful habit of shattering and disappearing.

**'Rhonda'** came from American breeder Lissmore in 1968. It is a modern climber, the result of a cross between 'New Dawn' x 'Spartan.' The flowers are dark carmine-rose, large, packed with petals, and in generous big clusters. They have only a hint of fragrance, but other points favor this as an outstanding climber to 10 feet high and 6 feet wide. As a cultivar, it has a reputation for growing vigorously and producing medium-green leaves with excellent disease resistance.

**'Royal Gold'** is a modern climber introduced by American breeder Dennison Morey in 1957. The result of a cross between 'Goldilocks' x 'Lydia,' it produces classic, high-centered hybrid tea roses in a bright yellow that is fade resistant. They are abundantly fragrant and appear continuously on canes to 8 feet tall and as broad.

**'Climbing Royal Sunset'** has buds like a classic hybrid tea, borne in profusion on heavy, reddish canes clad in coppery green foliage. The blossoms are a rich apricot color and delightfully fragrant.

**'Climbing Snow Bird'** has hybrid tea buds that become fully double, very fragrant, snowy white roses up to 5 inches across. These appear freely on new growth throughout the season, from early summer to fall frost.

**'Show Garden'** is a very tall, vigorous climber that is said by its marketers, Shumway, to be the hardiest of the class. The large flowers are a glowing dark pink to crimson over an extended season, most welcome for a frost belt climber.

**'Tempo'** (Jackson & Perkins; 1975) is a modern climber bred by Warriner out of a cross between 'Ena Harkness, Climber' x an unknown, a truly everblooming climber with ovoid buds that become large, petal-packed, high-centered, lightly fragrant, dark red roses. The unusually large leaves are glossy dark green, on canes that grow 6 to 8 feet long.

**'Climbing Viking Queen'** is an extremely hardy rose with medium-size blooms that are dark pink to crimson and endowed with heavy old-rose fragrance.

**'Climbing White Cherokee'** is the official flower of the state of Georgia and a favorite rose throughout the Southeast. Large, single, pure-white flowers in abundant clusters appear in spring. Glossy leaves clothe the canes in summer, highlighted in autumn by a profusion of brownish-red seed hips.

**'Climbing White Dawn'** was bred by L. E. Longley and introduced by the University of Minnesota in 1949. It is from a cross between 'New Dawn' x 'Lily Pons' and possibly the most loved of white climbing roses. The medium-size, snowy white, double flowers contain 35 petals arranged like those of a gardenia, in generous clusters recurrently. There is plenty of fragrance, and the vigorous canes climb readily to 6 or 8 feet, occasionally to 14 feet.

**'Climbing Yellow Blaze'** came from the Tyler, Texas, Co-Operative Rose Growers, Inc., in 1991. It is a medium yellow climber, sharing the vigorous habit and performance standards of the original 'Blaze.'

'Reine des Violettes'

# English garden roses

Beginning a decade or so before the introduction of 'Constance Spry' in 1961, David Austin's English roses have come to be seen by some as the single most important development in roses since the 19th-century hybrid teas and the 1930s floribundas. These new and thoroughly modern roses just happen to look like the most voluptuous, sensuously formed, subtly colored, and fragrant blossoms of the past, real or imagined.

The David Austin English roses represent what the hybrid musks offered earlier: a better shrub rose that has everything going for it, including habit restrained enough to make the plant happily manageable in a small space. As a class unto their own, these roses are universally vigorous, fragrant, completely double, disease resistant, repeat flowering (mostly), and low upkeep. Complex parentage yields perfumes varying from tea to myrrh, as in 'Constance Spry,' but always unmistakably rose.

Because they are repeat blooming, set as your goal to build a strong open-vase framework. When first planted, these roses need no pruning other than to remove dead tips, damaged canes, or broken roots. At the beginning of the following season, thin any weak or twiggy parts, any wood that is obviously dead, diseased, or discolored. Remove entirely the oldest, flowered canes, and cut back the remaining canes by about half. These roses are rated for Zones 5–9.

The David Austin roses make a stupendous appearance annually at the Chelsea Flower Show in London. The relatively compact bushes seen there are likely to reach considerably higher and wider in North American gardens. They are proving popular alone, as part of mixed shrubbery borders, and in cottage gardens of all types.

There are now a host of David Austin English garden roses on the market, available through catalogs and from local garden centers. Here are some of the choicest:

'Constance Spry' (1961) is a clear-pink old-fashioned rose that blooms superbly over an extended season from late spring to early summer. The plant can be handled as a medium to large shrub or a vigorous climber having canes to 15 feet. A wall covered with these, with a garden bench nestled in front, makes an unforgettable picture.

'Cottage Rose' (1991) is a modern rose in the English cottage garden tradition of Gertrude Jekyll. It blooms almost nonstop on strong canes to 5 feet tall and as wide, these clad in medium-green leaves that because of their disease resistance have a fair chance of being healthy even without special sprays. The high-pointed buds become cupped, 3-inch, pink, sweet-smelling, and all but irresistible roses.

'Fair Bianca' (1982) is the perfect pure white old rose, with big cupped, quartered, and petal-packed flowers that take your breath away, exquisite and scented of myrrh. The bushes grow a stocky 3 or 4 feet tall and as wide; they are ideal for small spaces and large pots.

'Gertrude Jekyll' (1986) honors the sublime garden maker of a century past. Rich, pink, 4-inch flowers have a damask fragrance on a bush that grows to 4 or 5 feet tall and as wide.

'Graham Thomas' (1983) is an exquisitely cupped yellow rose with red or apricot tinting. The tea-scented flowers appear constantly on canes 4 to 8 feet long to 5 feet wide, often vigorous enough to enjoy as a climber.

'The Squire' (1977) has thick petals in a big cupped rose with unfading crimson color and a large portion of old rose perfume. The bush grows to 4 feet. It is not floriferous, but flowers make up for this in size.

'Wife of Bath' (1969) is an upright small rose that grows to 4 feet tall and about 3 feet wide. It looks delicate but is actually strong and vigorous, ideally suited to a small space or even to growing in a container. The desirably cupped pink flowers smell of myrrh.

'Gertrude Jekyll'

# Hybrid musk roses

Tolerance for more shade than most other roses has made the hybrid musks unique in their appeal. They can be shrubs, hedges, pillars, or well-behaved climbers. The blended pastel colors are accompanied by abundant fragrance and strong, disease-resistant foliage. Some have decorative seed hips that add fall and winter color. It is no wonder "useful" is the adjective most often used to describe this class of roses, first developed early in the 20th century by an English minister, Joseph Hardwick Pemberton, through crosses of a *Rosa moschata* hybrid of unknown parentage with hybrid teas and polyanthas. 'Trier,' a 1904 white rambling rose, technically a hybrid multiflora, is said also to be involved, along with certain teas, Chinas, and hybrid perpetuals. When Pemberton died, his seedlings were passed along and his breeding work continued by his gardeners, Ann and John Bentall.

**'Aglaia,'** also known as 'Yellow Rambler,' dates from 1896 and figures prominently in Pemberton's breeding program. Small, pale yellow roses in clusters grow from nearly thornless canes

'Belinda'

clothed in bronze-tinted, bright green foliage. Measuring from 8 to 10 feet tall, this cultivar serves readily as a garden shrub or climbing rose.

**'Autumn Delight'** was introduced in 1933 by John Bentall, presumably directly from the Pemberton legacy. A shrub from 5 to 6 feet high and broad, 'Autumn Delight' is a nearly single, exceptionally large, off-white blossom having a large number of showy, eye-catching stamens.

**'Belinda'** was introduced in 1936 by Ann Bentall. The rounded bush grows 4 to 8 feet tall and as wide. It has white-eyed soft pink flowers with 10 petals and excellent fragrance. 'Belinda' repeats dependably, blooming heavily in spring but also intermittently in summer and often in a welcome surge as the fall season begins. The clusters of seed hips end the year on a bright note.

**'Bishop Darlington'** (Pemberton, 1926) grows naturally upright 4 to 6 feet and serves well as a hardy hedge rose. The buds are coral-pink opening to creamy semidouble flowers that smell of a true musk rose.

**'Bloomfield Dainty'** is a 1924 hybrid musk introduction from the American firm of Bobbink & Atkins. It has very large single flowers that open an intense yellow and then pale to near white. There is a light scent and not much repeat bloom.

**'Buff Beauty'** (Bentall, 1939) forms a spreading bush 4 to 6 feet tall covered with 2-inch, double apricot blooms, especially in spring and again in autumn. Few rosarians are disappointed by 'Buff Beauty,' and the pastel color gets on well in almost any setting with a variety of flowers.

**'Clytemnestra'** (Pemberton, 1915) has a procumbent habit that makes it especially pretty at the edge of a garden pool. Training as a pillar is another option. The blush to darker pink flowers are semidouble in great clusters. There is a touch of yellow at the petal bases and a pleasant musk fragrance. The bushes grow 4 to 6 feet tall and wide or can be climbers to twice this height.

'Cornelia' came from Pemberton's seedlings in 1925, a shrub that grows to 5 or 6 feet and can be enjoyed as a specimen or trained as a climber. The fragrance is different from others in the class, and the small, semi-double flowers are a distinctive pale coral that makes the golden stamens seem to shine.

'Danae' (Pemberton, 1913) has arching dark red canes set with small, dark green foliage. Intense yellow buds become clusters of creamy semidouble roses with a mild scent. As a bush this hybrid musk grows to 5 feet high and wide, or as a climber to twice this height. It performs well as hedging, interlacing through a fence or next to any water garden. The orange-red seed hips that finish the season look especially beautiful with the late blooms.

'Erfurt' (1939) grows 4 to 6 feet tall, becoming a cascading bush that makes a satisfying appearance in the garden. Its blooms are semi-double, dark rose, with creamy white markings at the petal bases and noticeable gold stamens. The scent is of true musk rose.

'Felicia' (Pemberton, 1928) is noteworthy for an outstanding performance in autumn when the many-petaled double flowers are most welcome. The color opens apricot-pink and then fades gracefully to cream and salmon. The bush itself is a medium-size shrub, from 4 to 6 feet high and wide.

'Kathleen' (Pemberton, 1922) produces a truly remarkable number of small five-petaled roses that look like old-fashioned apple blossoms. They are pale pink with a darker pink on the petal reverses. The yellow stamens stand out in a scintillating manner. There is also fragrance, both musk-rich and attar-of-roses sweet. The dark green foliage has a droopiness that is visually appealing, especially when 'Kathleen' is combined with a lattice garden structure. As a shrub, it can reach 4 feet tall by 6 feet wide, or to twice this as a climber.

'Lavender Lassie' (Kordes, 1960) is possibly the newest of the hybrid musks. Its color is on the lilac side of pink, with large clusters of semidouble, intensely fragrant roses. It performs ideally as a climber 8 to 12 feet tall and dependably carries a large amount of foliage. It also can be managed as a bush, to 5 feet high and nearly as wide, and is notably tolerant of semishade.

'Penelope' (Pemberton, 1924) won a Gold Medal from England's National Rose Society the year after it was introduced. A sturdy shrub 5 feet high and wide, this one can be smothered in blooms by the second or third year after planting. It has semi-double flowers in huge clusters, pale pink to peaches and cream, individually large and abundantly scented. Orange-pink, globular seed hips decorate the bushes in the cold seasons.

'Prosperity' (Pemberton, 1919) has a sweet scent that comes from its tea rose parent, 'Perle des Jardin.' Medium-size double flowers appear in clusters sufficiently large to weight the cane tips so that they arch attractively. As a shrub, 'Prosperity' reaches to 5 feet high by 4 feet across. It makes a superb pillar and when trained this way can reach to 8 feet. The color is from the pale pink of the developing buds to the ivory-white of the fully open blossoms, one of those subtle colorations best appreciated on an overcast day.

'Vanity' (Pemberton, 1920) can be a shrub to 6 feet tall and wide or a vigorous climber to 10 feet. It has large single flowers in a saturated cerise-pink that has high visual impact at some distance in the garden or when cut. There is a generous musk fragrance that makes it among the favorites of this class.

## Patience pays with hybrid musks

When you plant a hybrid musk rose, be prepared to cultivate a little patience in yourself. As a class, this one is slow to establish but will take off at the beginning of the second season, not unlike today's newly popular 'Bonica.' Pruning depends on the habit of the rose and on how it is being used in the garden. Climbers need to have the laterals cut back after the first flush of spring growth. In general, no other pruning is needed except to remove old canes or deadwood. Deadheading results in more flowers, but negates the formation of colorful seed hips.

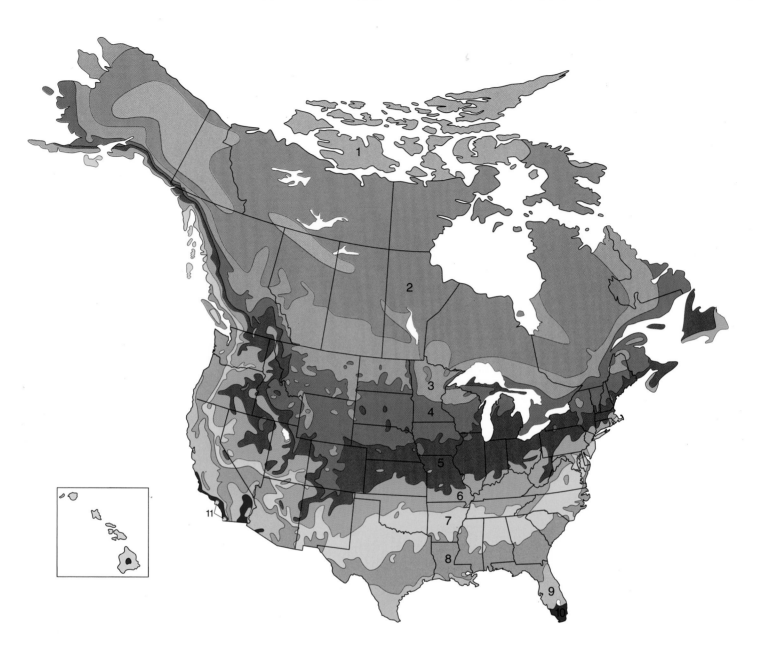

# The USDA Plant Hardiness Map of North America

The map, issued by the United States Department of Agriculture, lists average annual minimum temperatures for each zone. It relates directly to the cold-hardiness of plants, roses included, but does not address the other extreme, high temperatures. Special considerations with regard to high temperatures as they apply to roses are noted as appropriate throughout the pages of this book. A new map, in preparation by the USDA in cooperation with the American Horticultural Society, will treat equally matters of hot and cold and their effect on plants.

## RANGE OF AVERAGE ANNUAL MINIMUM TEMPERATURES FOR EACH ZONE

| | | |
|---|---|---|
| | ZONE 1 | BELOW -50° F |
| | ZONE 2 | -50° TO -40° |
| | ZONE 3 | -40° TO -30° |
| | ZONE 4 | -30° TO -20° |
| | ZONE 5 | -20° TO -10° |
| | ZONE 6 | -10° TO 0° |
| | ZONE 7 | 0° TO 10° |
| | ZONE 8 | 10° TO 20° |
| | ZONE 9 | 20° TO 30° |
| | ZONE 10 | 30° TO 40° |
| | ZONE 11 | ABOVE 40° |

# Glossary

**Asexual reproduction** A method of producing plants by rooting stems or leaves so that the offspring are identical to the parent. Patented plants may not be reproduced this way without the permission of the patent holder (usually the breeder or the breeder's company).

**Bud** Also known as an eye, it's a small node located at the intersection of the leaf and plant stem containing undeveloped stems, leaves, and flower structures as well as the unopened flower.

**Budding** This is the process of removing a bud from its stem and inserting that bud into another plant, generally on its stem. Also known as grafting, it allows, for example, a selected color variety to be budded to a thrifty rootstock.

**Bud union** The demarcation at the crown where the bud has joined with the rootstock.

**Budwood** Sections of woody stem from a variety that is to be budded to a rootstock to reproduce that variety. This section of wood contains several buds.

**Canes** The main stems of a rose plant.

**Crown** The point where the roots and stems are joined.

**Cultivar** As opposed to a variety that occurs naturally in the wild, a cultivar has been human-made through hybridizing or careful selection.

**Cuttings** The whips of rootstock after they have been sawed into 9-inch lengths (and subsequently will be rooted in the field).

**'Doctor Huey'** The name of a specific rootstock variety that is used generally for garden-variety roses. There are other commercial rootstocks, some suited to certain regions.

**Everblooming** Said of a rose that blooms constantly all season.

**Eye** See bud.

**Grafting** See budding.

**Hybrid** The result of crossing two different species or varieties by means of the pollen of one and the egg of another.

**Intermittent** Said of a rose that blooms several times each season at more-or-less regular intervals.

**Lateral** A stem that emerges from and grows sideways to a cane.

**Node** A slightly swollen spot on a stem where a branch or leaf would develop, given the right environmental conditions.

**Own-root** This term describes those varieties that do not need to be budded to a rootstock; they produce roots of their own that provide many of the same advantages of the rootstock. Most miniature roses are own-root plants.

**Remontant** Said of a rose that blooms more than once in a season, often in several waves rather than continuously, in which case it would be everblooming.

**Repeat** Said of a rose that blooms more than once in a season, often a major burst at the beginning of the season and another crescendo, though smaller, in early fall.

**Rootstock** A plant variety specially selected for its ability to provide superior roots, support a wide range of budded varieties, and resist diseases and pests. It is rooted from a cutting often stuck to grow right in the field and then a hybrid is budded on it.

**Rosarian** A gardener who specializes in growing roses.

**Rose hip** The seed pod, or fruit, of the rose; it changes color as the seeds inside ripen.

**Scion** See budwood.

**Shadehouse** A mesh-cloth-covered structure used to protect delicate varieties, such as miniatures, while they grow in commercial ranges.

**Sport** The offspring of a parent plant that is produced naturally by gene mutation and differs from the parent in enough characteristics to be recognized as a distinct variety.

**Standard** Also called a tree rose, this is a rose plant that is grown on an extended cane to increase its height. Those sold in commerce are almost always grafted. It is often possible to prune an established miniature rose into a tree-form standard.

**Stud** A term that is applied to any rose that has proven to be valuable in breeding for new roses that are somehow improved over those that preceded them. The stud passes along the desired genes through pollen or through seed.

**Sucker** A stem that arises from the rootstock rather than from the budded stock; it should be removed at the point where it originates.

**Tree-form roses** See standard.

**Two-Year** term used to describe plants grown for the home landscape market or garden-variety roses.

**Whips** The long canes of rootstock after they have been collected.

**X** This symbol stands for "cross-pollinated with," as in the parentage of 'Mister Lincoln': 'Chrysler Imperial' x (cross-pollinated with) 'Charles Mallerin.'

# Public gardens

**ALABAMA**

Birmingham Botanical Gardens
2616 Lane Park Rd.
Birmingham, AL 25223
205/879-1227
1,200 plants, 153 varieties

Fairhope City Rose Garden
1 Fairhope Ave.
Fairhope, AL 36533
205/928-8003
1,200 plants, 35 varieties. AARS Display
    Garden

David A. Hemphill Park of Roses
Mobile Public Rose Garden
Springdale Plaza, Airport Blvd.
Mobile, AL 36606
205/479-3775
800 plants, 300 varieties. AARS Garden

Bellingrath Gardens Rose Garden
Rte 1, Box 60
Theodore, AL 36582
205/973-2217
2,800 plants, 35 varieties. AARS Garden

**ARIZONA**

Saguaro Historical Ranch Rose Garden
9802 N. 59th Ave.
Glendale, AZ 85301
602/931-5321
1,000 plants, 97 varieties. AARS Garden

Fields D.D.S. & Associates Rose Garden
4491 W. Northern Ave.
Glendale, AZ 85301
602/931-5321
750 plants, 570 varieties

Encanto Park Rose Garden
15th Avenue and Encanto Boulevard
Phoenix, AZ 85007
1,500 plants, 100 varieties. AARS Garden

Valley Garden Center
1809 N. 15th Ave.
Phoenix, AZ 85007
602/252-2120
1,255 plants, 100 varieties. AARS Garden

Gene C. Reid Park
900 S. Randolph Way
Tucson, AZ 85716
602/791-4873
1,080 plants, 138 varieties. AARS Garden

**ARKANSAS**

State Capitol Rose Garden
State Capitol Building
Little Rock, AR 72201
501/324-9695
1,800 plants, 90 varieties. AARS Garden

**CALIFORNIA**

Arboreta and Botanic Gardens
301 N. Baldwin Ave.
Arcadia, CA 91007-2697
818/446-8251
80 plants

Virginia Robinson Gardens
Beverly Hills, CA
213/276-5367
200 plants, 70 varieties

Fountain Square Rose Garden
7115 Greenback Lane
Citrus Heights, CA 95621
916/969-6666
1,400 plants, 334 varieties. AARS Garden

Roger's Gardens
2301 San Joaquin Hills Rd.
Corona del Mar, CA 92625
714/640-5800
76 plants, 36 varieties. AARS Garden

Sherman Library and Gardens
2647 E. Coast Hghwy.
Corona del Mar, CA 92625
714/673-2261
42 plants, 18 varieties

Bella Rosa Winery Rose Garden
Pond Road and Highway 99
DeLano, CA 93215
805/831-5197
1,263 plants, 88 varieties. AARS Garden

Quail Botanical Gardens
230 Quail Gardens Dr.
Encinitas, CA 92024
619/436-8301
10 plants, 9 varieties

Descanso Gardens International Rosarium
1418 Descanso Dr.
La Canada Flintridge, CA 91011
818/952-4401
7,000 plants, 2,000 varieties

Exposition Park Rose Garden
701 State Dr.
Los Angeles, CA 90037
213/748-4772
15,000 plants, 145 varieties. AARS Garden

J. Paul Getty Museum
17985 Pacific Coast Hghwy.
Malibu, CA 90625
310/458-2003
130 plants, 4 varieties

Morcom Amphitheater of Roses
700 Jean St.
Oakland, CA 94610
415/658-0731
5,000 plants, 300 varieties. AARS Garden

South Coast Botanic Garden
26300 Crenshaw Blvd.
Palos Verdes Peninsula, CA 90274
310/544-1948
3,000 plants

Tournament of Roses Wrigley Gardens
391 S. Orange Grove Blvd.
Pasadena, CA 91184
818/449-4100
1,500 plants, 100 varieties. AARS Garden

Rose Bowl Rose Garden
1001 Rose Bowl Dr.
Pasadena, CA 91103
818/577-3100
2,500 plants. AARS Garden

Fairmont Park Rose Garden
2225 Market St.
Riverside, CA 92501
714/782-5401
1,350 plants, 78 varieties. AARS Garden

Capitol Park Rose Garden
1300 L St.
Sacramento, CA 85814
916/445-3658
1,500 plants, 60 varieties. AARS Garden

McKinley Park Rose Garden
601 Alhambra Blvd.
Sacramento, CA 95816
916/448-4273
1,200 plants, 158 varieties. AARS Garden

Inez Curant Parker Memorial Rose Garden
2130 Pan American Plaza
San Diego, CA 92101
619/236-5717
2,000 plants, 200 varieties. AARS Garden

Golden Gate Park Rose Garden
Golden Gate Park
San Francisco, CA 94117
415/666-7003
1,500 plants, 145 varieties. AARS Garden

San Jose Municipal Rose Garden
Nagles and Dana Avenues
San Jose, CA 95121
408/287-0698
4,500 plants, 158 varieties. AARS Garden

Huntington Botanical Gardens
1151 Oxford Rd.
San Marino, CA 91108
818/405-2100
4,000 plants, 1,800 varieties. AARS Garden

Hearst San Simeon State Historical
    Monument
750 Hearst Castle Rd.
San Simeon, CA 93452
805/927-2090
2,300 plants, 80 varieties

A.C. Postel Memorial Rose Garden
Los Olives and Laguna Streets
Santa Barbara, CA 93103
805/564-5437
1,300 plants, 130 varieties. AARS Garden

Wasco Community Garden
Barker Park
11th Street at Birch
Wasco, CA 93280
1,000 plants

Westminster Civic Center Rose Garden
8200 Westminster Blvd.
Westminster, CA 92683
714/895-2860
1,440 plants, 162 varieties. AARS Garden

Pageant of Roses Garden
Rose Hills Memorial Park
3900 S. Workman Mill Rd.
P.O. Box 110
Whittier, CA 90601
310/699-0921
7,000 plants, 600 varieties. AARS Garden

Filoli Center
Canada Road
Woodside, CA 94062
415/364-8300; 415/364-2880
560 plants, 250 varieties

COLORADO
Four Corners Rose Garden
E. 2nd Avenue and 12th Street
Durango, CO 81301
300 plants

War Memorial Rose Garden
5804 S. Bemis St.
Littleton, CO 80120
303/795-9856
800 plants, 120 varieties. AARS Garden

Longmont Memorial Rose Garden
Roosevelt Park
700 block of Bross Street
Longmont, CO 80501
303/651-8446
1,280 plants, 90 varieties. AARS Garden

CONNECTICUT
Norwich Memorial Rose Garden
Mohegan Park
Rockwell Street and Judd Road
Norwich, CT 06360
203/886-2381
2,500 plants, 200 varieties. AARS Garden

Elizabeth Park Rose Garden
150 Walbridge Rd.
Hartford, CT 06119
203/722-6543
1,500 plants, 800 varieties. AARS Garden

DELAWARE
Hagley Museum and Library
P.O. Box 3630
Wilmington, DE 19807
305/658-2400
95 plants, 20 varieties

DISTRICT OF COLUMBIA
Dumbarton Oaks
1703 32nd St., N.W.
Washington, DC 20007
202/342-3290
1,000 plants, 35 varieties

The George Washington University
2033 G St., NW, and 730 21st St.
Washington, DC 20052
202/994-7575
600 plants, 90 varieties. AARS Garden

United States Botanic Garden
245 First St., SW
Washington, DC 20024
180 plants, 30 varieties

FLORIDA
Florida Cypress Gardens
P.O. Box 1
Cypress Gardens, FL 33884
813/324-2111
200 plants, 12 varieties. AARS Garden

Giles  Rose Nursery
2611 Holly Hill Cutoff Rd.
Davenport, FL 33837
813/422-8103
8,000 plants, 350 varieties

Walt Disney World Resort
c/o Parks Horticulture
P.O. Box 10,000
Lake Buena Vista, FL 32830
407/824-6987
6,298 plants, 40 varieties. AARS Garden

Sturgeon Memorial Rose Garden
13401 Indian Rocks Rd.
Largo, FL 34644
813/595-2914
850 plants, 125 varieties. AARS Garden

Giles Ramblin' Roses Nursery
2968 SR 710
Okeechokee, FL 34974
813/763-6611
8,000 plants, 350 varieties

GEORGIA
Elizabeth Bradley Turner Memorial Rose
    Garden
The State Botanical Garden of Georgia
2450 S. Milledge Ave.
Athens, GA 30605-1624
706/542-1244
339 plants, 64 varieties. AARS Display
    Garden

Atlanta Botanical Garden
P.O. Box 77246
Piedmont Park at the Prado
Atlanta. GA 30367
404/876-5859
450 plants, 44 varieties. AARS Display
    Garden

Thomasville Nurseries, Inc. Rose Test
    Garden
1840 Smith Ave.
Thomasville, GA 31792
912/226-5568
2,000 plants, 250 varieties. AARS Garden

HAWAII
Maui Agricultural Research Center
University of Hawaii
209 Mauna Place
Kula, HI 96790
808/878-1213
460 plants, 29 varieties. AARS Garden

IDAHO
Julia Davis Rose Garden
Capital Boulevard and Julia Davis Drive
Boise, ID 83706
208/384-4327
2,000 plants

ILLINOIS
The Nan Elliott Memorial Rose Garden
The Gordon F. Moore Community Park
4550 College Ave.
Alton, IL 62002
618/463-3580
1,700 plants, 130 varieties. AARS Display
    Garden

Marquette Park
6700 S. Kedzie Ave.
Chicago, IL 60629
312//776-0728
4,500 plants, 75 varieties

Merrick Park Rose Garden
Southwest Corner of Oak Avenue and
    Lake Street
Evanston, IL 60204
708/866-2911
2,000 plants, 90 varieties. AARS Garden

The Bruce Krasberg Rose Garden
Chicago Botanic Garden
Lake Cook Road, P.O. Box 400
Glencoe, IL 60022
708/835-5441
5,000 plants, 162 varieties. AARS Garden

Park District of Highland Park
636 Ridge Rd.
Highland Park, Il 60035
312/831-3810
380 plants, 32 varieties

Lynn J. Arthur Rose Garden
Cook Memorial Park
Libertyville, IL 60064
312/937-7896
800 plants, 70 varieties. AARS Garden

The Morton Arboretum
Route 53
Lisle, IL 60532
708/968-0074
154 plants, 47 varieties

George L. Luthy Memorial Botanical Garden
2218 N. Prospect Rd.
Peoria, IL 61603
309/686-3362
1,000 plants, 128 varieties. AARS Garden

Sinnissippi Greenhouse and Gardens
1401 N. Second St.
Rockford, IL 61107
815/987-8858
3,500 plants, 74 varieties. AARS Garden

The Washington Park Botanical Garden
Fayette and Chatham Road
P.O. Box 5052
Springfield, IL 62705
217/753-6228
3,000 plants, 300 varieties

Cantigny Gardens
1 S. 151 Winfield Rd.
Wheaton, IL 60187
708/668-5161
1,000 plants, 100 varieties. AARS Garden

INDIANA
Lakeside Rose Garden
Lakeside Park
1500 Lake Ave.
Fort Wayne, IN 46805
219/427-1253
2,000 plants, 225 varieties. AARS Display
    Garden

Richmond Rose Garden
Glen Miller Park
Richmond, IN 47374
1,600 plants, 90 varieties. AARS Garden

IOWA
Iowa State University Horticulture Garden
Pammel Drive and Haber Road
Ames, IA 50011
515/294-0038
670 plants, 134 varieties. AARS Garden

Bettendorf Park Board Municipal Rose
Garden
2204 Grant St.
Bettendorf, IA 52722
319/359-0913
617 plants, 42 varieties. AARS Garden

Noelridge Park Rose Garden
4900 Council St. NE
Cedar Rapids, IA 52402
319/398-5101
540 plants, 43 varieties. AARS Garden

Bickelhaupt Arboretum
340 S. 14th St.
Clinton, IA 52732
319/242-4771
37 plants, 30 varieties

VanderVeer Park Municipal Rose Garden
215 W. Central Park Ave.
Davenport, IA 52803
319/326-7865
2,300 plants, 170 varieties. AARS Garden

Greenwood Park Rose Garden
4812 Grand Ave.
Des Moines, IA 50310
515/242-2993
2,500 plants, 100 varieties. AARS Garden

Dubuque Arboretum and Botanical Gardens
3125 W. 32nd St. and Arboretum Dr.
Dubuque, IA 52001
319/582-8621
725 plants, 200 varieties. AARS Display
    Garden

Weed Park Memorial Rose Garden
Weed Park
Muscatine, IA 52761
319/263-0241
1,300 plants, 85 varieties. AARS Garden

State Center Public Rose Garden
300 3rd St. SE
State Center, IA 50247
515/483-2081
1,200 plants, 70 varieties. AARS Garden

KANSAS
E.F.A. Reinisch Rose Garden
Gage Park
4320 W. 10th St.
Topeka, KS 66604
913/272-6150
6,500 plants, 400 varieties. AARS Garden

Lake Shawnee Gardens
West Edge Drive at E. 37th Street
Topeka, KS 66609
913/267-2000
680 plants

KENTUCKY
Louisville
Kentucky Memorial Rose Garden
Kentucky Fair and Exposition Center
Louisville, KY 40232
502/267-6308
1,300 plants, 100 varieties. AARS Garden

LOUISIANA
L.S.U. Agriculture Center
All-America Rose Display Garden
4560 Essen Lane
Baton Rouge, LA 70809
1,400 plants, 140 varieties. AARS Garden

Hodges Gardens
P.O. Box 900
Highway 171 South
Many, LA 71449
318/586-3523
1,757 plants, 125 varieties. AARS Garden

American Rose Center
8877 Jefferson-Paige Rd.
Shreveport, LA 71119
318/938-5402
500 plants, 32 varieties. AARS Garden

MAINE
City of Portland Rose Circle
Derring Oaks Park
Portland, ME 04101
207/775-5451
600 plants, 39 varieties. AARS Garden

MARYLAND
William Paca Garden
1 Martin St.
Annapolis, MD 21401
301/267-6656
100 plants, 13 varieties

Maryland Rose Society Heritage Rose
    Garden
The Cylburn Arboretum
4915 Greenspring Ave.
Baltimore, MD 21209
410/396-0180
31 plants, 13 varieties

Ladew Topiary Gardens
3535 Jarrettsville Pike
Monkton, MD 21111
410/557-9570
250 plants, 30 varieties

MASSACHUSETTS
James P. Kelleher Rose Garden
Park Drive
Boston, MA 02130
617/524-3362
2,000 plants, 103 varieties. AARS Garden

Arnold Arboretum of Harvard University
125 Arborway
Jamaica Plain, MA 02130
1,302 plants, 165 varieties

Berkshire Garden Center
P.O. Box 826, Route 102
Stockbridge, MA 01262
413/298-3926

Naumkeag
P.O. Box 792, Prospect Hill
Stockbridge, MA 01262
413/298-3239
128 plants, 16 varieties

The Stanley Park of Westfield
400 Western Ave.
Westfield, MA 01085
413/568-9312
2,000 plants, 50 varieties. AARS Garden

MICHIGAN
University of Michigan Matthaei Botanical
    Gardens
1800 Dixboro Rd.
Ann Arbor, MI 48105
313/998-7060 (recording)
313/998-7061 (receptionist)
165 plants, 55 varieties

Anna Scripps Whitcomb Conservatory
Belle Isle
Detroit, MI 48207
313/267-7133
85 plants, 10 varieties

Michigan State University Demonstration
    Gardens
Horticulture Department
East Lansing, MI 48823
517/355-0348
500 plants, 120 varieties. AARS Garden

Frances Park Memorial Rose Garden
2600 Moores River Dr.
Lansing, MI 48912
517/483-4207
1,100 plants, 155 varieties

Fernwood Botanic Garden
3988 Range Line Rd.
Niles, MI 49120-9042
616/695-6491 or 683-8653
150 plants, 80 varieties

MINNESOTA
Minnesota Landscape Arboretum
3675 Arboretum Dr.
P.O. Box 39
Channhassen, MN 55317
713/862-2520
1,000 plants, 408 varieties

Lyndale Park Municipal Rose Garden
4125 E. Lake Harriet Pkwy.
Minneapolis, MN 55409
612/348-4448
3,000 plants, 150 varieties. AARS Garden

Como Park Conservatory
1325 Aida Place
St. Paul, MN 55103
612/489-5378
110 plants, 13 varieties

MISSISSIPPI
Hattiesburg Area Rose SocietyGarden
University of Southern Mississippi
Hattiesburg, MS 39401
601/583-8848
1,200 plants, 40 varieties. AARS Garden

MISSOURI
Cape Girardeau Rose Display Garden
Park Street
Cape Girardeau, MO 63701
314/335-0706
700 plants, 40 varieties. AARS Garden

Laura Conyers Smith Municipal Rose Garden
Jacob L. Loose Memorial Park
5200 Pennsylvania
Kansas City, MO 64112
816/561-9710
3,500 plants; 200 varieties. AARS Garden

Gladney & Lehmann Rose Garden
Missouri Botanical Garden
4344 Shaw Blvd.
St. Louis, MO 63110
314/577-5100
5,000 plants, 200 varieties. AARS Garden

MONTANA
Missoula Memorial Rose Garden
Blaine and Brooks Street
Missoula, MT 59833
406/642-3340
326 plants, 52 varieties. AARS Garden

NEBRASKA
AARS Constitution Rose Garden
Father Flanagan's Boys' Home
Boys Town, NE 68010
402/498-1100
1,200 plants, 52 varieties. AARS Garden

Lincoln Municipal Rose Garden
Antelope Park
27th and C Street
Lincoln, NE 68502
402/471-7847
700 plants, 37 varieties, AARS Garden

Hanscom Park Greenhouse
1500 S. 32nd St.
Omaha , NE 68105
402/444-5497
1,582 plants, 175 varieties

Memorial Park Rose Garden
57th and Underwood Avenue
Omaha, NE 68104
402/444-5497
1,600 plants; 162 varieties, AARS Garden

NEVADA
Reno Municipal Rose Garden
2055 Idlewild Dr.
Reno, NV 89509
702/785-2270
2,400 plants, 560 varieties. AARS Garden

NEW HAMPSHIRE
Fuller Gardens Rose Gardens
10 Willow Ave.
North Hampton, NH 03862
603/964-5414
1,400 plants, 100 varieties. AARS Garden

NEW JERSEY
Rudolf W. van der Goot Rose Garden
Colonial Park
R.D. 1, Mettler's Road
East Millstone, NJ 08873
908/873-2459
3,000 plants, 225 varieties. AARS Garden

The Reeves-Reed Arboretum
165 Hobart Ave.
Summit, NJ 07901
908/273-8787
204 plants, 66 varieties

Lambertus C. Bobbink Memorial Rose
   Garden
Thompson Park
Newman Springs Road
Lincroft, NJ 07738
908/842-4000
770 roses, 63 varieties. AARS Garden

Freylinghuysen Arboretum
53 E. Hanover Ave., P.O. Box 1295
Morristown, NJ 07962
201/326-7600
150 plants, 27 varieties

Jack D. Lissemore Rose Garden
Davis Johnson Park & Gardens
137 Engle St.
Tenafly, NJ 07670
1,235 plants, 75 varieties. AARS Garden

NEW MEXICO
Prospect Park Rose Garden
8205 Apache Ave. NE
Albuquerque , NM 87110
505/296-8210
1,200 plants, 500 varieties. AARS Garden

NEW YORK
The Peggy Rockefeller Rose Garden
The New York Botanical Garden
Bronx, NY 10458
212/220-8767
2,700 plants, 238 varieties. AARS Garden

Cranford Rose Garden
Brooklyn Botanic Garden
1000 Washington Ave.
Brooklyn , NY 11225
718/622-4433
6,000 plants, 1,100 varieties. AARS Garden

Joan Fuzak Memorial Rose Garden
502 City Hall
Buffalo, NY 14202
716/815-4268
1,000 plants, 250 varieties. AARS Garden

Sonnenberg Gardens Rose Garden
151 Charlotte St.
Canaridaigua, NY 14424
716/394-2521
2,600 plants, 35 varieties. AARS Garden

Queens Botanical Garden
43–50 Main St.
Flushing, NY 11355
718/886-3800
230 plants, 42 varieties. AARS Garden

The Cloisters
The Metropolitan Museum of Art
Fort Tryon Park, NY 10040
212/923-3700
8 plants, 8 varieties

United Nations Rose Garden
United Nations
New York, NY 10017
212/963-6145
1,391 plants, 39 varieties. AARS Garden

Old Westbury Gardens
Old Westbury Road
P.O. Box 430
Old Westbury, NY 11568
516/333-0048
1,200 plants, 100 varieties. AARS Garden

Maplewood Rose Garden
100 Maplewood Ave.
Rochester, NY 14613
716/647-2379
4,000 plants, 300 varieties. AARS Garden

Central Park Rose Garden
Central Parkway
Schenectady, NY 12305
518/382-5152
3,000 plants, 50 varieties. AARS Garden

Dr. E.M. Mills Memorial Rose Garden
Thorden Park
Ostron Avenue and University Place
Syracuse, NY 13207
315/473-2631
2,500 plants, 112 varieties. AARS Garden

NORTH CAROLINA
Biltmore Estate
1 N. Park Square
Asheville, NC 28801
704/255-1776
2,000 plants, 80 varieties. AARS Garden

Tanglewood Park Rose Garden
Tanglewood Park
P.O. Box 1040
Clemmons, NC 27012
919/766-0591
837 plants, 72 varieties. AARS Garden

Fayetteville Rose Garden
Fayetteville Technical Community College
2201 Hull Rd.
Fayetteville, NC 28303
919/678-8304
960 plants, 38 varieties. AARS Display
    Garden

Raleigh Municipal Rose Garden
301 Pogue St.
Raleigh, NC 27607
919/821-4579
1,200 plants, 60 varieties. AARS Garden

Reynolda Rose Gardens of Wake Forest
    University
100 Reynolda Village
Winston-Salem, NC 27106
919/759-5593
1,050 plants, 90 varieties. AARS Garden

NORTH DAKOTA
International Peace Garden, Inc.
Rte.1, P.O. Box 116
Dunseith, ND 58329
701/263-4390
50 plants, 16 varieties

OHIO
Stan Hywet Hall and Gardens
714 N. Portage Path
Akron, OH 44303
216/836-0576
800 plants, 60 varieties. AARS Garden

Cahoon Memorial Rose Garden
Cahoon Memorial Park
Bay Village, OH 44140
216/871-5081
1,250 plants, 190 varieties. AARS Garden

Mary Anne Sears Swetland Rose Garden
Garden Center of Greater Cleveland
11030 East Blvd.
Cleveland, OH 44106
208 plants, 30 varieties

Columbus Park of Roses
3923 N. High St.
Columbus, OH 43214
614/645-3350
10,669 plants, 358 varieties. AARS Garden

Charles Edwin Nail Memorial Rose Garden
Kingwood Center
900 Park Ave. W.
Mansfield, OH 44906
419/522-0211
850 plants, 250 varieties. AARS Garden

Inniswood Metro Gardens
940 Hempstead Rd.
Westerville, OH 43081
614/895-6216
460 plants, 140 varieties

Secrest Arboretum
Ohio State University
1680 Madison Ave.
Wooster, OH 44691
216/263-3761
1,297 plants, 445 varieties

OKLAHOMA
J.E. Conrad Municipal Rose Garden
641 Park Dr.
Muskogee, OK 74401
918/682-6602
2,500 plants, 236 varieties. AARS Garden

Charles E. Sparks Rose Garden
3500 Pat Murphy Dr.
Will Rogers Park
Oklahoma City, OK 73112
405/943-4200
4,000 plants, 300 varieties. AARS Garden

Tulsa Municipal Rose Garden
Woodward Park
21st and Peoria
Tulsa, OK 74114
918/596-7255
9,000 plants, 278 varieties. AARS Garden

OREGON
Shore Acres Botanical Garden/State Park
13030 Cape Arago Hghwy.
Coos Bay, OR 97420
503/888-3732
726 plants, 65 varieties. AARS Garden

Corvallis Rose Garden
Avery Park
Corvallis, OR 97330
503/753-6879
1,400 plants, 300 varieties

Owen Memorial Rose Garden
300 N. Jefferson
Eugene, OR 97401
503/687-5334
4,500 plants, 450 varieties. AARS Garden

International Rose Test Garden
400 S.W. Kingston Ave.
Portland, OR 97201
503/248-4302
10,000 plants, 450 varieties. AARS Garden

PENNSYLVANIA
Malcolm W. Gross Memorial Rose Garden
2700 Parkway Blvd.
Allentown, PA 18104
215/437-7628
3,600 plants, 80 varieties. AARS Garden

Hershey Gardens
P.O. Box B6, Hotel Road
Hershey, PA 17033
717/534-3492
8,000 plants, 300 varieties. AARS Garden

Longwood Gardens, Inc.
Department of Horticulture
Rte 1, P.O. Box 501
Kennett Square, PA 19348
215/388-6741
1,200 plants, 100 varieties. AARS Garden

Marion Rivanus Rose Garden
Morris Arboretum
University of Pennsylvania
9414 Meadowbrook Ave.
Philadelphia, PA 19118
215/247-5777
1,000 plants, 50 varieties

Robert Pyle Memorial Rose Gardens
Rtes 1 and 796
West Grove, PA 19390
215/869-2426
2,100 plants, 100 varieties

RHODE ISLAND
Blithewolde Gardens and Arboretum
Ferry Road
Bristol, RI 02809
401/253-2707
70 plants, 10 varieties

Rosecliff
Bellevue Avenue
Newport, RI 02840
401/846-7718
200 plants, 4 varieties

SOUTH CAROLINA
Edisto Memorial Gardens
200 Riverside Dr.
Orangeburg, SC 29115
803/534-6376
3,100 plants, 75 varieties. AARS Garden

SOUTH DAKOTA
Rapid City Memorial Rose Garden
444 Mt. Rushmore Rd.
Rapid City, SD 57702
605/394-4175
1,100 plants, 90 varieties. AARS Garden

Halby Park
Rapid City, SD
500 plants

TENNESSEE
Warner Park Rose Garden
1254 E. Third St.
Chattanooga, TN 37404
615/757-5054
1,100 plants, 100 varieties. AARS Garden

Memphis Municipal Rose Garden of the
    Memphis Botanic Garden
750 Cherry Rd.
Memphis, TN 38117-4699
901/685-1566
1,500 plants, 105 varieties. AARS Garden

Cheekwood Botanical Gardens
200 Forrest Park Dr.
Nashville, TN 37205
615/353-2148
500 plants, 49 varieties

TEXAS
Mabel Davis Rose Garden
Zilker Botanical Gardens
2220 Barton Springs Rd.
Austin, TX 78749
512/478-6875
850 plants, 62 varieties. AARS Garden

Dallas Arboretum and Botanical Gardens
8617 Garland Rd.
Dallas, TX 75218
214/327-8263
100 plants

Samuell-Grand Municipal Rose Garden
6200 E. Grand Blvd.
Dallas, TX 75218
214/826-4540
4,750 plants, 270 varieties. AARS Garden

El Paso Municipal Rose Garden
1702 N. Copia
El Paso, TX 79904
505/755-2555
1,414 plants, 223 varieties. AARS Garden

Fort Worth Botanic Gardens
3220 Botanic Garden Dr.
Fort Worth, TX 76107
817/870-7688
3,820 plants, 190 varieties. AARS Garden

Houston Municipal Rose Garden
1500 Hermann Dr.
Houston, TX 77004
713/529-3960
2,400 plants, 97 varieties. AARS Garden

Tyler Municipal Rose Garden
420 S. Rose Park Dr.
Tyler, TX 75702
903/531-1200
30,000 plants, 400 varieties. AARS Garden

Victoria Rose Garden
480 McCright Dr.
Victoria, TX 77901
512/572-2767
1,000 plants, 110 varieties

UTAH
Utah Botanical Gardens
1817 N. Main St.
Farmington, UT 84025
801/451-2492
580 plants, 250 varieties

Fillmore
Territorial Statehouse State Park Rose
    Garden
50 West Capitol Ave.
Fillmore, UT 84631
801/743-5316
330 plants, 33 varieties. AARS Garden

Nephi Federated Women's Club Memorial
    Rose Garden
1 North 1 East
Nephi, UT 84648
801/623-2003
1,000 plants, 100 varieties. AARS Garden

Salt Lake Municipal Rose Garden
1602 E. 2100 S. Sugarhouse
Salt Lake Cuty, UT 84106
801/467-0461
1,330 plants, 170 varieties. AARS Garden

VIRGINIA
River Farm
American Horticultural Society
7931 E. Boulevard Dr.
Alexandria, VA 22308
703/768-5700
320 plants, 50 varieties. AARS Garden

Woodlawn Plantation
9000 Richmond Hghwy.
Alexandria, VA 22309
703/780-4000
190 plants, 41 varieties

Bon Air Memorial Rose Garden
Bon Air Park
Wilson Boulevard and Lexington Street
Arlington, VA 22152
703/644-4954
3,500 plants, 125 varieties. AARS Garden

Confederate Section
Old City Cemetery
Fourth and Taylor Street
Lynchburg, VA 24506
60 plants

Norfolk Botanical Garden Bicentennial
    Rose Garden
Azalea Garden Road
Norfolk, VA 23518
804/441-5831
4,000 plants, 213 varieties. AARS Garden

WASHINGTON
Cornwall Park Rose Garden
Cornwall Avenue
Bellingham, WA 98550
600 plants, 65 varieties

Fairhaven Park Rose Garden
Chuckanut Drive
Bellingham, WA 98225
1,000 plants, 105 varieties.

City of Chehalis Municipal Rose Garden
80 N.E. Cascade Ave.
Chehalis, WA 98532
206/748-0271
290 plants, 50 varieties. AARS Garden

Bert Ross Memorial Rose Garden
1611 Riverside Dr.
Hoquiam, WA 98227
300 plants

Tri-Cities Rose Garden
Lawrence Scott Memorial Park
Kennewick, WA 99337
200 plants

Carl S. English, Jr. Botanical Garden
3015 Northwest 54th St.
Seattle, WA 98107
206/783-7059
120 plants, 35 varieties

Woodland Park Rose Garden
5500 Phinney Ave. N.
Seattle, WA 98103
206/684-4803
4,800 plants, 260 varieties

Manito Gardens-Rose Hill
4 W. 21st Ave.
Spokane, WA 99203
509/625-6622
1,500 plants, 150 varieties. AARS Garden

WEST VIRGINIA
Centennial Rose Garden
Sunrise Museum
746 Myrtle Rd.
Charleston, WV
250 plants

Ritter Park Rose Garden
1500 McCoy Rd.
Huntington, WV 25704
304/696-5543
1,000 plants, 80 varieties. AARS Garden

WISCONSIN
Boerner Botanical Gardens
5879 S. 92nd St.
Hales Corner, WI 53130
414/425-1131
3,500 plants, 350 varieties

Longenecker Gardens of the University of
    Wisconsin (Madison) Arboretum
1207 Seminole Highway
Madison, WI 53711
608/262-2746
100 plants, 65 varieties

Olbrich Botanical Garden
3330 Atwood Ave.
Madison, WI 53704
608/246-4551
600 plants, 100 varieties

Paine Art Center and Arboretum
1410 Algona Blvd.
Oshkosh, WI 54901
414/235-4530
145 plants, 30 varieties

Gene Schindler
508 Macomber St.
Chippewa Falls, WI 54729
715/723-9089
100 hybrid teas, 75 miniatures

CANADA
Minter Gardens
52892 Bunker Rd.
Rosedale, British Columbia,Canada
V2P 6H7
604/794-7191
800 plants, 50 varieties

Montreal Botanical Gardens
4101 Sherwood St. East
Montreal, Quebec,Canada
H1X 2B2
514/872-1400
9,000 plants, 500 varieties

Niagara Parks Botanical Gardens
2565 Niagara Pkwy.
P.O. Box 150
Niagara Falls, Ontario,Canada
L2E 6T2
416/356-8554
2,250 plants, 78 varieties

Royal Botanical Gardens
Off Plains Road West
Burlington, Ontario, Canada
P.O. Box 399
Hamilton, Ontario,Canada
L8N 3H8
416//527-1158
5,000 plants, 400 varieties

University of British Columbia Botanical
    Gardens
601 N.W. Marine Dr.
Vancouver, British Columbia, Canada
V6T 1W5
604/228-2172
350 varieties

# Bibliography and Resources

## Bibliography

A Heritage of Roses, by Hazel LeRougetel. Stemmer House, Owings Mills, Maryland, 1988.

Antique Roses for the South, by William C. Welch. Taylor Publishing Company, Dallas, Texas, 1991.

Hortus Third, by the Staff of the L.H. Bailey Hortorium, Cornell University, Ithaca, New York. Macmillan Publishing Company, New York, 1976.

In Search of Los Roses, by Thomas Christopher. Summit Books, New York, 1989.

Landscaping with Antique Roses, by Liz Druitt and G. Michael Shoup. The Taunton Press, Newtown, Connecticut, 1992.

Roses, by Peter Beales. Henry Holt & Company, New York, 1992.

Roses, by Roger Phillips and Martyn Rix. Random House, New York, 1988.

Roses at the Cape of Good Hope, by Gwen Fagan. Breestraat-Publikasies, Capetown, South Africa, 1988.

Roses of America: The Brooklyn Botanic Garden's Guide To Our National Flower, by Stephen Scanniello and Tania Bayard; photography by Albert Squillace. Henry Holt & Company, New York, 1990.

The American Horticultural Society Illustrated Encyclopedia of Gardening: Roses, by the staff for The Franklin Library and Ortho Books. The American Horticultural Society, Alexandria, Virginia, 1980.

The Book of the Rose, by Laura Cerwinske. Thames and Hudson, New York, 1992.

## Resources

### Roses
Edmunds' Roses
6235 S.W. Kahle Rd.
Wilsonville, OR 97070
503/682-1476

Gardener's Supply Company
128 Intervale Rd.
Burlington, VT 05401-2850
802/863-1700

Garden Solutions
2535 Waldorf Ct., N.W.
Grand Rapids, MI 49550-0724

Gurney's Seed & Nursery Co.
110 Capitol St.
Yankton, SD 57079
605/665-1930

Inter-State Nurseries
1800 Hamilton Rd.
Bloomington, IL 61704
309/663-9551

Jackson & Perkins
1 Rose Lane
Medford, OR 97501-0702
1/800-USA-ROSE

Nor'East Miniature Roses, Inc.
P.O. Box 307
Rowley, MA 01969
1/800/426-6485

Roses of Thomasville
P.O. Box 7
Thomasville, GA 31799
912/226-5568

Roses of Yesterday and Today
Watsonville, CA 95076-0398
408/724-2755

Smith & Hawken
25 Corte Madera
Mill Valley, CA 94941
415/383-2000

Springhill Nurseries
110 W. Elm St.
Tipp City, OH 45371
309/691-4616

Stark Brothers Nursery
Louisiana, MO 63353

Wayside Gardens
1 Garden Lane
Hodges, SC 29695-0001
1/800-845-1124

White Flower Farm
Litchfield, CT 06759-0050
1/800-944-9624

### Rose Organizations
American Rose Society
P.O. Box 3900
Shreveport, LA 71130-0030
318/938-5402

All-America Rose Selections, Inc.
221 N. LaSalle St., Suite 3900
Chicago, IL 60601
312/372-7090

# Index